America's Best Pies

Nearly 200 Recipes You'll Love

American Pie Council with Linda Hoskins

Skyhorse Publishing

Editor's Note:

Crisco® is a trademark of The J.M. Smucker Company.

The Great American Pie Festival and the National Pie Championships are trademarks of American Pie Council.

10 9 8 7 6 5 4 3

Library of Congress Cataloging-in-Publication Data is available on file.
ISBN: 978-1-62087-165-2

Printed in China

Table of Contents

Introduction   v

American Pie Council's Tips for a Great Pie   vii

Apple   1

Cherry   33

Chocolate   59

Citrus   87

Cream   115

Cream Cheese   143

Custard   161

Fruit & Berry   181

Nut   211

Open   231

Peanut Butter   255

Pumpkin   275

Raisin   297

Special Categories   319

Special Dietary   343

Sweet Potato   363

American Pie Council Events   383

Special Thanks   385

Photography Courtesy of . . .   386

American Pie Council Board of Directors Member Companies. . .   386

Index   387

INTRODUCTION

When I tell people I'm the executive director of the American Pie Council, they think I'm kidding. "What a great job," they say. And it is a great job! The people I meet—from those who work at commercial pie manufacturing facilities to restaurant chefs to home bakers—are terrific, and we all have one thing in common—*We love pie!*

The American Pie Council, founded in 1983, is the only organization dedicated solely to pie, America's favorite dessert. We believe in the total enjoyment, consumption, and the pursuit of pie. We believe that the art of pie making shouldn't be forgotten. We believe that the enjoyment of pie should be continued. We believe that the search for the perfect pie should be eternal. And it is in this spirit that we hold the American Pie Council Crisco National Pie Championships every year to determine who's making the best pies in America.

In the months before the event, two hundred judges (food professionals, chefs, cookbook authors, food editors, suppliers to the pie industry, and every day pie lovers) are chosen, and in April each year, pie bakers from all over the country descend upon Celebration, FL, to compete. Pies are entered into five divisions: commercial, independent/retail bakers, amateur bakers, professional chefs, and junior chefs, and then further divided into price point and flavor categories. Then the judging begins. Close to 1,000 pies are judged each year over the course of three days, each entrant hoping his or her pie will be the best!

This book is a compilation of nearly 200 winning pie recipes from the American Pie Council Crisco National Pie Championships and is dedicated to pie lovers everywhere. I hope you enjoy!

To learn more about the American Pie Council and membership, visit www.piecouncil.org

AMERICAN PIE COUNCIL'S TIPS FOR A GREAT PIE

1. Read the recipe in its entirety before beginning. Make sure you have all the ingredients and utensils, and make sure that you understand all the directions. Many mistakes have been made by skipping steps.

2. Cold ingredients are essential to making a great pie crust. Keeping the shortening cold ensures a nice flaky crust! It helps to use cold bowls and utensils, and it's even a good idea to have cold hands before handling the dough. In addition, be sure to chill the dough for at least an hour before rolling it out.

3. Don't overwork or overhandle the dough. Your shortening/butter should be coated with the flour mixture, not blended with it. Overprocessing causes gluten to form, a substance that toughens the dough.

4. Make sure that all your ingredients are really fresh. Try making fruit pies when the fruit is in season to ensure a wonderful pie.

5. To ensure that your bottom crust is baked properly, bake the pie in the lower third of the oven. You may have to cover the edges with foil or a crust protector to avoid overbrowning the edges.

APPLE

"Apple pie is America's favorite pie! There are so many varieties of apples with distinct flavors that make them the perfect ingredient. They can be cooked with cherries, pecans, pumpkin, and even coconut. Some of our best baking varieties include Gala, Rome, Northern Spy, Fuji, and McIntosh."

—Denise Donohue
Executive Director, Michigan Apple Committee

Appealing Apple Caramel Pie	2	Gratz Grand Apple Pecan Caramel Pie	18
Apple Leaf Pie	4	Harvest Apple Pie	20
Apple Pie	6	Hilton's Apple Pie	22
Best Ever Caramel Apple Pecan Pie	8	Orchard-Fresh Apple Pie	24
Brightest Apple Pie	10	Simply Divine Cinnamon	
Butterscotch Pecan Apple Pie	12	Roll Raisin Apple Pie	26
Golden Apple Pie	14	Splendid Apple Pie	28
Grandma Haeh's Apple Pie	16	Sweet Cider Apple Pie	30

« *Apple Pie (recipe page 6)*

APPEALING APPLE CARAMEL PIE

Karen Panosian, Celebration, FL
2007 APC Crisco National Pie Championships Amateur Division 1st Place Apple

CRUST
2 cups all-purpose flour
½ teaspoon salt
⅔ cup Crisco shortening
1 teaspoon vanilla extract
6 tablespoons cold water
Additional milk, sugar, and butter

FILLING
8 apples, peeled, cored, and sliced
2 tablespoons flour

1 cup sugar
¼ teaspoon cinnamon
¼ teaspoon ginger
¼ teaspoon nutmeg
¼ teaspoon allspice
2 tablespoons butter
¼ cup caramel sauce

For the crust: Mix flour and salt in large bowl. Blend in Crisco and add vanilla extract and cold water. Mix until dough is moist. Form dough into a ball and divide in half. Wrap dough in plastic wrap and refrigerate for 30 to 40 minutes.

For the filling: Preheat oven to 400°F. In a medium-sized bowl, combine flour, sugar, mixed spices, and butter. Add apple slices and mix well.

Roll out bottom crust on wax paper, sprinkling the dough and wax paper with flour. Lift dough into 9-inch pie pan and gently press into the bottom of the pan. Place dots of butter on top of bottom crust. Add filling and dot with butter.

Roll out top crust on wax paper, sprinkling flour on the wax paper and dough. Cut the dough into approximately ½-inch strips. Lay the first two strips in an "X" shape in the center of the pie and lay the rest of the strips around the pie in alternating directions, overlapping and weaving each time. Trim the dough edges and fold the edge of the top crust lattice over the pie pan edge and pinch to seal. Brush top crust lattice with milk and sprinkle sugar on top.

Bake for about 50 minutes or until crust is golden. Just before serving, drizzle caramel sauce on top.

Appealing Apple Caramel Pie

APPLE LEAF PIE

Sarah Spaugh, Winston-Salem, NC
2004 APC Crisco National Pie Championships Amateur Division 2nd Place Apple

CRUST

3 cups all-purpose flour
1 teaspoon salt
¾ cup butter-flavored Crisco
¼ cup cold butter, cut into pieces
6 tablespoons cold water
1 tablespoon white vinegar
1 egg, beaten

FILLING

7 cups apples, peeled, cored, and
   sliced

¾ cup white sugar
¼ cup brown sugar
¾ cup apple juice
1 teaspoon cinnamon
¼ teaspoon allspice
2 tablespoons butter
2 tablespoons cornstarch
1 tablespoon maple syrup
Half and half to brush over crust

For the crust: Combine flour and salt in a mixing bowl. Cut in shortening and butter until coarse crumbs form. Combine water and beaten egg; add vinegar. Stir egg mixture into flour mixture with a fork. Divide dough into 2 balls. Roll one out for bottom crust. Roll out the other and make leaf cutouts for top of pie.

For the filling: Preheat oven to 400°F. Combine apples, spices, and sugars in a mixing bowl. Combine cornstarch and apple juice in a small saucepan. Bring to a slight boil. Add butter and maple syrup. Pour over apples and mix. Slowly heat mixture in a large saucepan until apples are barely tender. Spoon filling into unbaked pie shell. Moisten edges of crust with water. To assemble top crust over filling, start from the outside edge and cover the apples with a ring of leaves. Place a second ring of leaves above, staggering positions. Continue with rows of leaves until filling is covered. Place tiny balls of dough in center. Brush lightly with half and half. Bake at 400°F for 10 minutes, then 350°F for 30 to 40 minutes or until crust is golden brown.

Apple Leaf Pie

APPLE PIE

Michael Glodowski, Verona, WI
2011 APC Crisco National Pie Championships Amateur Division 3rd Place Apple

CRUST
2 cups flour
1 teaspoon salt
¾ cup butter
5 to 6 tablespoons water

FILLING
1 tablespoon lemon juice
6 cups apples (2 each Granny Smith, Braeburn, McIntosh, and Fuji), peeled, cored, and cut into small pieces

1½ cups sugar
2 tablespoons minute tapioca
1 teaspoon salt
1 teaspoon cinnamon
2 tablespoons flour
1 tablespoon cornstarch
3 tablespoons butter
1 egg
1 tablespoon sugar

To make the crust: Combine flour, salt, and butter by crossing 2 knives or using a pastry blender until the consistency of the mixture resembles pea-sized balls. Add water to blend. Roll out on a floured surface to form two 9-inch crusts. Place one crust in a 9-inch pie dish. Set the other aside for the top crust.

To make the filling: Preheat oven to 450°F. Combine lemon juice and apples to coat. Add sugar, tapioca, salt, cinnamon, flour, and cornstarch and combine. Pour filling into prepared bottom crust, top with butter and cover with prepared top crust. Score top crust to vent. Mix egg with pastry brush and spread over top crust to lightly coat. Sprinkle sugar over egg coating. Bake at 450°F for 15 minutes. Reduce heat to 350°F. Continue baking until filling bubbles in center of pie, approximately 45 to 60 minutes.

Apple Pie

BEST EVER CARAMEL APPLE PECAN PIE

Rumie Martinez, Farwell, MI
2010 APC Crisco National Pie Championships Amateur Division 3rd Place Apple

CRUST
1 cup flour
½ cup Crisco shortening
½ teaspoon salt
¼ cup cold milk (approximately)

FILLING
½ cup Kraft caramel bits from an 11
  oz. bag. Save the rest for garnish
  below.
  [Note: Kraft caramel bits work
  best, otherwise, unwrap and cut
  up 12 regular Kraft caramels each
  into 8 tiny pieces]
3 lbs, minimum 8 cups, of apples
  (Golden Delicious or Jonagold),
  peeled, cored, and sliced
⅔ cup firmly packed brown sugar
1 tablespoon fresh lemon juice
2 tablespoons granulated sugar

2 tablespoons cornstarch
1 teaspoon ground cinnamon
1 teaspoon pure vanilla extract
¼ teaspoon ground nutmeg

PECAN CRUMB TOPPING
¾ cup all-purpose flour
½ cup chopped pecan halves
½ cup granulated sugar
¼ teaspoon salt
8 tablespoons unsalted butter,
  slightly cold

CARAMEL GARNISH
Remaining Kraft caramels
4 tablespoons unsalted butter
1½ tablespoons water
¼ to ½ cup chopped pecans
12 pecan halves

For the crust: Cut shortening into the flour and salt until it resembles coarse crumbs about the size of a pea. Add in cold milk a little at a time. When it starts to ball up and you have no dry ingredients visible, then your crust is ready to roll out on a floured non-stick silicone mat (or floured surface). Put your bottom crust into a 9-inch pie dish, then trim and flute the edges of your crust. Layer ½ cup of caramel bits on the bottom crust in the pie dish and set this aside in your refrigerator to cool.

For the filling: Preheat oven to 400°F. Mix together apples, brown sugar, and lemon juice in a large bowl. Set aside for about 5 minutes to juice. Mix the granulated sugar and cornstarch together in a small bowl. Once mixed, combine with the apples and mix together. Add the cinnamon, nutmeg, and vanilla to the apples and mix well. Fill the chilled crust with apple mixture, mounding the apples in pie dish as high as you can. Pat down the fruit and smooth down the apples so none are sticking up. Place the pie on the center rack and bake for 30 minutes.

For the topping: While pie is baking, make the crumb topping by combining flour, chopped pecans, granulated sugar, and salt. Cut in butter. Once mixture is coarse, knead together with hands so butter is well blended and looks gravelly. Keep in refrigerator until the pie comes out of the oven.

After 30 minutes of baking, remove pie from oven, lower temperature to 350°F. Carefully pile the refrigerated pecan topping on top and in the center of pie. Spread crumb topping over entire pie

Best Ever Caramel Apple Pecan Pie

evenly to edge of crust. Tap down the crumb topping, and then return the pie to the oven for an additional 45 to 50 minutes. Juices will bubble thickly around the edge of pie toward the end of baking time. Place a baking sheet or tin foil sheet under the pie in oven to catch any juices. You can use a pie shield or tin foil if your pie is getting too dark. Remove pie from oven and cool for approximately 45 to 60 minutes on a wire rack.

For the garnish: While pie is cooling, prepare the caramel garnish. Using a double boiler, combine the butter, water, and remaining caramels. Slowly melt the caramels over simmering water. This should take about 10 to 15 minutes. As caramels are slowly melting, carefully press down and mix together with the melting butter and water. When melted and smooth, mix together and drizzle the caramel garnish mixture over the pie after it has cooled. Immediately sprinkle the chopped pecans over the top and place the pecan halves decoratively on top of pie. Let the pie finish cooling for at least 3 to 4 hours.

BRIGHTEST APPLE PIE

Jennifer Nystrom, Morrow, OH
2008 APC Crisco National Pie Championships Amateur Division 3rd Place Apple

CRUST
2¾ cups all-purpose flour
1 teaspoon table salt
¾ cup vegetable shortening
½ cup butter (not margarine)
1 egg, slightly beaten
⅓ cup cold buttermilk

FILLING
8 to 10 Granny Smith apples, peeled,
   cored, and thinly sliced

¾ cup packed brown sugar
½ cup granulated sugar
1 teaspoon cinnamon
½ teaspoon ground nutmeg
2 tablespoons tapioca
Zest and juice from 1 large lime
   (about 2 to 3 teaspoons zest and
   4 tablespoons juice)
Whipping cream
Sugar in the Raw (Demerara sugar)

For the crust: In a large bowl, mix together the flour and the salt. With a pastry blender, cut in shortening until flour resembles cornmeal. Cut in butter until mixture resembles small peas in consistency. In a small bowl, beat egg with a fork. Beat in buttermilk. At this point, mixture will look almost gelatinous. Quickly mix buttermilk mixture in with the flour until dough just begins to hold together. Separate dough into halves and form each half into a disc. Wrap each disc tightly with plastic wrap and refrigerate for at least an hour or up to two days before rolling out.

For the filling: Preheat oven to 375°F. While dough is chilling, put apples, brown sugar, granulated sugar, cinnamon, nutmeg, zest, juice, and tapioca in an 8-quart pot and mix thoroughly. Cook over medium-high heat until just beginning to soften, about 5 minutes. Remove from heat to cool. While apples are cooling, roll out one refrigerated dough disc to fit a 9-inch deep-dish pie plate. Roll out remaining dough for a top crust. Put cooled apples in the pie plate and cover with second crust. Crimp edges and cut slits in the top of the pie. Brush the top of the pie with whipping cream and sprinkle with Demerara sugar.

Bake for about one hour. Cover the edges of pie with foil if they begin to brown too quickly. Remove from oven and cool before serving.

BUTTERSCOTCH PECAN APPLE PIE

Bev Johnson, Crookston, MN
2009 APC Crisco National Pie Championships Amateur Division 3rd Place Apple

CRUST
1¼ cups flour
½ teaspoon salt
6 tablespoons unsalted butter
2 tablespoons lard
¼ cup plus 1 tablespoon (if needed) Ice water

FILLING
7 cups Golden Delicious apples, peeled, cored, and sliced
½ cup light brown sugar
1 tablespoon fresh lemon juice
2 tablespoons granulated sugar
1 tablespoon cornstarch
½ teaspoon cinnamon
1 teaspoon vanilla extract

CRUMB TOPPING
¾ cup flour
¾ cup pecan halves
½ cup light brown sugar
¼ teaspoon salt
6 tablespoons unsalted butter (cut into ¼ inch pieces)

BUTTERSCOTCH TOPPING
½ cup butterscotch ice cream topping
⅓ cup pecan halves
½ cup chopped pecans

For the crust: Pour water into a spray bottle and place in a bowl of crushed ice to chill. Cut butter and lard into small pieces. Place on two different plates and place in freezer. Place flour and salt in food processor and pulse to mix. Add chilled butter and pulse 8 to 10 times. Add lard lard and pulse 5 to 7 times. Spray a portion of the water on the mixture and pulse 3 times, wait 30 seconds and spray again. Continue until all the water is used. Form dough into a ball, knead once or twice, and flatten ball into a ¾ inch disc. Place in bowl and refrigerate for ½ hour. Roll out dough between 2 sheets of plastic wrap or waxed paper. Place in a 9-inch deep dish pie plate. Keep in freezer until ready to use.

For the filling: Preheat oven to 400°F. Combine apples, brown sugar, and lemon juice in a large bowl. Mix well and set aside for 10 minutes to juice. Mix the granulated sugar and cornstarch together and stir into apples along with cinnamon and vanilla.

Pour filling into the chilled pie shell and bake for 30 minutes.

For the crumb topping: Combine flour, pecans, brown sugar, and salt in food processor. Pulse several times, chopping nuts coarsely. Scatter butter over mixture and pulse until fine crumbs. Place in bowl and mix with fingers until crumbly. Refrigerate until ready to use.

Remove pie from oven and reduce oven temperature to 375°F. Place crumbs in center of the pie and then spread evenly over the top of pie. Tamp down lightly. Return pie to oven so that the part facing the front is now in the back. Bake 40 minutes. Cover the pie with tented foil for the last 15 minutes to keep from getting too brown. Place on wire rack to cool for one hour.

For the butterscotch topping: Warm butterscotch topping in microwave for 15 seconds. Drizzle the topping over pie, press pecan halves into the butterscotch, then sprinkle the chopped pecans over top.

GOLDEN APPLE PIE

Deborah Gray, Winter Haven, FL
2007 APC Crisco National Pie Championships Amateur Division 2nd Place Apple

CRUST
2½ cups all-purpose unbleached
   flour
1 teaspoon salt
½ teaspoon sugar
1 cup frozen Crisco, cut up
8 tablespoons ice water
1 oz milk
2 tablespoons sugar

FILLING
8 Golden Delicious apples, peeled,
   cored, and sliced
¾ cup sugar
3 tablespoons flour
2 teaspoons cinnamon
Dash of nutmeg
1 tablespoon lemon juice
1 tablespoon butter

For the crust: In a medium bowl, combine flour, salt, and sugar. Cut in Crisco. Add water until dough forms a soft ball. Divide dough in half. Roll out each half on a floured surface. Use one for a bottom crust and the other for a top crust. Spray 9-inch pie pan with non-stick spray. Place pastry in pie pan. Flute edges as desired.

For the filling: Preheat oven to 350°F. Place apples in large bowl and sprinkle with lemon juice. Combine sugar, flour, cinnamon, and nutmeg in small bowl. Sprinkle mixture over apples, gently turning to coat all the apples. Place one pie crust in bottom of 9-inch pan. Carefully layer the apples on the crust, forming a mound. Divide butter into fours and place on the apples. Place the top crust over the apples, pinching edges to seal the top of the pie. Make two slits in the center of the pie. Brush top crust with milk and sugar. Bake for 45 to 50 minutes.

Golden Apple Pie

GRANDMA HAEH'S APPLE PIE

Beverley Hari, Orlando, FL
2004 APC Crisco National Pie Championships Amateur Division 1st Place Apple

CRUST
15 oz. Armour Lard, room
    temperature
28 oz. Gold Medal all-purpose flour,
    sifted
1 teaspoon baking powder
2 teaspoons salt
¼ cup sugar
1 whole egg, beaten
1 tablespoon white vinegar
Cold water

FILLING
8 large Granny Smith apples, peeled,
    cored, and finely sliced
1½ cups granulated sugar
1 teaspoon cinnamon
2 teaspoons cornstarch
⅛ teaspoon salt
½ stick butter, finely sliced
1 egg white, whisked

For the crust: Blend all dry ingredients together thoroughly. Cut in lard with pastry cutter until pieces are the size of coarse meal. Beat egg in a 1-cup measuring cup. Add vinegar. Add ice-cold water to ⅔ cup mark. Add liquid slowly to dry ingredients while blending with pastry cutter to form a soft pliable ball. If you add liquid too quickly, the dough will be too wet to handle. Handle dough as little as possible. Dough will be a little moist, but it will dry while resting. Let rest by chilling at least 1 to 2 hours before rolling. Yields 3 double-crust pies, depending on thickness of crust.

Roll out bottom pie crust between 2 wide sheets of saran wrap. Place on 10-inch pie pan. Roll out top crust between 2 sheets of Saran Wrap. Cut vents and set aside.

For the filling: Preheat oven to 400°F. Peel and core apples. Cut each apple into quarters, then into 3 more sections. Slice apple sections very thinly and place on pie crust. Maneuver the slices so they are compactly layered and rounded above pie plate edges. Mix sugar, cinnamon, cornstarch, and salt together. Pour sugar mixture over top of apples, making sure all the apples are covered. Distribute butter slices over top of sugar and apple mixture. Brush whisked egg white on bottom crust edge. Place top crust on top and press edges together for a good seal. Crimp crust edge. Brush with whisked egg white. Place drip pan or foil on bottom oven rack below where pie will sit. Place pie on rack in center of oven.

Bake at 400°F for 15 minutes. Reduce temperature to 350°F and continue baking for another 80 minutes. Lower temperature if crust starts to get too brown, allowing a little more baking time for the lower temperature. Juices should start to bubble up through opening when ready.

GRATZ GRAND APPLE PECAN CARAMEL PIE

Heidi CV Neidlinger, Schuylkill Haven, PA
2006 APC Crisco National Pie Championships Amateur Division 3rd Place

CRUST
2 cups plus 4 tablespoons all-purpose flour
2 tablespoons sugar
1 teaspoon salt
8 tablespoons (4 oz.) cream cheese, chilled and cut into ½ inch cubes
8 tablespoons frozen butter
4 tablespoons frozen Crisco
6 to 10 tablespoons ice-cold water

GLAZE
¼ cup packed brown sugar
1 tablespoon butter, melted

1 tablespoon light corn syrup
1 cup whole pecan halves

FILLING
4 to 5 pounds Granny Smith apples, peeled, cored, and sliced
¼ cup sugar and a sprinkle of cinnamon
½ cup packed brown sugar
3 tablespoons flour
¾ teaspoon cinnamon
Dash ground nutmeg

For the crust: Mix flour, sugar, and salt in a medium bowl. Rub the cream cheese into the flour mixture until it resembles cornmeal. Shred the butter and shortening on a grater into the mixture. Mix again until it resembles cornmeal. Stir in the ice-cold water a little at a time with a fork until the dough clumps and you can form a ball. Make two balls, cover with plastic wrap, and refrigerate overnight.

For the glaze: Combine brown sugar, butter, and corn syrup. Spread this mixture evenly into greased glass pie plate. Arrange whole pecan halves in a pattern of circles by size around the entire dish, completely covering the glaze. Set aside.

Remove dough ball from refrigerator and shape into a disc. Roll out on a floured board into a 14-inch circle and then place into the glass dish on top of the prepared glaze and nuts, fitting sides and bottom of dish. Let edges hang over until filling is ready. Refrigerate until ready to use.

For the filling: Preheat oven to 425°F. Mix sliced apples with sugar and sprinkle with cinnamon. In a large skillet, cook apples about 10 minutes until slightly tender and set aside. In a small mixing bowl, mix brown sugar, flour, cinnamon, and nutmeg, then set aside. Remove prepared crust with glaze from refrigerator. Take half

Gratz Grand Apple Pecan Caramel Pie

of the cooked apples and spread evenly into the crust that is sitting on top of the nuts/glaze. Then sprinkle evenly with ½ of the flour/sugar mixture. Repeat this process with remaining apples and flour mixture.

Take second dough ball out of refrigerator and roll out onto floured surface into a 14-inch circle. Place on top of apples. Take sides of both crusts and tuck under. Flute edges of pie. With a knife, cut slits into top of pie to vent. Cover edges with pie ring and bake 50 to 60 minutes. Put pie on cooling rack when done baking. After only 5 minutes, flip pie onto a heat-proof plate, and let cool totally before serving (about 2 hours).

HARVEST APPLE PIE

Lana Ross, Indianola, IA
2009 APC Crisco National Pie Championships Amateur Division 1ˢᵗ Place Apple

CRUST
2 cups flour
1 teaspoon salt
2/3 cups Crisco
6–8 tablespoons ice-cold water
2 teaspoons vinegar

FILLING
3 Harrelson apples, peeled, cored,
  and sliced
3 Golden Delicious apples, peeled,
  cored, and sliced

1/3 cup flour
1 cup sugar
2 teaspoons cinnamon
1/2 cup dried cranberries

TOPPING
1 cup flour
6 tablespoons butter
1/2 cup brown sugar
2/3 cups toasted, sliced almonds
Ice water

For the crust: Mix together flour and salt. Mix the vinegar into the ice water. Cut the Crisco into the flour mixture and gradually add water until dough sticks together. Roll out half and place in a nine- or ten-inch pie pan. Trim and flute the edges. Roll out the remaining dough and make decorative leaf cutouts for top crust.

For the filling: Preheat the oven to 350°F. In a bowl, combine the flour, sugar, cinnamon, and cranberries. Add the apples. Toss to coat and place into prepared crust.

For the topping: Combine all topping ingredients and carefully cover the apples. Add the cut-out leaves around the crust. Dampen the crust edge with the ice water to help leaves stick. Bake at 350°F for 75 to 80 minutes.

HILTON'S APPLE PIE

Andy Hilton, Davenport, FL
2011 APC Crisco National Pie Championships Professional Division 1st Place Apple

CRUST
2½ cups all-purpose flour
½ cup butter
½ cup shortening
1 tablespoon sugar
½ teaspoon baking powder
8 to 9 tablespoons cold water
Egg wash and sugar for top crust

FILLING
7 or 8 of your favorite apples (Granny Smith and Northern Spys recommended) peeled, cored, and sliced
1 tablespoon lemon juice
1 cup sugar
2 tablespoons modified cornstarch
½ teaspoon cinnamon
¼ teaspoon nutmeg
2 tablespoons butter

For the crust: Whisk together the dry ingredients in a bowl. Place cold butter and cold shortening on top of the flour mixture. Cut in with a pastry blender until the butter and shortening are the size of small peas. Sprinkle with 4 tablespoons of cold water and fluff with a fork. Sprinkle with the remaining 4 or 5 tablespoons of water and fluff until the dough comes together. Form a ball with the dough, wrap in plastic, and place in the refrigerator for 30 minutes. Split dough in half and roll out one half for the bottom crust. Place in pie dish. Roll out the other half for the top crust. Set aside until ready to use.

For the filling: Preheat the oven to 400°F. Peel and slice apples and place in a large bowl, then sprinkle with lemon juice. In another bowl, mix together the dry ingredients. Pour dry ingredients over the apples and blend together. Place apple filling in the prepared pie crust and dot with butter. Cover with the top crust and cut in steam vents. Brush the top of the pie with an egg wash and sprinkle with sugar. Place the pie on a cookie sheet and bake at 400°F for 15 minutes. Lower oven temp to 350°F and bake for 45 minutes or until the top is golden brown and the pie juices are bubbling. Remove the pie and cool.

Hilton's Apple Pie

ORCHARD-FRESH APPLE PIE

Evette Rahman, Orlando, FL
2006 APC Crisco National Pie Championships Amateur Division 1st Place Apple

CRUST
2 cups flour
2 tablespoons sugar
1 teaspoon salt
½ teaspoon baking powder
⅓ cup shortening
⅓ cup very cold unsalted butter, cubed
2 teaspoons cider vinegar
1 tablespoon canola oil
5 tablespoons heavy cream
1 egg, beaten with 1 teaspoon water for brushing top crust

Sugar for sprinkling

FILLING
6 cups cooking apples, peeled, cored, and thinly sliced
1 cup sugar
4 tablespoons cornstarch
1 teaspoon ground cinnamon
Freshly ground nutmeg to taste
1½ tablespoons butter, cubed

For the crust: In a large bowl, mix together all dry ingredients for crust. Cut in shortening and butter until mixture is well blended but still has very small chunks of butter. Mix vinegar, oil, and cream together in a small bowl. Slowly add this to the flour mixture and stir together well. Pour this onto counter and further blend together with palms of your hands. Then form dough into two discs. Wrap in plastic wrap and refrigerate for one hour. Roll out one disc into a 10-inch round. Place in a 9-inch pie plate.

For the filling: Preheat oven to 400°F. In a large bowl, mix together apples, sugar, corn-starch, ground cinnamon, and nutmeg. Place filling in pie plate. Dot with butter. Roll out remaining disc to a 10-inch round and cover filling. Trim excess and seal edges of pie. Make slits in top of crust or cut a 1-inch round in center for ventilation. Brush some of the egg mixture on top crust and sprinkle with sugar.

Bake on center rack at 400°F for 20 minutes, then reduce heat to 375°F and bake for another 40 minutes or until juices are bubbling inside and pie crust is golden brown. Cover edges with foil if necessary to prevent burning.

SIMPLY DIVINE CINNAMON ROLL RAISIN APPLE PIE

Karen Hall, Elm Creek, NE
2011 APC Crisco National Pie Championships Amateur Division 1st Place Apple

CRUST
3 cups unbleached flour
1 cup plus 1 tablespoon butter-flavored Crisco, cold
½ teaspoon baking powder
1 egg
1 teaspoon sea salt
¼ cup plus 1 tablespoon ice water
1 tablespoon sugar
1 tablespoon rice vinegar

FILLING
7 apples, peeled, cored, and thinly sliced
⅓ cup butter, melted
¾ cup granulated sugar
½ cup light brown sugar, packed

1½ teaspoons cinnamon
2 tablespoons flour
½ cup raisins

CINNAMON ROLL TOP
8 oz. package refrigerated crescent rolls
2 tablespoons butter, melted
2 tablespoons sugar
2 teaspoons cinnamon

ICING FOR CINNAMON ROLL TOP
2 oz. cream cheese, softened
1 cup powdered sugar
1 tablespoon butter, softened
1 tablespoon milk

For the crust: In a large bowl, combine flour, baking powder, salt, and sugar. With a pastry blender, cut in Crisco until mixture resembles coarse crumbs. In a small bowl, beat egg, water, and vinegar together. Add egg mixture slowly to flour mixture while tossing with fork until mixture is moistened. Do not overmix. Divide dough and shape into 3 balls, flattening each to form 3 discs. Wrap each disc with plastic wrap and refrigerate at least 30 minutes before using. Makes 3 single crusts. Use one disc for this recipe.

For the filling: Preheat oven to 425°F. In a large skillet over low heat, melt butter. In a large bowl, blend together granulated sugar, brown sugar, cinnamon, and flour. Add apples and raisins to mixture and toss to coat apples. Turn apple mixture into skillet with melted butter; cook and stir over medium heat for 6 to 8 minutes or until apples are tender.

Roll out bottom crust and line 9-inch pie dish; flute edge.

Turn filling into pastry-lined dish; protect edge of pie with foil and bake at 425°F for 10 minutes. Reduce oven to 375°F and bake an additional 10 minutes.

Simply Divine Cinnamon Roll Raisin Apple Pie

For the topping: Unroll crescent rolls (do not divide); brush top side with 2 tablespoons melted butter. Blend together sugar and cinnamon in a small bowl; sprinkle mixture over melted butter. Roll crescent pastry up into a log lengthwise and pinch edge to seal. Cut log into ¼ inch miniature cinnamon rolls. Place miniature cinnamon rolls evenly on top of pie. Bake at 375°F degrees 18–20 minutes longer or until cinnamon roll top is golden brown. Cool pie on rack.

For the icing: In a small bowl, blend together until smooth the softened cream cheese, powdered sugar, butter, and milk. Pipe icing onto cinnamon rolls in a swirling pattern.

SPLENDID APPLE PIE

Therese "Josie" Chaffee, Longmont, CO
2010 APC Crisco National Pie Championships Amateur Division 1st Place Apple

CRUST
2²/₃ cups all-purpose flour
1½ teaspoons salt
1 cup (one stick) Crisco shortening
½ cup plus 1 tablespoon ice water

FILLING
7 medium Braeburn or sweet/tart
   apples, peeled, cored, and thinly
   sliced
1 tablespoon fresh lemon juice
²/₃ cup Splenda sugar blend
2 teaspoons ground cinnamon
3 tablespoons all-purpose flour
¼ teaspoon salt

CRUMB TOPPING
½ cup Splenda brown sugar blend
½ cup all-purpose flour
½ cup Quaker oats
¼ teaspoon salt
½ cup unsalted butter

CARAMEL PECAN FINISH
¼ cup Smucker's sugar-free caramel
   topping
¼ cup chopped pecans

Makes dough for two pie crusts. Use half for this recipe and save the rest for another pie.

For the crust: Working in a cool place and using cool utensils, sift together flour and salt. With a pastry blender or two knives, cut in half the shortening, until the size of peas, and then cut in the other half until small crumbs are achieved. Gradually drizzle most of the ice water over crumb mixture, while stirring and lifting with a fork to incorporate, until mixture begins to come together.

Gently form a ball and cut pastry in half with knife. Lightly flatten one half into a circular shape. Keeping work surface and rolling pin liberally dusted with flour, gently roll the dough from center out to an 11- to 12-inch circle, occasionally picking up the pastry and dusting the surface and rolling pin with additional flour. If freezing pastry, place unwrapped, formed pastry shell in freezer for 20 minutes before wrapping with foil or plastic. Otherwise, carefully fold pastry in half, place in 9-inch glass pie pan; unfold pastry and ease down into the pie pan; trim any excess, leaving about a ½ inch overhang; fold under edge of pastry; crimp edge.

For the filling: Preheat oven to 450°F. Drizzle lemon juice over sliced apples. Combine Splenda sugar blend, cinnamon, flour, and salt. Toss apples into this mixture. Arrange apple mixture in 9-inch unbaked pie shell.

Splendid Apple Pie

For the crumb topping: Combine Splenda brown sugar blend, flour, oats, and salt. Cut in butter with pastry blender until medium crumb is achieved. Carefully spoon mixture on top of apples and gently press onto pie.

Protect bottom of oven with a piece of foil or a pan just large enough to catch drips. Bake at 450°F for 15 minutes; reduce heat to 375°F, cover edge of pie crust with a pie protector or aluminum foil, and continue to bake for an additional 60 minutes. If top is browning too quickly, then loosely cover with foil tent during last 30 minutes of baking time. Remove from oven.

For the topping: While pie is still warm, heat the Smucker's topping and drizzle half the topping over the pie. Sprinkle with pecans, then drizzle the remaining warm Smucker's topping over the pie.

SWEET CIDER APPLE PIE

Phyllis Bartholomew, Columbus, NE
2010 APC Crisco National Pie Championships Professional Division 1st Place Apple

CRUST
2 cups flour
1 cup cake flour
1 cup Crisco
¼ teaspoon salt
¼ teaspoon baking powder
1 egg
1 tablespoon apple cider vinegar
½ cup ice water

FILLING
3 cups sweet apple cider
4 to 5 Granny Smith apples, peeled, cored, and sliced
2 tablespoons tapioca
¼ teaspoon salt
1 teaspoon cinnamon
⅔ cup sugar
2 tablespoons melted butter

For the crust: Mix all the dry ingredients together and then cut in the Crisco. Beat together egg, vinegar, and ice water. Add to the flour mixture. Mix only until all the flour is moistened. Form dough into a ball. Divide in half. Roll out one half for the bottom crust. Roll out the remaining half for a top crust.

For the filling: Preheat oven to 400°F. In a saucepan over medium heat, reduce the apple cider down to about ½ cup. Add the peeled and sliced apples and cook until the apples are about half-way done. Combine the remaining ingredients and add to the apples.

Pour filling into a pastry-lined pie dish. Add top crust, brush with warm milk and sprinkle with sugar. Bake at 375°F to 400°F for about an hour or until crust is a golden brown color.

Sweet Cider Apple Pie

CHERRY

"Many family traditions and memorable moments start with great recipes, and memorable pie recipes start with a great crust. That is why Crisco® has been a proud sponsor of the National Pie Championships Crisco Classic Cherry Pie category and long time supporter of the American Pie Council and the Great American Pie Festival. We are pleased the collection of award-winning pies found within this recipe book will have a broader opportunity to be shared at special gatherings and to become favorites of families and friends."

—Maribeth Badertscher,
Vice President of Corporate Communications,
The J.M. Smucker Company.

All American Sour Cherry Pie	34	Cherry Cherry Bang Bang Pie	46
Black Bottom Cherry Pie	36	Grammy J's Cherry Pie	48
Blue Ridge Cherry Pie	38	I'm So Cheery Cherry Pie	50
Cherry Streusel Pie	40	Classic Cherry Pie	52
Chocolate Cherry Cordial Pie	42	Sweet Tart Cherry Pie	54
Classic Cherry Strudel-Topped Pie	44	Tom's Cheery Cherry Berry Pie	56

‹‹ *Classic Cherry Pie (recipe page 52)*

ALL-AMERICAN SOUR CHERRY PIE

Jim Woodworth, Pueblo West, CO
2008 APC Crisco National Pie Championships Amateur Division 1st Place
Crisco Classic Cherry

CRUST
1¾ cups all-purpose flour
¾ cups butter-flavored Crisco
shortening
¾ teaspoon salt
½ teaspoon sugar
1 tablespoon vinegar
1 egg
1 to 2 tablespoons ice water

FILLING
1½ cups sugar (divided)
4 tablespoons cornstarch

⅛ teaspoon salt
1 cup cherry juice
1½ teaspoons lemon juice
¼ teaspoon almond extract
¼ teaspoon red food coloring
2 tablespoons butter
5 to 6 cups of frozen red sour pitted
cherries, thawed and drained
10 maraschino cherries cut in half
for decoration on top crust

For the crust: Combine all dry ingredients, then cut in Crisco and mix with a pastry blender. In a separate bowl, mix egg, vinegar, and ice water together and beat well. Then add about ½ to ¾ of the liquid mixture to dry ingredients. With a fork, toss the mixture well and let stand for a few minutes. Add more liquid as needed until dough just comes together in a ball. Divide in two. Roll out and press bottom crust into pie plate.

For the filling: Preheat oven to 450°F. In a large saucepan, stir together ¼ cup sugar, cornstarch, and salt. Add cherry juice. Cook this mixture over medium heat, bring to a boil, and continue stirring until thick. Then add the rest of the sugar, stirring and cooking for 2 to 3 minutes more. Remove from heat and add the butter, lemon juice, almond extract, red food coloring, and drained cherries. Mix gently and let cool. Pour cooled filling into prepared pie crust. Place and adjust top crust. Seal and flute edges of the pie crust. Cut slits to vent, or, for a special look, cut in a design and fill with maraschino cherries. Cover the edge with a pie shield to prevent over-browning. Bake at 450°F for 15 minutes. Then reduce heat to 350°F and continue to bake for 30–35 minutes or until bubbly.

BLACK BOTTOM CHERRY PIE

Johnna Poulson, Celebration, FL
2005 APC Crisco National Pie Championships Amateur Division 1st Place
Crisco Classic Cherry

CRUST
1 cup flour
½ cup unsweetened cocoa powder
⅓ cup sugar
¼ teaspoon salt
½ cup Crisco shortening
1 large egg yolk
3 to 4 tablespoons cold water

FILLING
½ cup plus 2 tablespoons sugar
¼ cup unsweetened cocoa powder
2 tablespoons cornstarch
2 cups heavy whipping cream
2 egg yolks

1½ oz. bittersweet chocolate
1½ oz. semi-sweet chocolate
1 tablespoon butter
1 teaspoon vanilla extract

TOPPING
(2) 15 oz. cans good-quality cherry
    pie filling
½ teaspoon almond extract
1 cup whipping cream
1 tablespoon powdered sugar
½ teaspoon vanilla extract
2 oz. milk chocolate bar (grated for
    garnish)

For the crust: Preheat oven to 425°F. Combine flour, cocoa powder, sugar, and salt. Blend in shortening with fingers until mixture resembles coarse meal. Add egg yolk and gently blend. Sprinkle cold water over ingredients until they are moist. Form into a ball and chill.

Roll dough between two sheets of waxed paper to 1/8 inch thickness. Place in pie tin. Dock bottom and sides of pastry shell by perforating dough with a fork. Use pie weights or dried beans to weigh down crust. Bake for 10–12 minutes. Remove from oven. Let cool to room temperature.

For the filling: Whisk together sugar, cocoa, and cornstarch in a saucepan over medium-high heat. Gradually whisk in heavy cream and egg

yolks, stirring constantly until mixture is thick, about 2 to 4 minutes. Remove from heat. Add chocolates, butter, and vanilla. Whisk together until well-blended. Pour into pre-baked pie shell. Press plastic wrap directly on top of pie and refrigerate 4 hours or overnight.

For the topping: Pour cans of cherry pie filling into a colander to strain off excess liquid. Place strained cherries in bowl. Fold in almond extract. Gently spoon the cherries onto the top of the chocolate layer. Beat together whipping cream, powdered sugar, and vanilla. With a pastry bag, pipe cream onto the top of the cherry layer leaving a small pool in the center of the pie without any cream. Grate chocolate bar on top of whipped cream for garnish.

Black Bottom Cherry Pie

BLUE RIDGE CHERRY PIE

Emily Spaugh, Yadkinville, NC
2010 APC Crisco National Pie Championships Amateur Division 1st Place
Crisco Classic Cherry

CRUST
3 cups all-purpose flour
1 tablespoon plus 1 or 1½ teaspoons
  sugar
1 teaspoon salt
1 cup plus 2 tablespoons Crisco
  shortening
½ cup ice water
1 egg slightly beaten
1 tablespoon vinegar

FILLING
1 cup cherry juice
1 cup sugar

¼ cup cornstarch
4 cups pitted red cherries
2 tablespoons butter
½ teaspoon almond extract
½ teaspoon vanilla
1 or 2 drops red food coloring

GLAZE
Brush with milk, sprinkle with sugar.

For the crust: Combine flour, 1 tablespoon plus 1 to 1 ½ teaspoons sugar and salt in large bowl. Cut in Crisco until all flour is blended to form pea-size chunks. Combine water, egg, and vinegar in small bowl. Sprinkle over flour mixture, 1 tablespoon at a time. Toss lightly with fork until dough forms a ball (you may not use all liquid). Divide dough into pieces. Flatten each piece and wrap in plastic. Refrigerate until chilled.

For the filling: Preheat oven to 375°F. In saucepan, combine cherry juice, sugar, and cornstarch. Cook until mixture begins to thicken, but it need not boil. Allow to cool slightly. Add cherries and flavoring. Roll bottom crust and place in 9-inch pie plate. Roll out top crust and cut into strips to form a lattice top. Spoon filling into pastry-lined pie pan. Dot with butter and top with lattice crust. Brush with milk and sprinkle with sugar. Bake 35 to 40 minutes or until filling in center is bubbly and crust is golden brown. Serve barely warm or at room temperature.

Blue Ridge Cherry Pie

CHERRY STREUSEL PIE

Grace Thatcher, Delta, OH
2011 APC Crisco National Pie Championships Amateur Division 2nd Place
Crisco Classic Cherry

CRUST
2 cups flour
½ teaspoon salt
10 tablespoons Crisco shortening
3 to 4 tablespoons cold water

STREUSEL
6 tablespoons sugar
4 tablespoons flour
2 teaspoons wheat germ
2 tablespoons almond flour
⅛ teaspoon cinnamon

5 tablespoons butter, melted
2 drops almond extract
¼ cup slivered almonds

FILLING
(2) 15 oz. cans tart cherries, drained,
    with juice reserved
1 tablespoon clear jel
1 cup dried tart cherries
2 tablespoons almond pastry filling
1 tablespoon butter

For the crust: Preheat oven to 425°F. In a large mixing bowl, sift together the flour and salt. Then add all of the shortening. Cut the Crisco shortening into the flour with a pastry blender until the mixture develops a coarse texture. Sprinkle the water over the mixture a spoonful at a time, and toss until the dough begins to come together. Gather the dough into a ball and press together with your hands, cover with plastic wrap, and refrigerate for at least one hour before using. Prepare pie crust in a 9-inch pie pan and prebake for 10 to 15 minutes.

For the streusel: Mix sugar, flour, wheat germ, almond flour, and cinnamon together in a medium bowl. Melt butter in a small bowl and add almond extract. Mix lightly, then incorporate into the dry mixture. Add almonds and lightly toss with fingertips to combine, then set aside.

For the filling: Preheat oven to 350°F. Prepare cherry filling by tossing both kinds of cherries together in a bowl. Put reserved cherry juice into a saucepan and reduce to ½ cup. Then add clear jel and simmer for approximately one minute or until thickened. Add to cherry mixture and stir until well-incorporated and allow to cool. In the meantime, mix almond filling with 1 tablespoon melted butter and spread evenly on the bottom of prepared Crisco classic crust.

Add cherry filling and bake for 30 minutes, then place streusel on top and bake an additional 10 minutes, or until slightly browned.

Cherry Streusel Pie

CHOCOLATE CHERRY CORDIAL PIE

Christine Montalvo, Windsor Heights, IA
2011 APC Crisco National Pie Championships Amateur Division 1st Place
Crisco Classic Cherry

CRUST
1¼ cups all-purpose flour
½ cup sugar
¼ cup unsweetened cocoa
½ teaspoon salt
½ cup Crisco shortening, frozen and
　cut into pieces
3 to 4 tablespoons ice water

FILLING
5 cups frozen cherries
1 cup sugar

¼ cup cornstarch
¼ teaspoon almond extract
2 cups semi-sweet chocolate morsels
½ cup whipping cream
¼ cup butter, cut into pieces
8 oz. package cream cheese,
　softened
⅓ cup powdered sugar
1 large egg
8 maraschino cherries with stems
1 cup whipped cream
2 tablespoons powdered sugar

For the crust: In food processor, add flour, sugar, cocoa, and salt. Pulse to blend. Add Crisco pieces and pulse until mixture resembles cornmeal. Add water and pulse until dough just comes together. Form dough into a disc, wrap in plastic wrap, and chill about 1 hour. Roll out dough to a 12-inch circle between 2 pieces of parchment paper. Spray bottom and sides of a deep-dish 9-inch pie plate with cooking spray. Ease crust into pie plate. Trim and flute edges. Prick bottom of crust with a fork. Line the crust with a piece of aluminum foil and add pie weights, dried beans, or uncooked rice to gently weigh it down. Bake at 425°F for about 20 minutes. Meanwhile, make filling.

For the filling: Preheat oven to 350°F. Place the cherries in 3-quart pot. In small bowl, mix the sugar and cornstarch until well-blended. Stir this into the cherries and stir until everything is evenly combined. Heat over medium heat, stirring constantly until mixture starts to thicken and boil. Let boil for 1 minute. Remove from heat and stir in the almond extract. Set aside and cool completely. Microwave chocolate morsels and cream in a bowl until chocolate begins to melt. Whisk in butter until smooth. Let cool, whisking occasionally for 5 to 10 minutes or until mixture is a spreadable consistency. Spoon half of chocolate mixture into the baked pie crust. Cover and chill remaining chocolate mixture. Spoon cooled cherry mixture evenly over chocolate mixture in pie crust. Set aside.

Chocolate Cherry Cordial Pie

Beat together cream cheese, sugar, egg, and almond extract at medium speed with an electric mixer until smooth. Pour evenly over cherry pie filling. Bake for 30 minutes or until center is set. Remove pie from oven and cool on a wire rack. Cover and chill for 8 hours.

Microwave reserved chocolate mixture for 1 minute. Stir until spreadable. Dip maraschino cherries in chocolate mixture and let them firm up on a sheet of wax paper for 15 minutes before decorating pie. Spread remaining chocolate evenly over top of pie. In a large bowl, whip cream and sugar until stiff peaks form. Pipe around edge of pie; place cherries decoratively around pie.

CLASSIC CHERRY STRUDEL-TOPPED PIE

Nikki Norman, Milton, TN
2009 APC Crisco National Pie Championships Amateur Division 1st Place
Crisco Classic Cherry

CRUST
1½ cups plus 2 tablespoons unbleached all-purpose flour
1 tablespoon fine granulated sugar
¾ teaspoon fine sea salt
½ cup plus 1 tablespoon butter-
   flavored Crisco shortening
4 tablespoons cold water

FILLING
1¼ cups granulated sugar
½ teaspoon fine sea salt
¼ cup cornstarch
2 cups canned pitted sour red cherries, drained, reserving 1 cup juice

Few drops of red food coloring
   (optional)
½ teaspoon pure almond extract

STRUDEL TOPPING
¾ cup unbleached all-purpose flour
¼ teaspoon baking soda
½ teaspoon fine sea salt
½ cup light brown sugar, packed
½ cup quick cooking oats
4 tablespoons unsalted butter

GARNISH (OPTIONAL)
¼ cup confectioner's sugar
1 to 2 tablespoons heavy cream

For the crust: In a medium bowl, combine flour, sugar, and salt. Stir with a pastry cutter. Add shortening; mix with pastry cutter for 2 minutes or until small lumps appear. Using a fork, gradually stir in cold water one tablespoon at a time. Shape dough into a ball and wrap in plastic wrap. Refrigerate at least one hour. Using remaining 2 tablespoons flour, dust work surface and roll out crust. Fit crust in 9-inch pie pan; fashion a decorative edge for crust if desired or leave plain. Freeze crust for at least one hour.

For the filling: In a small saucepan, combine sugar, salt, and cornstarch. Gradually whisk in reserved cherry juice. Cook over medium heat, whisking constantly until thickened. Remove from heat and add red food coloring if desired. Add almond extract and fold in cherries. Cool. Pour filling into pie crust.

For the topping: Preheat oven to 350°F. Using a pastry cutter, combine all ingredients in a small bowl until it is a crumb texture. Sprinkle evenly over cherry filling. Bake directly on oven rack for 45 minutes or until set. During last 15 minutes of baking, you may want to cover crust edge to prevent overbrowning.

For the garnish: If desired, combine ingredients in a small bowl. Use a teaspoon or fork to drizzle over pie.

CHERRY CHERRY BANG BANG PIE

Sandy Newcastle, Omaha, NE
2007 APC Crisco National Pie Championships Amateur Division 1st Place
Crisco Classic Cherry

CRUST
3 cups flour
1 teaspoon salt
1 teaspoon sugar
1 cup plus 2 tablespoons butter-
   flavored Crisco shortening
⅓ cup plus 1 tablespoon apple juice
1 extra large egg, well-beaten

FILLING
4 cups red tart pitted cherries
½ teaspoon almond extract
1 ¼ cups sugar
3 tablespoons cornstarch
Dash of salt
2 tablespoons unsalted butter, melted
2 tablespoons wild chokecherry jelly

For the crust: Sift together flour, salt, and sugar into a large mixing bowl. Cut in shortening with a pastry blender until mixture resembles cornmeal. Combine apple juice and egg. Add liquid, one tablespoon at a time, sprinkling over flour mixture and tossing with a fork to form soft dough. Shape into 3 discs. Wrap in plastic wrap and chill 3 to 24 hours. Extra pastry may be frozen for later use.

For the filling: Preheat oven to 425°F. Mix together all filling ingredients and set aside.

Roll out one pie pastry disc and line a 9-inch pie plate. Pour filling into pie plate. Roll out top crust and apply, or cut out lattice strips and apply. Flute and vent. Brush top crust with slightly beaten egg white and sprinkle with sugar. Bake for 10 minutes. Reduce oven temperature to 350°F and bake an additional 30 to 35 minutes. Remove from oven. Cool on a wire rack.

GRAMMY J'S CHERRY PIE

Therese "Josie" Chaffee, Longmont, CO
2010 APC Crisco National Pie Championships Amateur Division 2nd Place
Crisco Classic Cherry

CRUST
2⅔ cups all-purpose flour
1½ teaspoons salt
1 cup (one stick) Crisco shortening
Approximately ½ cup ice-cold water

FILLING
1¼ cups sugar
4 tablespoons cornstarch
¼ teaspoon salt
(3) 15-oz. cans tart pitted pie cherries, drained, reserving juice
¾ cup reserved juice from canned cherries

1 tablespoon fresh lemon juice
½ teaspoon almond extract
½ teaspoon cinnamon
Small amount of red food coloring if necessary
1 tablespoon unsalted sweet cream butter
Milk to moisten edge of pie and to brush over pie before baking
Sugar to sprinkle over finished pie before baking

For the crust: Preheat oven to 450°F. Sift together flour and salt. With a pastry blender or two knives, cut in half the shortening, until the size of peas, and then cut in the other half until small crumb is achieved. Gradually drizzle most of the ice water over crumb mixture, while stirring and lifting with a fork to incorporate, until mixture begins to come together. Gently form a ball and cut pastry in half with knife. Lightly flatten one half into a circular shape. Gently roll from center out to an 11- to 12-inch circle. Carefully fold pastry in half, place in 9-inch pie pan, then unfold pastry and ease down into the pie pan. Trim any excess, leaving about a ½ inch overhang. When ready to top the pie, flatten and roll remaining pastry to 11- to 12-inch circle. Using knife or pastry wheel, cut lattice strips. Moisten edge of bottom crust lightly with milk and weave lattice top over pie. Trim lattice edges. Fold bottom pastry over edge of Lattice. Crimp edge.

For the filling: Preheat oven to 450°F. In a heavy-bottomed saucepan, combine sugar, cornstarch, and salt. Stir in cherry juice until smooth.

Cook over medium-high heat, whisking often, until mixture comes to a boil. Remove from heat and stir in cherries, almond extract, lemon juice, and cinnamon. Return to heat and simmer over medium heat for about five minutes stirring occasionally. Remove from heat and cool slightly for about five to ten minutes, stirring a few times.

Pour cherry filling into prepared pie shell leaving some room for expansion of the filling. Do not overfill. Dot filling with butter. Lightly moisten edge of bottom crust with milk. Weave lattice of pastry strips over pie filling. Lightly brush milk on lattice top and lightly sprinkle lattice top with sugar.

Bake at 450°F for 15 minutes. Reduce heat to 375°F, cover edge of pie crust with a pie protector or aluminum foil, and continue to bake for an additional 25 to 30 minutes or until filling is bubbly and lattice is golden brown.

I'M SO CHEERY CHERRY PIE

Susan Boyle, DeBary, FL
2011 APC Crisco National Pie Championships Professional Division 1ˢᵗ Place
Crisco Classic Cherry

CRUST
2 cups all-purpose flour
¾ cup Crisco
1 teaspoon salt
6 tablespoons ice-cold water

FILLING
5 cups tart cherries
½ cup dried cherries

½ cup cherry juice concentrate
¼ teaspoon almond extract
½ teaspoon cinnamon
⅓ cup cornstarch
4 drops red food coloring

For the crust: Mix flour and salt in bowl. Add Crisco, and then use a pastry blender to cut in butter. Slowly add water one tablespoon at a time until mixture forms ball. Divide dough and place on floured surface. Shape like a pancake and roll out to fit upside-down pie plate. Fold into quarters and place in pie plate. Trim dough to ½ inch over edge of plate and flute. Refrigerate other half of dough for leaf designs to place on top of filling.

For the filling: Preheat oven to 425°F. Soak dried cherries in cherry juice about fifteen minutes. Do not drain. Add 5 cups of tart cherries, sugar, cornstarch, cinnamon, almond extract, and food coloring. Toss gently as not to break cherries and to coat well. Add filling to an unbaked pastry shell and flute. Cut leaf designs and lay on top of filling.

Bake at 425°F for 10 minutes, then reduce heat to 375°F for 50 minutes.

I'm So Cheery Cherry Pie

CLASSIC CHERRY PIE

Valarie Enters, Sanford, FL
2006 APC Crisco National Pie Championships Amateur Division 1st Place
Crisco Classic Cherry and Best of Show

CRUST
2 cups flour
½ cup butter-flavored Crisco
¼ cup butter
3 teaspoons powdered sugar
¼ cup ice water
2 teaspoons vinegar
1 egg

FILLING
4 cups drained Morello cherries
    (Trader Joe's brand), reserve juice

1¼ cups sugar
3 tablespoons tapioca
Pinch salt
1⅓ cups juice (reserved from
    cherries)
1 tablespoon amaretto flavoring
Tiny dab of red gel food coloring
    (Wilton)

For the crust: Combine flour and salt. Cut in Crisco and butter until texture resembles cornmeal. Beat egg, blend in vinegar and water, and sprinkle over flour mixture. Toss with fork. Chill before rolling. Makes two 9-inch pie crusts—a bottom crust and a top crust.

For the filling: Preheat oven to 425°F. Mix ingredients together and pour into a pie shell. Cover with top crust and bake at 425°F for 15 minutes. Reduce heat to 350°F and bake until golden brown, about 45 minutes.

Valarie Enters with Classic Cherry Pie

SWEET TART CHERRY PIE

Kathy Costello, Tallmadge, OH
2007 APC Crisco National Pie Championships Amateur Division 3rd Place
Crisco Classic Cherry

CRUST
1 egg
1 teaspoon clear vanilla
2 tablespoons powdered sugar
1¼ cups butter-flavored Crisco shortening
2¾ cups plus 2 tablespoons flour
¼ cup ice water

FILLING
¼ cup sugar
½ cup powder sugar
¾ cup cherry juice (drained from cherries; use an equal amount of juice from each type of cherry; make up difference with water)
2½ cups canned tart cherries in water, drained
2½ cups canned sweet cherries in water, drained
⅛ teaspoon nutty amaretto oil flavoring.

DECORATIVE GARNISH
Leftover pie dough
Red and green food coloring
Cocoa

For the crust: Mix egg, vanilla, powdered sugar, and Crisco until creamy. Mix until all ingredients are incorporated. Do not over mix dough. Form 2 discs and wrap in plastic wrap. Chill for an hour.

Remove dough from refrigerator. Place dough on a lightly floured piece of plastic wrap, sprinkle with flour, and cover with another sheet of plastic. Roll out dough to fit pie dish, then line bottom of pie dish with dough.

For the filling: Preheat oven to 375°F. Whisk sugar, powdered sugar, and cherry juice together and cook over medium heat. Stir until mixture begins to thicken. Add drained cherries and nutty amaretto oil flavoring. Continue to cook until mixture becomes thick and clear. Remove from heat, set aside to completely cool. After filling is cooled, place prepared filling in the pie dish and then cover with the other half of prepared rolled-out pie dough. Place small slits in top of pie for steam to escape. Beat 1 egg white until foamy and brush top of pie. Sprinkle lightly with sugar. Before placing pie in oven, place aluminum foil around the crimped edges of the pie to prevent overbrowning. Spray inner side of foil with flour cooking spray to prevent sticking when removing foil.

For decorative garnish: Use small amount of leftover pie dough and add several drops of red food coloring; well, then make 3 or more small marble-size balls to place on top of pie. Mix small amount of cocoa into dough to make stems to place under each cherry.

Mix small amount of green food coloring, press dough out on counter and cut out leafs, or use leaf cutter. Place leafs on stems.

Bake pie on bottom rack for 10 minutes. Then move pie up to middle rack for 40 to 45 minutes. Remove foil 5 minutes before pie is done.

Sweet Tart Cherry Pie

TOM'S CHEERY CHERRY BERRY PIE

Linda Hundt, DeWitt, MI
2009 APC Crisco Professional Cherry 1st Place Crisco Classic Cherry and Best of Show

CRUST
1½ cups flour
¼ teaspoon baking powder
½ teaspoon salt
1 teaspoon sugar
½ cup Crisco shortening

FILLING
4½ cups Montmorency tart cherries
   (frozen)
1 cup sugar
¼ cup cornstarch

½ teaspoon real almond extract
1 teaspoon fresh-squeezed lemon
   juice
½ teaspoon orange zest
½ cup dried Michigan cherries
1½ cups frozen blueberries

CRUMB TOPPING
1 cup sugar
1 cup all-purpose flour
¼ teaspoon salt
1 stick butter, softened

For the crust: Mix all ingredients in a stand mixer on medium speed swiftly until dough texture appears "pea-like." Carefully sprinkle ice cold water in crust mix until it just starts to be fully moistened and gathers together. Pat into disc; wrap and refrigerate for at least one half hour. Roll out on floured surface and make and crimp piecrust. Freeze until ready to use.

For the filling: Preheat oven to 400°F. Combine frozen cherries, dried cherries, sugar, and cornstarch. Stir constantly on medium-high heat until boiling. Boil for one minute or until thickened. Add almond extract, lemon juice, and zest. Pour blueberries on bottom pie shell and pour cherry mixture over them.

For the topping: Mix together all crumb topping ingredients by hand or with a pastry blender until crumbly. Cover filling with crumb topping. Bake for 45 minutes to one hour or until filling is bubbling over crust.

Tom's Cheery Cherry Berry Pie

CHOCOLATE

"The American Pie Council Crisco National Pie Championships has become one of the most favorite competitions that chefs in the Central Florida region truly look forward to judging. From the commercial category to junior chefs, no less than twenty-eight kinds of pies will be judged by professional chefs, food industry professionals, food editors, cookbook authors, as well as home cooks.

As chairman emeritus of the Florida Restaurant and Lodging Association, Central Florida chapter and a thirty-year member of the American Culinary Federation, I regard this competition as one of the best for those competing, as well as those judging. The American Pie Council is to be commended on a competition well-done."

—Jim Whaples,
Chairman Emeritus,
Florida Restaurant and Lodging Association, Central Florida

Caramel-Pecan Chocolate Pie	60	Chocolate Raspberry Delight Pie	70
Chocolate Caramel Nut Pie	62	Dark Chocolate Raspberry Glacier Pie	74
Chocolate Raspberry Silk and Cream Pie	64	German Chocolate Pie	76
		Shades of Chocolate Pie	78
Double Chocolate Raspberry Dream Pie	66	Silky, Rich & Smooth Chocolate Pie	80
Oh My Ganache! Chocolate Cream Pie	68	Three Blind Mice Chocolate Cheese Pie	82

‹‹ Double Chocolate Raspberry Dream Pie (recipe page 66)

CARAMEL-PECAN CHOCOLATE PIE

Veselina Iovanovici, Lakewood, CA
2011 APC Crisco National Pie Championships Amateur Division 2nd Place
Crisco Classic Chocolate

CRUST
2 cups all-purpose flour
1 cup butter-flavored Crisco shortening
¼ cup granulated sugar
½ cup brown sugar
1 tablespoon lemon juice
1 tablespoon vanilla
½ teaspoon salt
¼ teaspoon cinnamon
¼ teaspoon chili pepper
½ cup chopped pecans
⅓ cup chopped semi-sweet chocolate

FILLING 1
13.4 oz. can Dulce de Leche
3 cups pecan halves, lightly toasted

FILLING 2
⅓ cup cornstarch
⅔ cup granulated sugar
⅛ teaspoon salt

3 cups milk
6 oz. semi-sweet baking chocolate
1 tablespoon vanilla
3 egg yolks (pasteurized)
1 envelope unflavored gelatin
4 tablespoons cold water
8 oz. cream cheese
1 cup confectioner's sugar
2 cups whipping cream

CHOCOLATE GANACHE
4 oz. milk baking chocolate
2 oz. semi-sweet baking chocolate
½ cup whipping cream

GARNISH
Whipped cream
Pecan halves
Shaved chocolate

This recipe makes two pies.

For the crust: Preheat oven to 375°F. In a bowl mix together flour, cinnamon, chili pepper, and salt. In a separate bowl, whip together Crisco shortening, sugar, brown sugar, lemon juice, and vanilla. Slowly mix in pecans, chocolate, and flour mixture with an electric mixer. Divide dough in two. Roll it out and cover bottom and sides of two 9-inch-bottom pie pans. Bake for about 13 to 16 minutes. Cool the pie crust completely before filling.

For Filling 1: Reserve Dulce de Leche and pecan halves for assembly of pie.

For Filling 2: In a small cup, sprinkle the gelatin over 4 tablespoons cold water and let it bloom. In a heavy saucepan, whisk cornstarch, granulated sugar, salt, and milk. Cook over medium heat until bubbling, then add the chocolate and stir until chocolate is melted. In a separate small bowl, whisk the egg yolks and gradually add 4 to 5 spoons of hot chocolate pudding to temper the eggs. Return everything into the hot pudding, stir a few times, then add the gelatin and continue to stir until gelatin is dissolved. Remove from heat, transfer to a chilled bowl, cover with plastic wrap, and chill in refrigerator. Whip together cream cheese and confectioner's sugar. Add chilled pudding to mixture, and then add vanilla.

Caramel-Pecan Chocolate Pie

For the chocolate ganache: Melt the chocolate and the cream in a double boiler just before ready to assemble the pies.

To assemble the pies, divide Dulce de Leche and spread on the bottom of the two pans. Layer with toasted pecans, chocolate ganache, and chocolate cream (filling 2).

Garnish with whipped cream, pecan halves, and shaved chocolate. Chill pies in refrigerator for at least one hour.

CHOCOLATE CARAMEL NUT PIE

Todd Welveart, Battendorf, IA
2006 APC Crisco National Pie Championships Amateur Division 1st Place
Crisco Classic Chocolate

CRUST
1½ cups all-purpose flour
½ cup butter-flavored Crisco
½ pinch of salt
3 tablespoons water
1 tablespoon apple cider vinegar

CHOCOLATE LAYER
6 tablespoons all-purpose flour
½ teaspoon baking powder
½ pinch of salt
4 oz. semi-sweet chocolate chips
½ cup butter, diced
½ cup sugar
1 egg

1 egg white
1 teaspoon vanilla extract
1 Snickers bar (super-sized) thinly
    sliced, about ¼ inch thick

CREAM CHEESE LAYER
9 oz. cream cheese, softened
⅓ cup white sugar
1 teaspoon vanilla extract
3 oz. macadamia nuts (diced finely,
    toasted in oven)

GARNISH
2 oz. semi-sweet chocolate chips
2 tablespoons heavy whipping cream

For the crust: Preheat oven to 375°F. Mix flour and salt in a large mixing bowl. Cut in Crisco with a pastry blender. Mix water and vinegar in a spray bottle, adding 3 or 4 ice cubes to keep water mixture cold. Spray flour mixture lightly with water solution, mixing to combine. Repeat just until piecrust comes together. Put crust in a Ziploc bag and bring together into a ball. Place in refrigerator for 10 minutes. Pull crust out of the refrigerator and roll out to size of pie pan. Poke holes in the bottom and sides of the crust. Bake for 7 minutes. Remove from oven and let cool 5 minutes.

For the chocolate layer: In a medium mixing bowl, combine flour, baking powder, and salt. Mix well. In a double boiler, melt semi-sweet chocolate and ½ cup of butter, stirring until smooth. Cool for 10 minutes. Meanwhile, beat sugar, whole egg, and egg white in a medium bowl until slightly thickened. To this mixture add vanilla and cooled chocolate. Mix until well blended. Stir in dry ingredient mixture and mix until just combined. Pour mixture into crust and bake in a 375°F oven for about 19 minutes. Cool on rack for 10 minutes. Place candy layer (sliced Snickers bars) on top.

For the cream cheese layer: In a mixing bowl, beat cream cheese and sugar until blended. Add vanilla extract and beat until smooth. Spread mixture over candy bars, sprinkle macadamia nuts over cream cheese, and bake for 20 minutes or until set. Cool on rack.

For the garnish: In a small saucepan, stir chocolate and whipping cream over low heat until smooth. Drizzle over pie. Refrigerate, and serve chilled.

CHOCOLATE RASPBERRY SILK AND CREAM PIE

Emily Lewis, Mt. Dora, FL
2004 APC Crisco National Pie Championships Amateur Division 2nd Place
Crisco Classic Chocolate

CRUST
1½ cups chocolate cookie crumbs
²/₃ cup browned butter, melted
3 oz. dark chocolate ice cream topping, hardening type (optional)

FILLING
12 oz. semi-sweet chocolate, melted
8 tablespoons butter, room temperature
¾ cup unsifted powdered sugar
2 eggs (use pasteurized eggs), 6 tablespoons total

1 cup heavy whipping cream
1 teaspoon vanilla
½ cup raspberry jam (seedless)

TOPPING
1 cup whipping cream
1 teaspoon gelatin softened over 2 tablespoons water
2 tablespoons confectioner's sugar
1 teaspoon vanilla
Chocolate curls
12 fresh raspberries

For the crust: Mix crumbs and melted browned butter together. Press into 9-inch pie pan.

Optional: Squirt chocolate on bottom of crust. Spread evenly and chill.

For the filling: Melt chocolate; set aside. Mix butter with confectioner's sugar until fluffy. Add chocolate to butter mixture. Add eggs, 3 tablespoons at a time, mixing 5 minutes after each addition. Whip cream, add vanilla, and combine with chocolate mixture. Spread raspberry jam on bottom of crust. Top with chocolate filling. Chill for 3 hours.

For the topping: Melt gelatin in water in a small pan over low heat until dissolved. Cool slightly. Whip cream until soft peaks form. Add sugar, vanilla, and liquefied gelatin. Continue beating until stiff. Top pie with whipped cream. Sprinkle with chocolate curls and arrange raspberries decoratively on pie.

DOUBLE CHOCOLATE RASPBERRY DREAM PIE

Alberta Dunbar, San Diego, CA
2011 APC Crisco National Pie Championships Amateur Division 1st Place
Crisco Classic Chocolate

CRUST
1 ⅓ cups all-purpose flour
½ teaspoon salt
½ stick Crisco all-vegetable
  shortening
3 to 6 tablespoons ice water

FILLING 1
8 oz. cream cheese, softened
1 teaspoon raspberry extract
12 oz. semi-sweet chocolate, melted
  and cooled
¾ cup heavy cream, whipped

FILLING 2
8 oz. cream cheese, softened
1 teaspoon raspberry extract
12 oz. milk chocolate, melted and
  cooled
¾ cup heavy cream, whipped

TOPPING
2 cups fresh raspberries
1 cup raspberry jam, melted and
  cooled
2 cups heavy whipping cream
¼ cup powdered sugar, sifted
1 teaspoon rum extract

For the crust: Preheat oven to 400°F. Spoon flour into measuring cup and level. Mix flour and salt in a medium bowl. Cut in shortening using pastry blender or 2 knives until flour is blended and forms pea-size chunks. Sprinkle with water 1 tablespoon at a time. Toss lightly with a fork until dough forms a ball. Roll on lightly floured board to fit a 9-inch pie plate with ½ inch overlap. Turn into pie plate, flute edges, and prick bottom with fork. Bake for 10 minutes or until golden brown. Cool on rack completely before filling.

For filling 1: Place cream cheese and extract in a medium bowl and beat on high with electric mixer until smooth. Beat in cooled chocolate. Use wooden spoon to fold in whipped cream.

Carefully spread in cooled pie shell. Smooth top and chill for 30 minutes.

For filling 2: Repeat instructions for first filling, using milk chocolate instead of semi-sweet chocolate.

For the topping: In small bowl, combine raspberries and jam. Spread evenly over second layer. Chill for 30 minutes. In medium bowl, combine whipped cream, powdered sugar, and rum extract; beat on high speed until stiff. Fill pastry bag with whipped cream. Using a small rosette tip, make basket weave strips over raspberries. Fit bag with large rosette tip and pipe large swirls around outer edge of pie. Chill until ready to serve.

Double Chocolate Raspberry Dream Pie

OH MY GANACHE! CHOCOLATE CREAM PIE

Evette Rahman, Orlando, FL
2007 APC Crisco National Pie Championships Amateur Division 1st Place
Crisco Classic Chocolate

CRUST
1¼ cups chocolate cookie crumbs
¼ cup unsalted butter, melted

FILLING
1 cup heavy cream
1 cup semi-sweet chocolate morsels
½ cup chocolate hazelnut spread
2 oz. unsweetened chocolate, cut
   into pieces

½ cup unsalted butter
¾ cup sugar
¼ teaspoon kosher salt
1 teaspoon pure vanilla extract
1 cup pasteurized liquid eggs
3 cups whipped cream
Shaved chocolate

For the crust: Preheat oven to 350°F. Mix ingredients together and press into deep-dish pie plate. Bake for 8 minutes. Cool completely.

For the filling: In small saucepan, heat heavy cream until hot. Place morsels in small bowl, pour cream over, and let rest for five minutes. Stir gently to combine. Let cool slightly. Spread over bottom and sides of prepared pie shell. In saucepan over low heat, melt unsweetened chocolate. Remove from heat and stir in hazelnut spread. In another bowl, beat butter until fluffy. Slowly beat in sugar until fluffy. Beat in cooled chocolate mixture and vanilla until well blended. Add ¼ cup of eggs at a time, beating 2 minutes after each addition. Beat until fluffy. Pour onto ganache layer in prepared pie shell. Refrigerate until well chilled. Spread or pipe whipped cream over pie and garnish with shaved chocolate.

CHOCOLATE RASPBERRY DELIGHT PIE

Michelle Stuart, Norwalk, CT
2011 APC National Pie Championships Professional Division Honorable Mention
Crisco Classic Chocolate

CRUST
2 cups flour
1 teaspoon salt
¾ cup Crisco
5 tablespoons very cold water
Cream to brush on pie crust edge

FILLING 1
¾ cup plus 2 tablespoons sugar
3½ tablespoons cornstarch
⅛ teaspoon salt
2½ cups whole milk
4 large egg yolks
2 tablespoons unsalted butter
2 teaspoons vanilla
3 oz. unsweetened chocolate, chopped
⅛ cup semi-sweet chocolate chips
½ cup raspberry glace (recipe below)

½ cup brownie chunks (recipe below)
Chocolate whipped cream (recipe below)
Raspberries for garnish

RASPBERRY GLACE
1 cup fresh raspberries, mashed
1 cup sugar
3 tablespoons cornstarch
½ cup water

BROWNIE CHUNKS
4 oz. unsweetened chocolate
¾ cup butter
1⅓ cups flour
½ teaspoon salt
1 teaspoon baking powder
4 eggs
2 cups sugar

2 teaspoons vanilla
1 cup chocolate chips

CHOCOLATE WHIPPED CREAM
2 cups heavy cream
1 teaspoon vanilla
Confectionary sugar to taste
¼ cup cooled hot fudge sauce
(recipe below)

HOT FUDGE SAUCE
1 cup sugar
3 cups heavy cream
¼ cup light corn syrup
4 oz. unsweetened chocolate
¼ cup butter
1 tablespoon vanilla extract

For the crust: Combine flour and salt in a mixing bowl. Cut Crisco into the flour mixture until coarse crumbs form. Add water 1 tablespoon at a time, mixing gently until incorporated and dough can form a ball. Wrap dough in plastic and refrigerate for at least 30 minutes. Preheat oven to 425°F. Divide dough in half. Use only half the dough for this recipe. Roll out and place pastry in a 9-inch pan. Brush the edge of pie crust with cream. Bake for 15 to 20 minutes or until golden brown. Let the crust cool completely before filling.

For the raspberry glace: Combine the mashed raspberries, sugar, cornstarch, and water in a medium-sized saucepan over high heat. Stir while the ingredients cook, for about 10 minutes or until the mixture attains a thick consistency. Be patient, this does take time, but it is worth it! Let the glace cool to room temperature and then place in the refrigerator prior to use.

For the brownie chunks: preheat oven to 350°F. Grease ½ sheet pan. Melt chocolate and butter in saucepan over low heat, stirring constantly until smooth. Remove from heat and set aside. Mix flour, salt, and baking powder in a separate bowl. In another bowl, beat eggs thoroughly. Gradually beat sugar into eggs until thoroughly combined. Add the flour mixture to the egg mixture and combine well. Blend in chocolate mixture and vanilla. Stir well. Add chocolate chips, mixing well. Bake for 25 minutes. Cool in pan. Cut into chunks.

For the filling: Combine the sugar, cornstarch, and salt in a saucepan. Whisk to mix thoroughly. Whisk in egg yolks and milk. Place over medium heat and cook. Whisk nonstop until mixture starts to bubble and thicken. Once it thickens, add butter, one tablespoon at a time. Then add the vanilla. Once all mixed together, add the chocolate, ⅓ of the amount at a time. Remove from heat once all the chocolate is melted and

Chocolate Raspberry Delight Pie

mixture has thickened. Allow the cream to cool in a bowl in the refrigerator for about 15 minutes. Add the chocolate chips and brownie chunks, mixing until combined.

Spread raspberry glace evenly on the bottom of the pie shell. Pour chocolate mixture in pie shell over the raspberry glace. Cover with wrap and refrigerate for at least 3 hours.

Once chilled, remove plastic wrap from pie.

For the whipped cream: Mix together cream, vanilla, and sugar with an electric mixer on high speed until creamy.

For the hot fudge sauce: Combine all the ingredients except the vanilla in a medium saucepan. Bring the mixture to a boil over medium-high heat. Whisk constantly for 5 minutes over heat. Once it looks like the sauce is separating, remove from heat and add vanilla. Chill sauce until it thickens, about 5 hours.

Add hot fudge sauce to whipped cream mixture and beat until stiff peaks form.

Top pie with chocolate whipped cream and raspberries for garnish. Serve cold.

DARK CHOCOLATE RASPBERRY GLACIER PIE

Stan C. Strom, Gilbert, AZ
2010 APC Crisco National Pie Championships Amateur Division 1st Place
Crisco Classic Chocolate

CRUST
2 cups all-purpose flour (slightly tossed with fork in bag, gently scooped and leveled, but not sifted)
1 cup Soft As Silk cake flour
½ teaspoon kosher salt
½ cup Crisco butter-flavored vegetable shortening, chilled
½ cup butter or lard, chilled
3 tablespoons sugar
1 tablespoon cider vinegar
1 large egg, beaten
⅓ cup ice water

CHOCOLATE RASPBERRY CUSTARD LAYER
1 egg white, lightly beaten, plus 4 large eggs
1 cup International Delight chocolate raspberry coffee creamer (or substitute French vanilla creamer)

2 cups heavy cream
¾ cup sugar
¼ teaspoon salt
1½ teaspoon pure Watkins vanilla extract
1 teaspoon Watkins raspberry extract
12 oz. Hershey's special dark chocolate chips, melted

DARK CHOCOLATE GANACHE
1 cup heavy cream
6 oz. (½ bag) Hershey's semi-sweet or special dark chocolate chips

RASPBERRY TOPPING & GLAZE
2 to 3 pints fresh raspberries
¼ cup raspberry seedless jam
1 tablespoon water

For the crust: After measuring, sift flour, sugar, and salt. Cut in shortening and butter with a pastry blender until coarse in texture (pea-sized bits). Mix vinegar, beaten egg, and ice water in a small bowl, then add liquid to flour bits until just dampened, mixing with fork. Divide. Place on wide plastic wrap and gather into ball from the outside corners. Chill for at least 30 minutes. Roll out between two layers of wide plastic wrap and fit into 9-inch (deep-dish) glass pie pan. Flute with fork or fingers. Chill for 30 minutes or freeze 15 minutes. Preheat oven to 350°F. This recipe will make enough for one large 9-inch deep-dish pie with cutouts or one 9-inch double-crust pie. Bake for 20 to 22 minutes until slightly browned.

For the custard filling: In a heavy saucepan, combine the creamer and cream and heat until mixture just comes to a simmer. Whisk the 4 large eggs, ¾ cup sugar, salt, and vanilla together to combine. Add the hot milk mixture to the egg-sugar mixture and whisk to blend.

Transfer custard mixture to the blind-baked pie shell and bake at 350°F until the custard is set but still slightly wobbly in the center, 40 to 45 minutes. Transfer to a wire rack to cool. When cooled, transfer to the refrigerator to chill.

For the chocolate ganache: Heat cream in a saucepan over medium heat until hot, but not boiling. Remove pan from heat and stir in chocolate chips. Let rest for 7 to 10 minutes and then stir until smooth. Allow ganache to cool to room temperature, then stir again until smooth and pour over cooled custard.

For the raspberry topping and glaze: In a small saucepan, simmer the jam and water for five minutes, but do not boil. Remove from heat and cool. Brush raspberries with glaze and arrange berries upright on top of ganache. Refrigerate overnight.

GERMAN CHOCOLATE PIE

Rick Johnson, Belleville, IL
2010 APC Crisco National Pie Championships Amateur Division 2nd Place
Crisco Classic Chocolate

CRUST
2 cups flour
2 tablespoons sugar
½ cup butter
½ teaspoon salt
1 cup roasted chopped pecans
Cold water

FILLING 1
3 tablespoons butter
½ cup butter-flavored Crisco
1¼ cups powdered sugar
⅓ cup cocoa powder
4 eggs
¼ cup cream

FILLING 2
1 cup butter
2¼ cups powdered sugar
2 tablespoons molasses
½ teaspoon vanilla
2 egg yolks
1½ teaspoons coconut extract
½ cup cream

GARNISH
Whipped cream and/or shaved
    chocolate

For the crust: Preheat to oven to 375°F. Combine flour, salt, sugar, and butter in a food processor and process until gravelly. Add pecans and water a little at a time until dough just starts coming together. Press into a disc and refrigerate for at least 1 hour, then roll out into crust. Blind-bake crust for 20 minutes or until browned. Cool in refrigerator.

For filling 1: To make first filling, combine butter, butter-flavored Crisco, and powdered sugar. Mix on high speed for 5 minutes. Add cocoa powder and 2 eggs, and beat on high speed for 5 minutes. Add 2 remaining eggs and beat on

high for 3 minutes, then add cream and beat for 2 minutes and pour into prepared crust.

For second filling: Combine butter, powdered sugar, and molasses and beat on high for 5 minutes. Add vanilla, coconut extract, and 1 egg yolk and beat on high for 5 minutes. Add second egg yolk and beat for 3 minutes on high, then add cream and beat for 2 minutes. Pour on top of the first filling.

Garnish with whipped cream and shaved chocolate as desired.

SHADES OF CHOCOLATE PIE

Jeanne Ely, Polk City, FL
2009 APC Crisco National Pie Championships Amateur Division 2nd Place
Crisco Classic Chocolate

CRUST

3 cups flour
1 teaspoon salt
¼ cup shortening
1 cup butter-flavored Crisco
   shortening
1 egg
5 tablespoons cold water
1 tablespoon vinegar

FILLING

½ Ghirardelli 4 oz. white chocolate
   bar
1 cup milk chocolate chips
½ Ghirardelli 3.17 oz. dark chocolate
   bar
1 cup powdered sugar
1 stick butter, softened
1½ packages extra creamy Cool Whip

To make the crust: Preheat oven to 350°F. Cut together flour, salt, and shortening until texture is oatmeal-like in consistency. Beat egg in cup, add water and vinegar, beat all and pour into flour mixture. Blend well. Roll out dough and place in 9-inch pie plate. Bake about 12–15 minutes or until golden brown. Cool.

To make the filling: Place white chocolate in medium mixing bowl and melt in microwave.

Add ⅓ stick of butter and ⅓ cup powdered sugar. Beat until completely blended. Add 1 egg and beat until fluffy. Fold in ⅓ of the Cool Whip. Spoon into baked pie shell and refrigerate until firm. Repeat the above with the milk chocolate and refrigerate until firm, then repeat with the dark chocolate until firm. Garnish as desired.

Shades of Chocolate

SILKY, RICH & SMOOTH CHOCOLATE PIE

Susan Boyle, DeBary, FL
2011 APC Crisco National Pie Championships Professional Division 1st Place
Crisco Classic Chocolate

CRUST
4 cups crushed Oreo chocolate
  sandwich cookies
½ cup butter-flavored Crisco, melted

FILLING
8 oz. package cream cheese
1 cup confectionary sugar
1 teaspoon vanilla
4 tablespoons chocolate pudding

½ cup cocoa
2 ¼ cups heavy whipping cream
1 cup chocolate chips, melted

TOPPING
2 cups heavy whipping cream
2 tablespoons sugar
¼ cup milk

For the crust: Mix ingredients well together and press hard into pie pan. Chill until ready to use.

For the filling: In a cold mixing bowl, whip cream cheese, sugar, and vanilla until smooth. Slowly add chocolate pudding, cocoa, and whipping cream. Mix well. Add melted chocolate chips. Continue whipping on medium speed until filling is well-blended and firm. Spoon into chilled cookie crust and garnish with whip topping.

For the topping: Whip ingredients together on medium until stiff peaks form. Pipe a border around pie. Optional: chocolate curls /cookie crumbs to garnish pie

Silky, Rich & Smooth Chocolate Pie

THREE BLIND MICE CHOCOLATE CHEESE PIE

Diane Selich, Vassar, MI
2010 APC Crisco National Pie Championships Professional Division 1st Place
Crisco Classic Chocolate

CRUST
1 ⅓ cups flour
½ teaspoon salt
½ cup Crisco
3 to 4 tablespoons cold water

BROWNIE LAYER
¼ cup butter
½ cup sugar
½ teaspoon vanilla
1 egg
¼ cup cocoa
⅛ teaspoon baking powder
⅛ teaspoon salt

CHEESECAKE LAYER
4 oz. cream cheese, softened
¾ cup sugar
2 eggs
½ cup sour cream
¼ cup flour

1 teaspoon clear vanilla
⅓ cup whole milk

GANACHE
1 cup semi-sweet chocolate chips
⅔ cup heavy whipping cream

CHOCOLATE FILLING
2 cups whole milk, divided
¾ cup sugar
¼ cup cornstarch
2 egg yolks
¼ cup sifted cocoa
½ teaspoon vanilla
1 teaspoon butter

MICE AND CHEESE
¼ pound grey fondant
2 oz. black fondant
¼ cup melted chocolate

Continued on page 84.

Three Blind Mice Chocolate Cheese Pie

For the crust: Preheat oven to 350°F. Combine flour and salt in a small mixing bowl. Cut in Crisco, forming a coarse mixture. Add water a little at a time. Work the dough into a ball. Roll on floured board 1 ½ inches larger than pie plate. Pinch and trim the edges. Line crust with tin foil and bake for 20 to 25 minutes. Remove foil and bake another 5 to 8 minutes so the crust will be golden brown. Cool before using.

For the brownie layer: In a small mixing bowl, blend the butter, sugar, and vanilla. Add egg and beat together. Combine the dry ingredients and add to the butter mixture. Spread in a greased pie plate. Bake at 350°F for 8 to 10 minutes. Cool and set aside.

For the cheesecake layer: Blend cheese and sugar together. Add milk and mix in the eggs. Add sour cream, vanilla, and flour. Mix until smooth. Pour into a greased pie plate and bake at 350°F for 20 to 25 minutes. Let cool. Remove from plate and place in the freezer to set before using.

For the ganache layer: Melt chocolate and cream in a double boiler. When chips are melted, pour into a bowl and cool before using

In the baked pie shell, spread 4 tablespoons of ganache. Add the brownie layer. Spread 4 tablespoons of ganache over the brownie layer and add the cheesecake layer. Set aside.

For the chocolate filling: On low heat, place 1 cup of the milk with the sugar, vanilla, and the butter in a saucepan. In a mixing bowl, add the other cup of milk with the egg, cornstarch, and cocoa. Whip until smooth. Add slowly to the heated mixture, stirring to prevent lumps. Pour over the cheesecake layer. Cool and top with 4 cups of whipped topping and chocolate curls.

For the mice and cheese: Divide the grey fondant into 8 one-inch balls (like a truffle). Pull one side of the ball to a point (like a Hershey's kiss); set aside. Roll out the rest of the grey fondant thinly and cut 16 circles, using the wide end of a #12 decorator tip. Pinch the end to form the ear, and place two ears on the heads of each mouse. Roll the black fondant thin and cut out 6 eyes for the blind mice, using the small end of a # 12 tip.

For the eyes: Melt ¼ cup of chocolate and place some in a decorator tip. Cut a small hole in a baggie and make dots for the eyes and the nose on 5 of the mice. Place a small dot of chocolate on the back of the black eyes and place on 3 of the mice. Any leftover grey fondant can be rolled thin to make tails for the mice.

For the cheese, cut a sheet of Rice Krispies Treats into triangles about 2 inches wide; dip them into yellow coating chocolate and allow to dry. Set the mice on top of the Rice Krispies triangles and place on each slice of pie. You should have 8 pieces of cheese with 8 mice for the 8 pieces of pie.

Tip: Roll fondant on a thin layer of powdered sugar.

CITRUS

"Each year, the All-American community of Celebration, FL eagerly anticipates the Great American Pie Festival and National Pie Championships. We love having the opportunity to try out dozens of delicious, creative pies, taking part in the judging of the championships, and welcoming competitors back each year. The pie buffet is a favorite among our residents and visitors, and becoming a member of the 'pie police' has become a much-coveted position! Our favorite kind of pie? Why, key lime, of course!"

—Patricia A. Wasson, CMCA, PCAM
Executive Director, Celebration Town Hall

Cream Cheese Lemon Pie	88	Raspberry Lemonade Pie	104
Girl Scout Cookie Lemonade Pie	90	Razzilicious Key Lime Pie	106
Grandma's Zesty Lemon Sponge Pie	92	Support Group Key Lime Pie	108
Key Lime–Raspberry Pie	94	U. S. Route 1 Pie: Florida Key Lime with Maine Blueberries	110
Lemon–Lime Meringue Pie	96	When God Hands You Lemons, Make a Lemon Pie	112
Lemon Raspberry Twist	98		
Mandarin Sunrise Pie	100		
Orange Coconut Pie	102		

‹‹ *US Route 1 Pie: Florida Key Lime Pie with Maine Blueberries (recipe page 110)*

CREAM CHEESE LEMON PIE

Bobbie Allen, Canyon, TX
2005 APC Crisco National Pie Championships Amateur Division 3rd Place Citrus

CRUST
2 cups sifted flour
2/3 cup Crisco
1 teaspoon salt
4 to 5 tablespoons cold water

FILLING
1 cup sugar
½ cup cornstarch
2 ½ cups cold water
1/3 cup lemon juice, divided in half

1 small (3.4 oz.) package instant
   lemon pudding
1/8 teaspoon salt
3 tablespoons butter
14 oz. sweetened condensed milk
8 oz. cream cheese
3 egg yolks

GARNISH
Whipped cream
Lemon slices

For the crust: Preheat oven to 450°F. Combine flour and salt in mixing bowl. Cut in shortening with pastry blender until texture resembles coarse cornmeal. Sprinkle with water, 1 tablespoon at a time, tossing mixture lightly with a fork. The dough should be just moist enough to hold together when pressed gently with a fork. Shape dough into smooth ball before rolling. Roll out crust and place in pie pan. Bake at 450°F until lightly browned. Chill until ready to fill.

For the filling: Combine sugar and cornstarch. Gradually stir in water, mixing until smooth.

Cook and stir over medium heat until thickened and translucent. Quickly stir in egg yolks. Boil 1 minute. Remove from heat, stir in half of lemon juice, salt, and butter. Cool thoroughly. In mixing bowl, blend sweetened condensed milk with cream cheese until smooth. Stir in pudding mix and remaining lemon juice. Fold pudding mixture together with chilled egg mixture and pour into pie shell. Chill.

Garnish with whipped cream and lemon slices as desired.

Cream Cheese Lemon Pie

GIRL SCOUT COOKIE LEMONADE PIE

Beth Welveart, Bettendorf, IA
2007 APC Crisco National Pie Championships Amateur Division 2nd Place Citrus

CRUST
1/3 cup butter, melted
1/4 cup sugar
2/3 cup graham crackers, crushed
2/3 cup "Lemonades" Girl Scout Cookies, crushed

LEMON FILLING 1
1 1/2 cups sugar
1/2 teaspoon salt
6 tablespoons cornstarch
1 1/4 cups water
2 tablespoons butter
2 teaspoons lemon zest
4 drops yellow food coloring
2/3 cup lemon juice, preferably fresh

FILLING 2
11 oz. cream cheese, softened
3/4 cup powdered sugar
1 tablespoon lemon juice
5 tablespoons lemon curd
1/2 teaspoon vanilla
1 1/2 cups heavy cream, whipped (makes 3 cups whipped cream; save half for garnish)

GARNISH
Remaining whipped cream
Lemon peel
Lemonades cookies

For the crust: Preheat oven to 375°F. Combine all ingredients and press into a 9-inch pie plate. Bake for 5 minutes. Cool.

For the lemon filling: In a saucepan, combine sugar, salt, and cornstarch. Stir in water; bring to a boil over medium-high heat. Reduce heat; cook and stir for 2 minutes until thick and bubbly. Remove from heat. Stir in butter, zest, and food coloring. Gently stir in lemon juice until just combined. Cool to room temperature.

For filling 2: In a mixing bowl, beat cream cheese and sugar until smooth. Mix in lemon juice, lemon curd, and vanilla. Gently fold in 1½ cups whipped cream.

Spread cream cheese filling in bottom of crust; top with lemon filling. Chill overnight. Top with reserved whipped cream.

Garnish with lemon, lemon peel, and/or Lemonades cookies as desired.

Girl Scout Cookie Lemonade Pie

GRANDMA'S ZESTY LEMON SPONGE PIE

Jean Sprenkle, Hanover, PA
2010 APC Crisco National Pie Championships Amateur Division 2nd Place Citrus

CRUST
1½ cups of Gold Medal flour plus 3
    tablespoons of additional flour
½ teaspoon of salt
9 tablespoons refrigerated Crisco
4 tablespoons ice-cold milk

FILLING
½ cup freshly squeezed lemon juice,
grated lemon rind from one lemon

1 cup milk
2 tablespoons butter, melted
2 egg yolks, beaten
2 egg whites
1½ cups sugar
3 tablespoons flour
¼ teaspoon salt

For the crust: Preheat oven to 375°F. Mix all ingredients. Gather dough together and press into a ball. Roll dough out into a circle one inch larger than pie plate. Lay dough onto pie plate and press down and crimp edges.

For the filling: Preheat oven to 375°F. In a blender, blend together lemon juice, lemon rind, melted butter, and egg yolks. Combine flour and sugar in a bowl, and add salt to this mixture. Mix together with a fork. Then add the dry ingredients to the blender mixture and mix well.

Pour blender mixture into mixing bowl and save for later use.

In separate mixing bowl, beat the 2 egg whites until soft peaks form. Fold egg whites into the blender mixture in the mixing bowl. Pour this into unbaked prepared crust.

Bake for 40 to 45 minutes or until crust is nicely browned and filling is set. Remove from oven to cake rack to cool at least 2 hours before cutting the pie.

KEY LIME–RASPBERRY PIE

George Yates, Dallas, TX
2011 APC Crisco National Pie Championships Amateur Division 1st Place Citrus

CRUST
1½ cups crushed gingersnap crumbs
½ cup crushed vanilla wafer crumbs
¼ cup toasted almonds, ground
3 tablespoons sugar
5 tablespoons unsalted butter, melted
1 teaspoon key lime juice

KEY LIME CURD
3 eggs plus 4 egg yolks
1 cup sugar
1 tablespoon grated lime zest
½ cup fresh key lime juice
4 tablespoons unsalted butter, softened
⅛ teaspoon salt

KEY LIME FILLING
1 tablespoon unflavored gelatin
⅔ cup water
1 cup sugar, divided

⅔ cup fresh key lime juice
5 eggs, separated
1 tablespoon freshly grated key lime zest
4 oz. white chocolate, melted

RASPBERRY FILLING
1 cup fresh raspberries
1 cup water, divided
1 cup sugar
3 tablespoons cornstarch
3 tablespoons raspberry gelatin
2 tablespoons seedless raspberry jam
2 teaspoons key lime zest

GARNISH
2 cups whipping cream
4 tablespoons confectioner's sugar,
raspberries, sliced limes, sliced almonds, raspberry jam

For the crust: Preheat oven to 350°F. In a medium bowl, combine crumbs, ground almonds, and sugar. Stir key lime juice into melted butter until combined. Add butter mixture to crumb mixture until well-blended. Press crumb mixture into 10-inch deep-dish pie pan with 2-inch sides and bake for 10 minutes. Cool completely before filling.

For the curd: Whisk eggs, yolks, and sugar in a saucepan until thick. Whisk in zest, juice, butter, and salt. Cook over medium-low heat, stirring constantly until very smooth and thick. Remove from heat. Cool to room temperature. Refrigerate.

For the key lime filling: In a heavy-bottomed saucepan, sprinkle the gelatin over the water and let stand for a few minutes to soften. Add ½ cup sugar and the key lime juice. Mix well. Then add the egg yolks and whisk until blended. Place over moderate heat and cook, stirring constantly, until the mixture thickens slightly and barely reaches a simmer, 5 to 10 minutes; do not allow it to boil. Stir in the key lime zest and the melted white chocolate. Pour the gelatin mixture into a bowl and refrigerate, stirring occasionally, for about 1 hour.

In a medium bowl, beat the 5 egg whites until soft peaks form, then gradually add the remaining ½ cup sugar and beat until stiff peaks form. Gently fold the key lime mixture into the whites and pour half the filling into pie crust. Chill until firm. Mix raspberry filling (follows) and assemble.

Key Lime–Raspberry Pie

For the raspberry filling: Place raspberries and ⅔ cup water in a saucepan. Simmer for 3 minutes. Whisk sugar, cornstarch, and remaining ⅓ cup water in a small bowl until smooth; add to raspberry mixture. Boil one minute, whisking constantly. Remove from heat Add gelatin, whisking until smooth. Stir in jam until smooth. Strain through a sieve to remove seeds and stir in key lime zest. Cool to room temperature. Spread over the chilled key lime filling layer in pie crust. Spread the remaining key lime filling over raspberry filling. Chill until firm.

Spread curd over filling. Chill again for several hours or overnight.

For the garnish: Beat together whipping cream and confectioner's sugar. Garnish pie with whipped cream, raspberries, sliced limes, and sliced almonds. Drizzle with raspberry jam.

LEMON–LIME MERINGUE PIE

Beth Campbell, Belleville, WI
2007 APC Crisco National Pie Championships Amateur Division 1st Place Citrus

CRUST
1 cup flour
½ cup shortening
¼ cup cold water
Dash of salt

FILLING
1½ cups sugar
⅓ cup cornstarch
1½ cups water
3 egg yolks (slightly beaten)

3 tablespoons butter
⅛ cup lemon juice
⅛ cup lime juice
1 tablespoon grated lemon rind
1 tablespoon grated lime rind
Meringue
¼ teaspoon salt
¼ teaspoon vanilla
1 teaspoon lemon juice
3 egg whites
6 tablespoons sugar

For the crust: Preheat oven to 475°F. Cut the shortening into the flour and salt until texture resembles coarse meal. Gradually add the water to the flour mixture until dough can be formed into a ball. Roll the pastry two inches larger than the pie plate. Ease the pastry into the pie plate, pressing firmly against the bottom and the sides, crimping the edges. Prick the bottom and sides of crust. Bake until light brown, about 8–10 minutes. Cool.

For the filling: Mix the sugar and cornstarch in a saucepan and gradually stir in the water. Cook over medium heat, stirring constantly until mixture thickens and boils. Boil for one minute.

Slowly stir ½ of the hot mixture into the slightly beaten egg yolks. Then blend this mixture back into the other half of the thickened mixture in the saucepan. Boil for one minute longer, stirring constantly. Remove from the heat. Add butter, lemon juice, lime juice, and the grated lemon and lime rinds. Pour into the baked pie shell and cover with meringue.

For the meringue: Preheat oven to 350°F. Add vanilla, salt, and lemon juice to the egg whites. Beat until foamy. Add 6 tablespoons of sugar, one at a time. Beat until the sugar dissolves. Spread on top of lemon–lime filling. Bake 10 to 15 minutes until the meringue is lightly browned.

Lemon–Lime Meringue Pie

LEMON RASPBERRY TWIST

Michele Stuart, Norwalk, CT
2011 APC Crisco National Pie Championships Professional Division 1st Place Citrus

CRUST
2 cups flour
1 teaspoon salt
¾ cup Crisco
5 tablespoons very cold water
Cream to brush on pie crust edge
Raspberry Glace
1 cup fresh raspberries, mashed
1 cup sugar
3 tablespoons cornstarch
½ cup water

LEMON CHIFFON FILLING
1 whole egg
2 egg yolks
½ cup sugar
¼ cup cornstarch
Pinch of salt
1 cup lemon juice

1 cup hot water
2 tablespoons unsalted butter
1 tablespoon lemon zest
1 teaspoon water, room temperature
  (for the gelatin)
1 teaspoon gelatin

MERINGUE
4 large egg whites, room
  temperature
¼ teaspoon cream of tartar
Pinch of salt
½ cup sugar
1 teaspoon vanilla

GARNISH
Whipped cream
Lemon zest
Raspberries

For the crust: Preheat oven to 425°F. Combine flour and salt in a mixing bowl. Cut Crisco into the flour mixture until coarse crumbs form. Add water 1 tablespoon at a time, mixing gently until incorporated and dough can form a ball. Wrap dough in plastic and refrigerate for at least 30 minutes. Divide dough in half. Use only half the dough for this recipe. Roll out and place pastry in a 9-inch pan. Brush the edge of pie crust with cream. Bake for 15 to 20 minutes or until golden brown. Let the crust cool completely before filling.

For the raspberry glace: Combine the mashed raspberries, sugar, cornstarch, and water in a medium-sized saucepan over high heat. Stir while the ingredients cook, for about 10 minutes or until the mixture attains a thick consistency. Be patient, this does take time, but it is worth it! Let the glace cool to room temperature and then place in the refrigerator prior to use. Spread 1 cup raspberry glace on bottom of prepared pie shell.

For the lemon chiffon filling: In a small bowl, add the teaspoon of water to the gelatin. Set aside so gelatin can soften while filling is prepared.

Whisk the egg, egg yolks, and sugar together in a medium bowl. Still whisking, add the cornstarch and salt. Mix in the lemon juice, hot water, butter, and lemon zest.

Transfer the filling to a medium saucepan and cook over medium heat, scraping the sides of the

Lemon Raspberry Twist

pan frequently to prevent any burning. Whisk continuously until the mixture becomes bubbly and thick, for about 5 minutes. Add the gelatin to the filling, folding it in until all ingredients are combined.

For the meringue: In a separate mixing bowl, beat the egg whites until foamy. Add cream of tartar and salt. Beat until soft peaks form. Then add the sugar 1 tablespoon at a time. After all the sugar has been added, mix in the vanilla, beating for about 30 seconds. Once complete, gently fold the meringue into the lemon filling so that they are thoroughly combined. Place the lemon filling over the raspberry glace. Chill pie overnight.

Garnish with whipped cream, lemon zest, and raspberries.

MANDARIN SUNRISE PIE

Joretta Allen, Pueblo West, CO
2007 APC Crisco National Pie Championships Amateur Division 3rd Place Citrus

CRUST
1 1/3 cups all-purpose flour
1 teaspoon orange zest
½ teaspoon salt
½ cup Crisco shortening
3 to 4 tablespoons cold orange juice

FILLING
1½ cups sugar
1/3 cup + 1 tablespoon cornstarch
1½ cups water
3 egg yolks, lightly beaten
3 tablespoons butter

2 tablespoons grated orange peel
½ cup frozen orange juice concentrate, thawed
2 to 3 drops orange food coloring (optional)
2 cans (15 oz.) mandarin oranges, drained and separated—reserve ½ cup for garnish

GARNISH
4 oz. Cool Whip
Reserved mandarin orange slices
Mint leaves (optional)

For the crust: Preheat oven to 450°F. In a mixing bowl, stir together flour, zest, and salt. Cut in shortening until pieces are the size of small peas. Sprinkle juice over the mixture; gently toss with a fork until all is moistened. Form dough into a ball. Wrap in plastic wrap and chill. On a lightly floured surface, roll dough into a circle about 12 inches in diameter. Wrap dough around rolling pin. Unroll onto a 9-inch pie plate. Ease pastry into pie plate being careful not to stretch pastry. Trim to ½ inch beyond edge of plate; fold under extra pastry. Flute. Prick bottom and sides of pastry generously with tines of a fork. Bake for 10 to 12 minutes or until golden. Cool.

For the filling: Mix sugar and cornstarch in a 1½ quart saucepan. Gradually stir in water.

Cook over medium heat, stirring constantly until mixture boils and thickens. Boil and stir one minute. Stir at least half the hot mixture gradually into the egg yolks. Blend egg mixture into the hot mixture in saucepan. Boil and stir 1 minute. Remove from heat. Stir in butter, orange peel, orange juice, and food color. Cut orange slices each in half (except those for garnish). Stir orange pieces into hot mixture. Pour into cooled pie shell. Cool completely.

Pipe whipped topping with a pastry bag around edge of pie. Garnish with remaining orange slices and mint leaves if desired.

ORANGE COCONUT PIE

Marles Riessland, Riverdale, NE
2003 APC Crisco National Pie Championships Amateur Division 2nd Place Citrus

CRUST
3 cups all-purpose flour
1 teaspoon salt
1 teaspoon sugar
1 cup plus 1 tablespoon butter-flavored shortening, chilled
1/3 cup ice water
1 tablespoon vinegar
1 egg, beaten

FILLING
1 cup sugar
1/3 cup cornstarch
1/4 teaspoon salt

1½ cups water
3 egg yolks, slightly beaten
2 tablespoons butter
1 teaspoon finely shredded orange peel
1/4 cup fresh-squeezed orange juice
4 oz. cream cheese
½ cup powdered sugar
1 cup whipped topping

GARNISH
Shredded coconut and additional whipped topping for garnish

For the crust: Chill all ingredients, including the flour and vinegar. Combine the flour, salt, and sugar. Cut in shortening with a pastry blender until the mixture resembles cornmeal. In another bowl, mix water and vinegar with the beaten egg. Add the liquid mixture, one tablespoon at a time, to the flour mixture, tossing with a fork to form a soft dough. Shape into three discs. Wrap in plastic wrap and chill in refrigerator. Use one disc when making this pie. Freeze remaining dough for later use. Roll out one pastry and place into a 9-inch pie dish for bottom crust. Line the crust with a piece of aluminum foil and add pie weights, dried beans, or uncooked rice to gently weigh it down. Bake at 425°F for about 20 minutes.

For the filling: In a saucepan, combine sugar, cornstarch, and salt. Gradually stir in water. Cook and stir until thickened and bubbly. Reduce heat, cook and stir 2 minutes more. Remove from heat. Gradually stir 1 cup hot mixture into yolks. Add egg mixture to mixture in saucepan, and bring to a gentle boil. Cook and stir 2 minutes more. Remove from stove. Stir in butter, orange peel, and orange juice. Turn into pastry shell. Refrigerate. Meanwhile, prepare next layer by combining 4 oz. cream cheese and ½ cup powdered sugar until well blended. Beat in 1 cup whipped topping until light and fluffy. Spread over orange filling. Top with whipped topping and sprinkle with shredded coconut as desired. Chill until serving.

RASPBERRY LEMONADE PIE

Patricia Lapiezo, LaMesa, CA
2006 APC Crisco National Pie Championships Amateur Division 1st Place Citrus

CRUST
3 cups all-purpose flour
1¼ cups Crisco shortening
1 teaspoon salt
5 tablespoons ice water
1 tablespoon vinegar
1 egg, slightly beaten

FILLING
10 oz. box frozen sweetened
   raspberries, thawed
1 tablespoon cornstarch
1 tablespoon granulated sugar
½ cup fresh raspberries
12 oz. cream cheese, softened
6 oz. can frozen raspberry lemonade
   concentrate, thawed
14 oz. can sweetened condensed milk
1½ cups heavy cream, stiffly beaten

GARNISH
Sweetened whipped cream
Lemon slice
Raspberries

For the crust: Preheat oven to 400°F. Combine flour and salt in large bowl. Cut in shortening. In a small bowl, combine egg, water, and vinegar. Gradually add liquid to flour mixture until dough comes together. Refrigerate 1 hour. Roll out one half of dough to fit a 10-inch-deep pie pan. Prebake crust for 12–15 minutes or until golden brown. Cool.

For the filling: Puree the thawed raspberries until smooth. Strain. Place puree, cornstarch, and sugar in a small saucepan and stir until combined. Cook over medium heat until mixture thickens. Reserve ¼ cup and pour remaining mixture in bottom of crust.

In a large mixing bowl, beat the cream cheese until softened. Beat in sweetened condensed milk until well blended. Add raspberry lemonade, reserved ¼ cup raspberry puree, and ½ cup fresh raspberries, beating until blended. Fold in whipped cream. Pour over first layer, smoothing top.

Decorate with sweetened whipped cream, a lemon slice, and raspberries, if desired.

Refrigerate 1 hour.

RAZZILICIOUS KEY LIME PIE

Christine Fiedorowicz, Denver, CO
2010 APC Crisco National Pie Championships Amateur Division 1st Place Citrus

CRUST
9 honey graham crackers, crushed
5 tablespoons unsalted butter (½ stick), melted
⅓ cup finely chopped pecans
Dash of salt

FILLING
4 large egg yolks
16 oz. sweetened condensed milk
½ cup lime juice
2 tablespoons lime zest

RASPBERRY TOPPING
6 oz. Smucker's seedless raspberry preserves
1 tablespoon butter
1 teaspoon lemon juice
½ teaspoon vanilla extract

GARNISH
1 cup whipping cream
2 tablespoons confectioner's sugar
½ teaspoon vanilla extract
1 drop red food color (optional)
Lime wedges and raspberries

For the crust: Preheat oven to 350°F. Mix ingredients together and press into 9-inch pie pan. Prebake crust for 11 minutes.

For the filling: Preheat oven to 350°F. Beat yolks with zest, then add condensed milk. Add lime juice and whip 1 minute. Pour into pie crust. Bake for 12 minutes.

For the topping: Heat the raspberry preserves in a saucepan; add butter and lemon juice.

Remove from heat and add the vanilla extract, stirring well. Spread over key lime pie. Chill until set, about 4 hours.

For the garnish: Combine whipping cream, sugar, and vanilla. Beat well, then add food coloring if desired. Mix well. Pile sweetened whipped cream over pie. Decorate pie with lime wedges and raspberries.

Razzilicious Key Lime Pie

SUPPORT GROUP KEY LIME PIE

John Michael Lerma, St. Paul, MN
2011 APC Crisco National Pie Championships Professional Division
Honorable Mention Citrus

CRUST
²/₃ cup toasted slivered almonds
1 cup graham cracker crumbs
¼ cup white granulated sugar
1 pinch sea salt
¼ cup unsalted butter, melted

FILLING
4 egg yolks
14 oz. can sweetened condensed milk

½ cup key lime juice
¾ cup cold heavy whipping cream
1 tablespoon confectioner's sugar
1 teaspoon pure vanilla extract or
    vanilla bean paste
½ teaspoon grated lime zest

For the crust: Preheat oven to 350°F. Pulse the almonds in a food processor until finely ground. Combine the almonds with the graham cracker crumbs, sugar, and salt.

Pour in the melted butter and mix until evenly moistened. Press into a 9-inch pie dish. Bake the crust until golden brown, about 10 to 13 minutes.

For the filling: While the crust is baking, beat the egg yolks in a large mixing bowl with the condensed milk, cream, and lime zest. Whisk in the lime juice a little at a time to thicken the custard.

Pour the custard into the pie crust and return to the oven.

Bake in the oven for 15 minutes to help the custard begin to set. Cool to room temperature on a wire rack before covering loosely with plastic wrap and refrigerating overnight.

In a chilled medium mixing bowl beat cream to soft peaks. Add confectioner's sugar and vanilla. Continue beating until stiff peaks form. Decorate top of pie with puff of sweetened whipped cream and lime zest.

Support Group Key Lime Pie

U. S. ROUTE 1 PIE: FLORIDA KEY LIME WITH MAINE BLUEBERRIES

John Sunvold, Winter Springs, FL
2008 APC Crisco National Pie Championships Amateur Division 1st Place Citrus and Best of Show

CRUST
1½ cups graham cracker crumbs
½ cup sugar
4 tablespoons butter

KEY LIME LAYER
(2) 14 oz. cans sweetened
    condensed milk
2 eggs
¾ cup key lime juice

BLUEBERRY PRESERVES LAYER
¾ cup Smucker's blueberry
    preserves

WHITE CHOCOLATE MOUSSE LAYER
2 ½ cups heavy cream
¼ pound white chocolate, broken into
    small pieces

GARNISH
Fresh blueberries
Grated lime peel

For the crust: Preheat oven to 375°F. Mix all ingredients together and press mixture in a 9-inch pie plate. Bake for 8 minutes, or until golden brown. Allow to cool down to room temperature.

For the key lime layer: Mix all of the ingredients together and pour the mixture in the cooled pie shell. Bake in a 375°F oven for 15 minutes. Remove from oven. Chill the pie in the refrigerator for 2 hours.

For the blueberry preserves layer: Spread preserves on the top of the key lime layer. Cover fully from crust to crust. Do not let preserves touch the crust, as it may get soggy with contact. Chill.

For the white chocolate mousse layer: Bring ½ cup of cream to a boil over medium heat. Add white chocolate and stir constantly until the chocolate is melted and the mixture is combined. Remove from heat and let cool to room temperature. Refrigerate for at least 4 hours.

In a large bowl, beat the rest of the heavy cream with an electric mixer on high speed. Beat until soft peaks form. Slowly add the white chocolate mixture and continue to beat until stiff. Cover and refrigerate for 2 hours. Top the blueberry preserves layer with the white chocolate mousse.

Garnish with fresh blueberries and grated lime peel (for color). Chill for 2 hours.

U.S. Route 1 Pie: Florida Key Lime With Maine Blueberries

WHEN GOD HANDS YOU LEMONS, MAKE A LEMON PIE

Matt Zagorski, Arlington Heights, IL
2010 APC Crisco National Pie Championships Professional Division
Honorable Mention Citrus

CRUST
½ cup unsalted butter, melted
1 cup plus 1 tablespoon all-purpose
    flour
1 cup pecans, finely chopped in a
    food processor
1 tablespoon superfine sugar

CREAM CHEESE LAYER
1 cup powdered sugar
8 oz cream cheese, room
    temperature
1 cup Cool Whip

LEMON CURD LAYER
¾ stick unsalted butter, room
    temperature
½ cup superfine sugar
3 large eggs
¾ cup lemon juice

TOP LAYER
3 cups whipping cream
6 tablespoons superfine sugar
3 tablespoons lemon zest, for garnish
1 to 2 lemons, zested into the whip-
    ping cream for flavor

For the crust: Preheat oven to 375°F. In the bowl of a food processor, combine all the ingredients. Roll the crust out to ⅛ inch thickness and place it in the bottom of a 9-inch pie pan. Be careful not to make the sides too thick. Bake for 18 to 20 minutes until the crust is no longer wet and does not give off crumbs when touched. The edges will be lightly browned. Remove from oven and set aside to cool completely.

For the cream cheese layer: Place all the ingredients in a stand mixer and combine. Do not do by hand. Place the cream cheese mixture in the bottom of the cooled pecan pie crust. You may have to use your fingers to spread it around so it does not tear the pie crust. Refrigerate for at least 1 hour so the cream cheese is firm.

For the lemon curd layer: In the bowl of a stand mixer, cream the butter and sugar until fluffy. Once fluffy, add the eggs one at a time. Do not add another egg until the previous one is completely integrated with the butter and sugar. Once all the eggs have been added and integrated with the butter and sugar, add the lemon juice. Pour the uncooked lemon curd mixture into a saucepan and set over medium heat. Stir until the curd thickens. Do not let the curd boil. Small bubbles breaking the surface is all right. Remove the cooked curd from the pan and place ½ cup in one non-reactive bowl and the balance into a second non-reactive bowl. Cover the surfaces with plastic wrap so a skin does not form, and refrigerate until ready to use.

For the top layer: In the bowl of a stand mixer, beat the whipping cream and sugar to stiff peaks. Add the lemon zest and reserved ½ cup of the lemon curd. Mix one more time to combine. Set aside.

Once the cream cheese layer is firm, top with the cooled lemon curd. It is ideal to let this set for an hour before topping this with the whipped cream. Once set, top with the lemon curd whipped cream mixture. Decorate with the lemon-flavored whipped cream. Garnish the top of the whipped cream with fresh lemon zest. Place in the refrigerator 2 hours before serving.

CREAM

"Anyone with a passion for pies shouldn't miss the Great American Pie Festival and the National Pie Championships!!!"

—Dennis Dipo, Dr. Pieology
President, Fresh Foods Corporation of America
Cyrus O'Leary's Pies
Brown's Fruit Juice Sweetened Pies
"We've Got a Passion for Pies"

Butterscotch Crunch Pie 116
Creamy Coconut Cream Pie 118
Hula Hula Pineapple Cream Pie
    with Fried Pie Crust 120
Island Breeze Pineapple–
    Blueberry Cream Pie 122
Max's Coo-Coo for Coconut Cream Pie 124
Oh, So Sweet, Olivia's Maple Pie 126

Olalla Coconut Supreme Pie 128
Paradise Pineapple Cream Pie 130
Piña Colada Pie 132
Raspberry Smoothie Cream Pie 134
Toasted Coconut Cream Pie 136
Bananas Foster Cream Pie 138
Creamy Guava Pie 140

« *Raspberry Smoothie Cream Pie (recipe page 134)*

BUTTERSCOTCH CRUNCH PIE

Barbara Polk, Albuquerque, NM
2009 APC Crisco National Pie Championships Amateur Division 3rd Place Cream

CRUST
1½ cups crushed graham crackers,
  cinnamon-flavored
⅓ cup melted butter
3 tablespoons granulated sugar

FILLING
¾ cup dark brown sugar
⅓ cup cornstarch
¼ teaspoon salt
2 cups milk

3 egg yolks, large
3 tablespoons butter
1 teaspoon vanilla

CRUNCH TOPPING
1 cup quick cooking oats
¼ cup brown sugar
¼ cup butter, melted
½ cup chopped pecans
½ cup butterscotch chips

For the crust: Preheat oven to 350°F. Mix graham crackers, butter, and sugar. Press into a 9-inch pie plate, bottom and sides. Bake for 10 minutes. Let cool.

For the filling: Preheat oven to 350°F. In a small bowl, beat yolks and set aside. In medium saucepan, add sugar, flour, and salt. Stir until well mixed. Slowly add milk, cook over medium heat, stirring constantly for 2 minutes or until thick. Remove from heat and pour about a cup of the mixture slowly into yolks, beating constantly. Return to pan and stir constantly for 2 more minutes. Remove from heat and add butter and vanilla, then mix. Pour into shell. Cool while cooking the crunch topping.

For the topping: In a bowl, mix the oats, brown sugar, melted butter, and pecans. Spread in a 13 x 9-inch dish and bake for 10 minutes. When cool, crumble with a fork. Add the butterscotch chips and put a 1-inch layer around the edge of the cooled pie. Add a row of piped whipping cream inside that and then another 1-inch layer of crunch, one more cream layer, and finally the remainder of crunch in the center. Refrigerate.

CREAMY COCONUT CREAM PIE

Sarah Spaugh, Winston Salem, NC
2002 APC Crisco National Pie Championships Amateur Division 1st Cream &
Best of Show

CRUST

2 cups all-purpose flour
1 teaspoon salt
¾ cup Crisco shortening
5 tablespoons cold water
3 oz. semi-sweet chocolate chips

FILLING

3½ cups milk
½ cup cream of coconut
1 teaspoon pure vanilla
8 egg yolks

1 ⅓ cups sugar
½ cup cornstarch
2 tablespoons butter
¾ cup heavy cream, whipped
¾ cup sweetened coconut

TOPPING

½ cup heavy cream, whipped
3 tablespoons pulverized sugar
¾ cup lightly toasted coconut

For the crust: Preheat oven to 400°F. Combine flour and salt in bowl. Cut in shortening until all flour is blended in and pea-sized chunks form. Sprinkle water, one tablespoon at a time. Toss lightly with fork until dough forms a ball. Press dough between hands to form a 5- to 6-inch pancake. Flour rolling surface and pin lightly. Roll in circle one inch larger than upside-down pie plate. Place dough in deep 9-inch or 10-inch pan. Prick bottom and sides with fork. Bake until golden brown. In the meantime, melt semi-sweet chocolate chips. When pie crust is removed from oven, brush melted chocolate on inside of crust. Cool.

For the filling: Scald milk, then add cream of coconut. Whip egg yolks with sugar until light and fluffy. Add ½ cup of cornstarch and 2 tablespoons butter. Gradually add to milk mixture and cook, stirring constantly until mixture thickens. Add vanilla. Cool and strain through wire sieve if there are any lumps. Add whipped cream and sweetened coconut. Pour into prepared pie shell.

For the topping: Mix whipped cream, sugar, and coconut thoroughly and spread on top of pie. Refrigerate.

HULA HULA PINEAPPLE CREAM PIE WITH FRIED PIE CRUST

Andrea Spring, Bradenton, FL
2010 APC Crisco National Pie Championships Professional Division 1st Place Cream

CRUST
½ cup butter
½ cup shredded coconut
1 cup all-purpose flour
3 tablespoons light brown sugar

FILLING
20 oz. can crushed pineapple with juice
12 oz. tub Cool Whip
6 oz. package Jell-O pineapple gelatin
6 oz. whipped cream cheese

For the crust: Combine butter, coconut, flour, and brown sugar in saucepan. Cook on medium heat until mixture is medium brown, stirring frequently. Pour into 10-inch pie pan and press to cover bottom and sides. Chill 10 minutes before filling.

For the filling: Drain pineapple. Reserve juice. Combine gelatin with juice and microwave for one minute. In medium bowl, mix whipped topping and cream cheese until smooth. Add pineapple and gelatin mixture. Blend well. Spoon into pie shell. Refrigerate for 4 hours or until set.

Hula Hula Pineapple Cream Pie with Fried Pie Crust

ISLAND BREEZE PINEAPPLE–BLUEBERRY CREAM PIE

Carol Socier, Bay City, MI
2009 APC Crisco National Pie Championships Amateur Division 2nd Place Cream

CRUST
2 cups finely ground vanilla wafers
1 tablespoon sugar
6 tablespoons unsalted butter, melted and cooled
1 teaspoon vanilla extract

FILLING 1
4 oz. cream cheese, softened
½ cup powdered sugar
1 teaspoon vanilla
⅛ teaspoon salt
1 cup whipping cream, whipped
1 cup Smucker's blueberry preserves

FILLING 2
¾ cup sugar
¼ cup cornstarch
1½ cups water
3 oz. package Island Pineapple Jell-O
1 cup crushed pineapple, cooled

GARNISH
1 cup whipping cream, whipped for garnish
1 slice pineapple
2 cups fresh blueberries

For the crust: Preheat oven to 350°F. Combine crumbs, sugar, butter, and vanilla in bowl and stir until crumbs are moist. Press evenly into a 9-inch pie plate. Bake in preheated oven 6 to 8 minutes or until golden and crisp. Cool before filling.

For filling 1: Combine cream cheese, powdered sugar, vanilla, and salt. Beat until smooth. Gently fold in whipped cream. Place half of mixture in cooled crust. Refrigerate 15 minutes. Top with blueberry preserves and second layer of cream mixture. Refrigerate.

For filling 2: Combine sugar, cornstarch, and water. Cook over medium heat, stirring until thick and clear. Add Jell-O and mix until dissolved. Stir in cooled crushed pineapple and place in refrigerator until mixture begins to thicken. When thick, pour over the cream cheese layer in pie crust. Place in refrigerator until set.

Garnish with whipped cream, pineapple, and blueberries.

MAX'S COO-COO FOR COCONUT CREAM PIE

Matt Zagorski, Arlington Heights, IL
2010 APC Crisco National Pie Championships Professional Division Honorable Mention Cream

CRUST
½ cup unsalted butter, melted
1 cup plus 1 tablespoon all-purpose flour
½ cup macadamia nuts
½ cup Nilla Wafers
1 tablespoon superfine sugar

FILLING
2 tablespoons cornstarch
⅔ cup granulated sugar
¼ teaspoon fine salt
6 large egg yolks
2 cups coconut milk
4 teaspoons vanilla bean paste or vanilla extract, divided*

5 teaspoons coconut extract, divided*
2 tablespoons cold unsalted butter, cut into pieces
3 oz. white chocolate, finely chopped (about ½ cup)
2 cups whipping cream
5 tablespoons sugar
1 cup coconut, shredded and toasted

*DIVIDED ingredients means the item is used more than once in the recipe. The total specified in the ingredient list is the total needed to complete the whole recipe.

For the crust: Preheat oven to 375°F. In the bowl of a food processor, combine all the ingredients. Roll the crust out to ⅛ inch thickness and then place it in the bottom of a 9-inch pie pan. Be careful not to make the sides too thick. Bake for 15 minutes until the crust is no longer wet and does not give off crumbs when touched. The edges will be slightly browned. Remove from oven and set aside to cool completely.

To toast coconut: Preheat oven to 350°F. Spread shredded coconut on a rimmed baking sheet and bake, stirring once or twice, until golden, about 5 to 10 minutes. If you are toasting sweetened coconut, check and stir more frequently because the added sugar causes irregular browning. Be careful not to let it burn. Set aside to cool. This can be done a day ahead.

For the filling: Whisk together the cornstarch, sugar, and salt in a medium mixing bowl. Add the egg yolks, and whisk to combine. Heat the coconut milk in a medium saucepan over medium-high heat; bring to a boil. Pour half the hot coconut milk into the egg mixture to temper, whisking constantly to combine.

Pour the tempered egg mixture back into the saucepan, then place over medium-high heat. Bring the mixture to a boil, whisking constantly and vigorously until thickened and pulling away from the sides of the pan, about 3 minutes. Remove from heat.

Whisk 3 teaspoons of the coconut and vanilla extracts, butter, and white chocolate into the

custard until completely smooth. Strain through a fine sieve into a clean bowl, if necessary. Press a sheet of plastic wrap directly onto the surface of the pastry cream, then place in the refrigerator to cool until ready to use.

Fill the cooled pie shell with the cooled filling. If you have time, cover the filling with plastic wrap and put the pie back in the refrigerator for 2 to 3 hours to set. Whip the 2 cups of whipping cream with 4 to 5 tablespoons of sugar and the remaining 2 teaspoons of the coconut and vanilla extracts until you achieve soft peaks. Taste frequently and adjust to your personal preference.

Remove the chilled and filled pie from the refrigerator, remove the plastic wrap, and put the whipped cream on top of the coconut cream filling. Sprinkle the toasted coconut on top of the whipping cream for a finishing garnish.

OH, SO SWEET, OLIVIA'S MAPLE PIE

Naylet LaRochelle, Miami, FL
2008 APC Crisco National Pie Championships Amateur Division 3rd Place Cream

CRUST
1½ cups vanilla wafers, finely crushed
6 tablespoons butter or margarine, melted
¼ cup granulated sugar

FILLING
1 ½ teaspoons unflavored gelatin
½ cup milk
¼ cup granulated sugar
½ cup pure maple syrup
¼ teaspoon salt

1 teaspoon maple extract
½ cup white chocolate chips, melted and cooled (to melt quickly, microwave chocolate chips with 1 tablespoon of Crisco vegetable shortening for about 1 minute)
1 cup heavy whipping cream

TOPPING
Walnuts, chopped in small pieces and lightly toasted
Oatmeal cookies, crushed
Pure maple syrup, for drizzling

For the crust: In a medium bowl, combine the vanilla wafer crumbs, butter, and sugar. Press onto the bottom and up the sides of a greased 9-inch pie plate. Refrigerate for 30 minutes.

For the filling: In a small saucepan, sprinkle gelatin over milk. Let stand for 2 minutes. Cook and stir over low heat until gelatin is completely dissolved, 2 to 3 minutes. Add sugar, syrup, maple extract, and salt. Cook and stir for 8 to 10 minutes or until sugar is dissolved. Remove from heat. Pour melted white chocolate into the maple mixture. Stir until mixture is smooth and silky. Transfer to a large bowl and let cool 15 to 20 minutes.

In a medium mixing bowl, beat 1 cup cream until stiff peaks form. Fold into maple mixture. Spread evenly on crust. Refrigerate for 4 hours or until set.

Before serving, sprinkle walnuts and cookies and drizzle syrup over pie.

OLALLA COCONUT SUPREME PIE

Terri Beaver, Olalla, WA
2008 APC Crisco National Pie Championships Amateur Division 2nd Place Cream

CRUST
10 tablespoons butter-flavored Crisco shortening
6 tablespoons Crisco shortening
½ cup ice water
1 ice cube
1 tablespoon apple cider vinegar
2¾ cups flour (plus extra for rolling)
1 teaspoon salt
1 tablespoon sugar

FILLING
14 oz. can coconut milk
1 cup heavy cream
2 tablespoons butter
2 eggs
½ cup sugar
1/8 teaspoon salt
½ cup milk
¼ cup potato starch
1 cup miniature marshmallows
1 teaspoon vanilla extract
1 teaspoon coconut extract
3½ oz. flaked coconut (about 1 1/3 cup), divided

TOPPING
1 cup heavy whipped cream
¼ cup powdered sugar
1 teaspoon vanilla extract
1/3 cup toasted coconut

For the crust: Preheat oven to 400°F. Combine flour, salt, and sugar in a large bowl. Cut in both shortenings until texture is the size of peas. Mix water and vinegar in a small bowl. Add ice cube to keep it cold (you will not use all of this). Add 6 to 8 tablespoons water mixture to flour mixture, using a fork to stir in a little at a time. Divide into 2 equal portions and wrap with plastic wrap, making 2 discs. Refrigerate at least 30 minutes. Remove one disc and roll out on a well-floured board. Carefully place in pie plate and flute edges. Place in freezer while oven is preheating, or refrigerate at least 30 minutes. Freeze the other disc for another time.

Line pie shell with parchment paper and bake with pie weights for 15 minutes. Remove pie weights and prick bottom with a fork. Lower oven temperature to 375°F and bake for 15 to 17 minutes. Cover edges with pie guard if needed.

For the filling: In a saucepan, heat together coconut milk, cream, and butter. Bring just to a boil over medium heat. In a medium-size bowl, beat together eggs, sugar, and salt until light lemon-colored. Combine milk and potato starch in a small bowl and set aside. Slowly beat 1 cup of the hot milk mixture into the egg mixture to temper the eggs. Pour all of the egg mixture into the saucepan with the milk mixture, stirring

Olalla Coconut Supreme Pie

constantly. Add starch with milk mixture and stir until thick and bubbly. Add marshmallows and stir until melted and combined. Remove from heat and add extracts and 1 cup coconut. Let cool 5 minutes, stirring twice.

Pour into prepared crust. Place plastic wrap on top and refrigerate a minimum of 2 hours. Toast remaining 1/3 cup coconut to use for topping. To toast coconut, spread coconut in a thin layer on a baking sheet. Bake at 300 for about 20 minutes, stirring occasionally. Cool.

For the topping: Whip cream until almost done. Whip in sugar and vanilla. Spread over cooled pie. Top with toasted coconut.

PARADISE PINEAPPLE CREAM PIE

Marles Riessland, Riverdale, NE
2006 APC Crisco National Pie Championships Amateur Division 1st Place Cream

CRUST
1 cup pastry flour
2 cups all-purpose flour
1 teaspoon salt
1 teaspoon sugar
½ teaspoon baking powder
1 cup plus 1 tablespoon butter-flavored Crisco shortening, chilled
⅓ cup water (ice cold)
1 tablespoon vinegar
1 egg, beaten
¼ cup finely chopped macadamia nuts

FILLING 1
20 oz. can crushed pineapple (juiced pack, divided)
4 egg yolks, slightly beaten
1 tablespoon water
⅓ cup firmly packed cornstarch

1 ⅓ cups white chocolate chips
¼ teaspoon salt
2 cups milk
2 tablespoons butter
1 teaspoon vanilla

FILLING 2
8 oz. package cream cheese
½ cup powdered sugar
½ teaspoon vanilla
⅓ cup reserved pineapple juice

TOPPING
1 cup whipping cream, whipped
¼ cup macadamia nuts, chopped and toasted.

GARNISH (AS DESIRED)
Lemon peel or macadamia nuts

For the crust: Preheat oven to 425°F. In large bowl, combine the flours, salt, sugar, and baking powder. Cut in shortening with a pastry blender until the mixture resembles cornmeal. In a small bowl, mix water and vinegar with the beaten egg. Add the liquid mixture, one tablespoon at a time, to the flour mixture, tossing with a fork to form a soft dough. Shape into three discs. Wrap in plastic wrap and chill in refrigerator. Use one disc for this recipe. Roll out one disc of dough to fit 9-inch pie pan. Sprinkle macadamia nuts evenly over the crust. Using rolling pin, lightly roll nuts into crust. Adjust crust into pan, flute edge, and prick bottom. Bake 15 to 20 minutes or until golden brown. Cool.

For filling 1: Drain pineapple, reserving ⅓ cup juice for cream cheese layer. Combine the egg yolks and water in small bowl; stir in cornstarch. Set aside. Combine white chocolate, salt, milk, and remaining pineapple in saucepan. Cook and stir on medium heat until mixture almost boils. Reduce heat to low. Slowly stir in egg yolk mixture. Cook and stir until thickened. Add butter and vanilla. Remove from heat. Cover surface with plastic wrap. Refrigerate 30 minutes or longer, stirring once or twice.

For filling 2: Beat together cream cheese and powdered sugar until smooth. Add vanilla and the ⅓ cup of pineapple juice. Mix well. Spread filling over bottom of cool baked pie shell. Cover with pineapple cream filling.

For the topping: Spread whipping cream on top of pie. Sprinkle with the macadamia nuts.

To garnish: Place lemon peel or macadamia nuts decoratively on top of pie.

Refrigerate pie before serving.

PIÑA COLADA PIE

Jeanne Ely, Mulberry, FL
2005 APC Crisco National Pie Championships Amateur Division 1st Place Cream and
Best of Show

CRUST
3 cups flour
1 teaspoon salt
½ cup butter-flavored Crisco
   shortening
¾ cup regular-flavored Crisco
   shortening
1 egg
5 tablespoons cold water
1 tablespoon vinegar

FILLING
1 can Coco Goya Piña Colada mix
   (12 oz.)
½ cup coconut
½ cup crushed pineapple, drained
2 teaspoons rum extract
½ cup sugar
2 tablespoons cornstarch
¼ cup pineapple juice
6 oz. extra creamy Cool Whip

For the crust: Preheat oven to 475°F. Cut together flour, salt, and shortening until oatmeal-like consistency. Beat egg in cup, add water and vinegar. Beat all and pour into flour mixture. Blend well. Form dough into ball. Roll out on a floured surface and place in pie pan. Bake for 8 to 10 minutes until golden brown.

For the filling: Combine Piña Colada mix, coconut, pineapple, rum extract, and sugar in a small saucepan. Bring to a boil and boil 2 minutes. Dissolve cornstarch in pineapple juice and add to mixture. Cook until thickened. Remove from heat and cool. When completely cooled, fold in Cool Whip. Spoon into pie shell. Chill 3 to 4 hours and garnish as desired.

Piña Colada Pie

RASPBERRY SMOOTHIE CREAM PIE

Carol Socier, Bay City, MI
2010 APC Crisco National Pie Championships Amateur Division 1ˢᵗ Place Cream

CRUST
1½ cups all-purpose flour
1 tablespoon sugar
¼ teaspoon salt
½ cup Crisco shortening
¼ cup toasted almonds, finely
    crushed
¼ cup white chocolate chips
3 to 4 tablespoons ice cold water
2 teaspoons light cream

FILLING
4.6 oz. package Jell-O Cook & Serve
    vanilla pudding mix
1½ cups half and half
8 oz. raspberry cream cheese spread
10 oz. carton frozen raspberries in
    syrup
1 tablespoon cornstarch
3 cups fresh raspberries, divided
1 cup whipping cream, whipped and
    sweetened

For the crust: Preheat oven to 450°F. Combine flour, sugar, and salt. Cut in shortening until pea-sized pieces form. Stir in crushed almonds. Sprinkle in water, l tablespoon at a time, gently tossing with a fork until mixture is moistened and forms a ball. On lightly floured surface, roll out dough into a 12-inch circle; transfer to a 9-inch pie plate. Trim ½ inch from the edge. Fold under the extra pastry and flute the edge. Prick bottom and sides of the crust. Bake 12 to 15 minutes or until golden brown. Cool. Melt chips and cream; brush bottom and sides of cooled crust.

For the filling: Cook the pudding mix according to package directions, but use 1½ cups half and half for the liquid. Cool for 20 minutes. Beat in the cream cheese spread. Spread into bottom of prepared pie crust. Chill for 1 hour.

Meanwhile, prepare the glaze. Puree the frozen raspberries. In a small saucepan, combine berries and cornstarch. Cook and stir over medium heat until thick and bubbly. Cool to room temperature. Assemble the pie by placing half the fresh raspberries stem side down, over the cream layer. Drizzle glaze over the berries. Garnish with whipped cream and remaining raspberries.

Raspberry Smoothie Cream Pie

TOASTED COCONUT CREAM PIE

Dawn M. Viola, Orlando, FL
2011 APC Crisco National Pie Championships Professional Division Honorable Mention Cream

CRUST
8 oz. shortbread cookies
1 cup sweetened coconut, toasted
3 tablespoons European-style butter,
 melted
¼ teaspoon pure vanilla extract
1 egg white

CUSTARD FILLING
1½ cups whole milk
1½ cups heavy cream
1 vanilla bean, split, seeds scraped

2 cups sweetened coconut, toasted
3 large eggs
2 egg yolks
¾ cup organic sugar
½ teaspoon fresh lemon juice

COCONUT CREAM TOPPING
2 pints heavy cream
1½ cups sweetened coconut, toasted,
 divided
½ cup powdered sugar
1 teaspoon pure vanilla extract

For the crust: Preheat oven to 400°F. Place the cookies and coconut in the bowl of a food processor and pulse until a fine crumb is produced. Add the butter, vanilla extract, and egg white. Pulse until well combined and moist. Press the mixture into a pie plate to form a ¼ inch thick bottom crust. Bake for 25 minutes, or until the crust is golden brown and set. Remove from the oven and allow to cool.

For the filling: While the crust is cooling, heat the milk, cream, coconut, and vanilla on low heat in a medium saucepan for 45 minutes, stirring occasionally. Remove from heat and strain the mixture, reserving the liquid. Discard the vanilla bean and coconut.

Boil water for a water bath and preheat oven to 350°F.

In a large glass or ceramic bowl, whisk the eggs and sugar until thick. Whisk a small amount of the cream mixture into the eggs to temper the eggs. Continue to whisk in the rest of the cream mixture. Whisk in the lemon juice. Skim any air bubbles off the surface of the custard.

Place the pie plate with crust into a larger baking dish. Pour the custard into the pie crust until it just reaches the top of the crust. Place the baking dish on the oven rack. Fill the baking dish with boiling water ¾ of the way up the sides of the pie plate.

Toasted Coconut Cream Pie

Bake the custard until just set and still slightly jiggly in the center, about 36 minutes. Carefully remove the custard from the water bath and allow to cool at room temperature. When the custard has cooled, place in the refrigerator.

For the topping: In a large non-reactive bowl, combine cream with 1 cup of the toasted coconut. Steep 8 hours. Strain cream mixture; discard steeped coconut. Using a hand mixer on low speed, whip cream until it begins to thicken, about 2 minutes. Add sugar and vanilla extract; whip until stiff peaks form. Spoon or pipe the coconut cream on top of the custard filling, spreading it to the edges of the crust. Sprinkle remaining ½ cup of toasted coconut over the cream. Refrigerate until ready to serve.

BANANAS FOSTER CREAM PIE

Dionna Hurt, Longwood, FL
2008 APC Crisco National Pie Championships Professional Division 1st Place Cream and
Best of Show

COOKIE CRUST
3 cups Nilla Wafer cookies
½ cup butter, melted
2 to 3 tablespoons sugar

FILLING
3 tablespoons cornstarch
1 ⅔ cups heavy cream

14 oz. can Eagle sweetened
  condensed milk
3 egg yolks, beaten
1 tablespoon butter
1 teaspoon rum extract
2 medium bananas, sliced
3 tablespoons Dulce de Leche
Sweetened whipped cream

For the crust: Preheat oven to 350°F. In a food processor, grind cookies into crumbs. Transfer crumbs to a mixing bowl. Add sugar and melted butter. Toss with fork. Pour into a pie dish and press into the bottom and up the sides. Bake for 15 minutes and let cool.

For the filling: In a heavy saucepan, dissolve the cornstarch in the cream, then stir in sweet-ened condensed milk and egg yolks. Cook and stir until thick and bubbly. Remove from heat. Add butter and rum extract. Pour half of custard into cookie crust, top with sliced bananas and Dulce de Leche. Top with remaining custard and chill for 2 or more hours. Top with sweetened whipped cream and drizzle with additional Dulce de Leche.

Bananas Foster Cream Pie

CREAMY GUAVA PIE

Devin Davis, Plant City, FL
2011 APC Crisco National Pie Championships Junior Chef Division 1st Place Cream and Best of Show

CRUST
1 ⅓ cups all-purpose flour
½ teaspoon salt
1 tablespoon sugar
½ cup cold Crisco butter-flavored shortening, cut into cubes
2 to 3 tablespoons ice-cold water

FILLING
¾ cup heavy whipping cream
3 tablespoons powdered sugar
1 teaspoon vanilla extract
6 oz. cream cheese, room temperature
½ cup sugar

GUAVA TOPPING
1¼ cups water
1 cup guava paste, cut in small cubes
3 oz. package lemon-flavored Jell-O
1 tablespoon sugar
5 drops red food coloring

WHIPPED CREAM TOPPING
1 cup heavy whipping cream
4 tablespoons powdered sugar
1 teaspoon vanilla

For the crust: Preheat oven to 425°F. Position knife blade in food processor bowl; add flour, salt, and sugar, then pulse. Add in Crisco and pulse until it looks like peas. Then add water one tablespoon at a time and then process until it forms into a ball. Press with floured hands to a 5- to 6-inch circle. Place dough between floured wax paper and roll out to desired thickness. Remove top piece of wax paper and flip dough into 9-inch deep-dish pie plate. Remove other sheet. Fit in pie plate with hands and trim excess dough from around edge. Prick with fork all over sides and bottom. Bake for 10 to 15 minutes. Let cool completely.

For the filling: In medium-size bowl add heavy whipping cream and beat with an electric mixer until soft peaks form. Then add powdered sugar and vanilla, and continue beating until firm peaks form. Set aside. In separate bowl add cream cheese and sugar, blend until sugar dissolves. Then fold whipped cream into cream cheese mixture. Spread on bottom of pie crust and refrigerate.

For the guava topping: Put the water in medium-size saucepan and bring to a simmer on top of stove over medium heat. Then add guava cubes, stirring constantly until cubes are melted, then remove from heat and add the Jell-O, sugar and food coloring, stirring until well blended. Then pour gently over cream filling and place in refrigerator till set. For fast setting, put in freezer for 30 minutes then into the refrigerator until set.

For the whipped cream topping: Put cream in medium-size bowl and beat with electric mixer until soft peaks form. Add powdered sugar and vanilla, continuing to beat until firm. Spoon topping into pastry bag and decorate as desired once pie has set, leaving some of the guava top showing.

Creamy Guava Pie

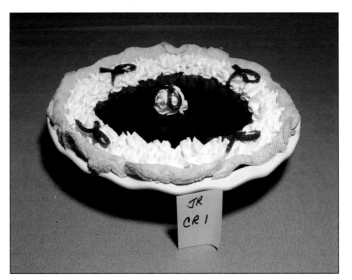

CREAM CHEESE

"For over 40 years, Legendary Baking has been perfecting the art of creating gourmet pies and baked desserts for our customers. Since 2001, over 300 of our pies have taken top honors, more than once, at the APC/Crisco® National Pie Championships, earning them the prestigious distinction of being called the Best Pies in America. We're proud of our association with the APC and look forward to many more years of collective success for the pie industry."

—Mary Pint,
HR Director "Pie Lady"
Legendary Baking

Chocolate Hazelnut Dream Pie 144
Dark Chocolate Raspberry Truffle Pie 146
Double Chocolate Caramel Macchiato Pie 148
Lemon Swirl Cream Cheese Pie 150
Pineapple Cream Delight 152
Double Strawberry Malt Shop Pie 154
Royal Macadamia Raspberry Pie 156
White and Milk Chocolate
Raspberry Mousse 158

« *Lemon Swirl Cream Cheese Pie (recipe page 150)*

CHOCOLATE HAZELNUT DREAM PIE

Jennifer Nystrom, Morrow, OH
2009 APC Crisco National Pie Championships Amateur Division 3rd Place Cream Cheese

CRUST
1½ cups chocolate graham cracker crumbs (about 10 whole graham crackers)
5 tablespoons butter, melted
2 tablespoons sugar

FILLING:
8 oz. package cream cheese, room temperature

⅓ cup granulated sugar
1 cup Nutella
2 cups heavy whipping cream, divided
1 teaspoon vanilla
2 tablespoons confectioner's sugar

GARNISH
Toasted hazelnuts
Chocolate curls

For the crust: Preheat oven to 350°F. Mix thoroughly together chocolate graham cracker crumbs, melted butter, and sugar. Put in 9-inch pie pan that has been sprayed with cooking spray and press evenly on bottom and up sides of dish. Bake in preheated oven for 15 minutes or until set. Remove from oven and cool on cooling rack.

For the filling: In a large bowl with an electric mixer, beat together cream cheese and sugar until smooth. Beat in Nutella until thoroughly combined and smooth. In a separate, clean, metal or glass bowl, beat 1 cup of whipping cream until medium peaks form. Lightly fold ½ of whipped cream into cream cheese mixture until incorporated. Gently fold in second half of whipped cream until completely combined, being careful not to deflate cream.

Spoon into cooled pie crust. Refrigerate for at least 4 hours. Whip together remaining 1 cup of cream, vanilla, confectioner's sugar. Spread on top of pie. Garnish with toasted hazelnuts and chocolate curls.

DARK CHOCOLATE RASPBERRY TRUFFLE PIE

Amy Clemons Mills, Babson Park, FL
2009 APC Crisco National Pie Championships Amateur Division 2nd Place Cream Cheese

OREO ALMOND CRUST
24 Oreo cookies
1 cup almond slivers
4 tablespoons butter, melted

FILLING
8 oz. cream cheese, softened and cut in half
4 oz. dark chocolate melted in the microwave at 15- to 30-second intervals

4 oz. milk chocolate melted in the microwave at 15- to 30-second intervals; do not melt until ready to prepare 3rd layer
¾ cup Cool Whip
12 oz. jar red raspberry preserves (seedless)
1 cup Cool Whip, chocolate curls, and shavings for garnish

For the crust: Preheat oven to 350°F. Grind cookies and almonds in a food processor. Add 4 tablespoons melted butter. Press into pie tin. Blind-bake for 10 minutes. Allow to cool before filling.

For the filling: Beat 4 oz. cream cheese until smooth. Add melted dark chocolate. Beat until smooth. Spread onto chocolate crust. Freeze until set. Meanwhile, microwave preserves 30 to 45 seconds or until liquid. Allow to cool slightly. Pour over chocolate truffle layer. Freeze until preserves are cool and have returned to a gel state. Beat remaining cream cheese until smooth. Add melted milk chocolate. Beat until smooth. Beat in Cool Whip. Spread over raspberry layer. Freeze until set.

Garnish with Cool Whip rosettes, chocolate curls, and shavings.

Dark Chocolate Raspberry Truffle Pie

DOUBLE CHOCOLATE CARAMEL MACCHIATO PIE

Amy Clemons, Babson Park, FL
2008 APC Crisco National Pie Championships Amateur Division 1st Place Cream Cheese

CRUST
10 Stella Dora almond toasts
3 tablespoons sugar
5 ½ tablespoons margarine, melted

FILLING
8 oz. package Philadelphia Cream
   Cheese, room temperature
4 oz. Hershey's special dark
   chocolate, broken into pieces

¼ cup cold strong coffee or espresso
4 oz. Hershey's milk chocolate,
   broken into pieces
¾ cup Smucker's caramel topping
3 tablespoons corn starch
⅔ cup powdered sugar
2 ½ cups Cool Whip topping
1 tablespoon water
Chocolate shavings for garnish

For the crust: Preheat oven to 350°F. Crush almond toasts in food processor (should yield 1½ cups crumbs). Mix together crumbs, sugar, and melted margarine. Press into a 9-inch pie tin. Bake for 10 minutes. Cool completely before filling.

For the bottom layer: Beat 4 oz. cream cheese until smooth. Add ⅓ cup powdered sugar and mix well. Add ½ cup Cool Whip and mix well. Melt dark chocolate in microwave (should take approximately 1 minute depending on microwave). Mix chocolate into cream cheese mixture. Mix in cold coffee. Spread into pie crust and freeze/chill until firm.

For the second layer: Stir together cornstarch and water. Microwave ½ cup caramel topping for 45 seconds. Stir together caramel and cornstarch mixture. Return to microwave for 1 minute or until thickened. Spread over dark chocolate layer. Refrigerate until firm.

For the third layer: Beat 4 oz. cream cheese until smooth. Add ⅓ cup powdered sugar and mix well. Add ½ cup Cool Whip and mix well. Melt milk chocolate in microwave (should take approximately 1 minute depending on microwave). Mix chocolate into cream cheese mixture. Spread over caramel layer. Freeze/chill until firm.

For the top layer: Microwave ¼ cup caramel topping for 15 seconds. Allow to cool but not set. Stir into 1 ½ cups Cool Whip. Spread over milk chocolate layer. Refrigerate overnight.

Before serving, sprinkle top with chocolate shavings.

Double Chocolate Caramel Macchiato Pie

LEMON SWIRL CREAM CHEESE PIE

Kate Stewart Rovner, Plano, TX
2010 APC Crisco National Pie Championships Amateur Division 1st Place
Cream Cheese and Best of Show

VANILLA WAFER CRUMB CRUST

1½ cups vanilla wafer crumbs
¾ cup almonds, finely ground and toasted
2 teaspoons lemon zest
Pinch of salt
7 tablespoons melted butter

LEMON CURD

1 teaspoon finely grated lemon zest
½ cup fresh lemon juice
½ cup sugar
3 eggs, lightly beaten
¼ cup butter, cut into small cubes

LEMON CREAM CHEESE FILLING

(2) 8 oz. packages cream cheese, softened
⅔ cup sugar
2 eggs
½ cup sour cream
½ teaspoon vanilla
½ teaspoon lemon extract
Reserved lemon curd

GARNISH

½ cup heavy whipping cream
2 tablespoons powdered sugar
½ teaspoon vanilla
About 12 to 15 fresh raspberries
1 lemon, cut into thin slices and quartered

For the crust: Preheat oven to 350°F. Spray a 9-inch pie plate with Crisco No-Stick spray. In a medium mixing bowl, use a fork to toss together vanilla wafer crumbs, almonds, lemon zest, and salt. Stir in melted butter. Press mixture onto bottom and sides of prepared pie plate. Bake for 12 minutes on bottom oven rack. Remove from oven and set aside.

For the lemon curd: In a 1½-qt saucepan, whisk together lemon zest, lemon juice, and sugar. Whisk in eggs and butter. Cook over medium-low heat, whisking frequently for 7 minutes or until curd is thick. Remove from heat and use a food mill or sieve to strain curd into a small bowl. Remove ½ cup of lemon curd, reserving remaining lemon curd. Press plastic wrap directly onto surfaces. Cool 30 minutes.

For the lemon cream cheese filling: In a medium mixing bowl, beat cream cheese and sugar at medium speed for 2 minutes or until smooth. Add eggs, one at a time, and beat at low speed until incorporated. Beat in sour cream, vanilla, and lemon extract. Beat in reserved lemon curd. Pour into baked crust. Dollop remaining ½ cup lemon curd onto filling and swirl into filling with a small knife. Bake at 350°F for 30 minutes or until center is nearly set. Remove from oven and place on a wire rack. Cool for 2 hours. Cover and refrigerate overnight.

For the garnish: In a chilled, medium mixing bowl, beat whipping cream, powdered sugar, and vanilla with a hand-held electric mixer, starting at lowest speed and increasing gradually each minute, until stiff peaks are formed. Using a #32 tip pipe whipped cream decoratively around border of pie. Decorate with fresh raspberries and lemon slices. Refrigerate until serving time.

Lemon Swirl Cream Cheese Pie

PINEAPPLE CREAM DELIGHT

Debbie Gray, Winter Haven, FL
2008 APC Crisco National Pie Championships 2nd Place Cream Cheese

PRETZEL CRUST
¾ cup flour
¾ cup finely chopped pretzels
1 tablespoon sugar
½ teaspoon salt
6 tablespoons butter
3 tablespoons ice water

FILLING
6 tablespoons sugar
2 tablespoons cornstarch
¾ cup water
2 extra large egg yolks
1 extra large egg
Dash of salt
3 tablespoons pineapple juice

2 tablespoons butter
8 oz. can pineapple tidbits, drained

CREAM CHEESE LAYER
8 oz. Philadelphia Cream Cheese,
   softened
½ cup powdered sugar
1 teaspoon almond extract
½ cup toasted coconut

TOPPING
1¼ cups heavy cream
⅓ cup powdered sugar
⅛ cup toasted coconut
⅛ cup sliced almonds

For the crust: Preheat oven to 425°F. Combine flour, pretzels, sugar, and salt. Cut in butter. Add ice water. Spray 9-inch pan with non-stick spray. Press dough evenly up sides and on bottom. Bake for 15 minutes.

For the filling: Combine sugar, cornstarch, and water in a medium saucepan. Cook on medium-high heat, stirring constantly until thick, about 10 minutes. In separate bowl, whisk egg yolks, egg, and salt. Whisk thickened cornstarch mixture into egg mixture. Pour back into saucepan. Add pineapple juice and butter until mixture thickens, about 5 minutes. Add drained pineapple and refrigerate for 30 minutes.

For the cream cheese layer: In a mixing bowl, combine softened cream cheese, powdered sugar, and almond extract until smooth. In a separate mixing bowl, whip heavy cream and powdered sugar until stiff. Add ¾ whipped cream and ½ cup toasted coconut to cream cheese mixture.

Spread the cream cheese layer onto bottom cooled crust. Place cooled pineapple filling over cream cheese layer.

To garnish: Decorate top of pie with remaining whipped cream. Sprinkle with almonds and toasted coconut.

DOUBLE STRAWBERRY MALT SHOP PIE

Christine Montalvo, Windsor Heights, IA
2011 APC Crisco National Pie Championships 2nd Place Cream Cheese

CRUST
6 tablespoons unsalted butter, at room temperature
¼ cup granulated sugar
1 cup all-purpose flour
1 cup finely ground shortbread cookies
2 to 3 tablespoons ice water

FILLING
5 cups sliced fresh strawberries, divided
6 oz. good quality white chocolate
1¾ teaspoon unflavored gelatin

1 tablespoon hot water
8 oz. package Philadelphia Cream Cheese
1 teaspoon vanilla
1½ cups powdered sugar
⅓ cup malted milk powder
2 cups heavy whipping cream, whipped

TOPPING
1½ cups heavy whipping cream
3 tablespoons sugar

For the crust: Preheat oven to 350°F. Using an electric mixer, cream the butter and sugar together on medium-high speed until fluffy. Add flour and ground shortbread cookies to the mixture and blend until fully incorporated. Add enough ice water so dough can come together. Press the mixture evenly into the bottom of a 9-inch deep-dish pie plate. Bake the crust for 20 to 25 minutes, or until golden brown. Allow the crust to cool completely.

For the filling: Put 2½ cups of strawberries in a food processor and puree. Set aside. Put all of the chocolate in a large microwave-safe bowl and melt in the microwave, being careful not to burn the chocolate. Cool slightly. Add cream cheese and vanilla, and beat until smooth. In a small bowl, combine gelatin and hot water. Stir and then let sit for 5 minutes. Microwave 15 seconds. Beat into cream cheese mixture until completely mixed. Beat in the powdered sugar and malted milk powder until smooth. Stir in the puree. Fold in the whipped cream. Fold in remaining sliced strawberries. Pour into cooled pie crust. Arrange the additional sliced strawberries over pie.

Whip cream in a large bowl with sugar until stiff peaks form. Pipe decoratively over pie.

Double Strawberry Malt Shop Pie

ROYAL MACADAMIA RASPBERRY PIE

Phyllis Szymanek, Toledo, OH
2011 APC Crisco National Pie Championships 1st Place Cream Cheese and Best of Show

CRUST
1½ cups Pillsbury all-purpose flour
½ cup Crisco
½ teaspoon salt
3 tablespoons butter (chilled)
3 to 4 tablespoons ice water
2 tablespoons chopped macadamia
 nuts

GLAZE
1 cup sugar
2½ tablespoons corn starch

1¼ cups water
Pinch of salt
3 oz. box raspberry Jell-O
3 cups raspberries

CREAM CHEESE FILLING
8 oz. package cream cheese
 (softened)
½ cup powdered sugar
½ teaspoon lemon juice
8 oz. Cool Whip
½ cup chopped macadamia nuts

For the crust: Preheat oven to 425°F. In a mixing bowl, combine flour and salt; cut in Crisco and butter until crumbly. Add water one tablespoon at a time until dough forms into a ball. Chill for one hour. Roll out on floured surface to fit a 9-inch pie dish. Lightly press macadamia nuts into pie crust. Place in pie dish and bake for 12 to 15 minutes or until lightly brown. Set aside to cool.

For the glaze: In a small saucepan, combine sugar, cornstarch, water, and salt over medium heat. Bring to a boil. Boil until thick and clear. Remove from heat and add Jell-O. Mix well. Set aside and cool for 15 to 20 minutes

For the cream cheese filling: Place cream cheese in a medium mixing bowl and beat on low speed until creamy. Add powdered sugar until mixed well. Add lemon juice. Fold in ½ of the Cool Whip. Spread ½ of the cream cheese mixture onto bottom cooled pie crust. Spread ½ of raspberries over cream cheese. Pour ½ glaze over raspberries. Refrigerate for 15 to 20 minutes. Then add remaining cream cheese over raspberries; top with remaining raspberries, then the rest of the glaze. Chill for about an hour. Put remaining Cool Whip in a pastry bag with a star tip to garnish top of pie, making three circles around outer edge of pie. Sprinkle with nuts.

Royal Macadamia Raspberry Pie

WHITE AND MILK CHOCOLATE RASPBERRY MOUSSE

Veselina Iovanovici, Lakewood, CA
2011 APC Crisco National Pie Championships 3rd Place Cream Cheese

CRUST
12 oz. shortbread chocolate striped cookies
1/3 cup melted butter
1/2 cup chopped white chocolate

WHITE CHOCOLATE FILLING
5 oz. white baking chocolate or chocolate chips
1½ cups whipping cream
2/3 cup confectioner's sugar
1 tablespoon vanilla
4 oz. cream cheese

MILK CHOCOLATE FILLING
5 oz. milk baking chocolate or chocolate chips
1½ cups whipping cream
2/3 cup confectioner's sugar
1 tablespoon vanilla
4 oz. cream cheese

RASPBERRY MOUSSE FILLING
12 oz. frozen raspberries
1 cup granulated sugar
1/8 teaspoon salt
1 envelope unflavored gelatin
4 tablespoons cold water
2 cups whipping cream
8 oz. cream cheese
1 cup confectioner's sugar

GARNISH
Whipped cream
Fresh raspberries

For the crust: Preheat oven to 375°F. In a food processor, pulse the cookies until they resemble cornmeal in consistency. Add melted butter and the chopped white chocolate. Pulse until all ingredients are incorporated. Cover bottom and sides of two 9-inch-bottom pie pans, pressing the mixture gently. Bake for 9 to 11 minutes. Chill in refrigerator.

For the white chocolate cream: Melt the white chocolate and 4 tablespoons cream in a double boiler and let it cool. With a Mixer, whip cream cheese and confectioner's sugar until fluffy. Mix in the white chocolate mixture and vanilla. In a separate bowl, beat the remaining cream and gently fold into the cream cheese and white chocolate mixture and refrigerate.

For the milk chocolate cream: Repeat all the steps for the white chocolate cream and use milk chocolate instead of white chocolate.

For the raspberry mousse filling: In a small saucepan, combine frozen raspberries, sugar, and salt. Cook over medium heat until sugar is melted and raspberries are soft. Remove raspberries from heat and strain to remove most of the seeds. In a cup, sprinkle gelatin over 4 tablespoons cold water. Let it bloom for a few minutes and add to the raspberry mixture. Return to heat, and stir until gelatin is melted. Set aside and let it cool. In a bowl, whip cream cheese and confectioner's

White and Milk Chocolate Raspberry Mousse Pie

sugar until fluffy and mix in the raspberry sauce. In a separate bowl, beat the whipped cream and gently fold into the cream cheese/raspberry mixture.

To assemble the pie: First place white and chocolate cream in separate piping bags. Cut about 1 inch off the tip of the bags. Take each of the 2 crusted pie pans and start piping a circle of white chocolate around the bottom of the pans, starting with the exterior. Then next to that pipe a milk chocolate circle. Repeat until bottom of each pan is covered. It should look like a dart target. On top of that, gently spoon and spread the raspberry mousse. Garnish the pie with whipped cream and fresh raspberries. Refrigerate the pies for at least one hour.

CUSTARD

"Pie, an All-American dessert, is admired throughout the world. If there is a celebration, there is pie. If there is pie, there is a celebration. Just like the story of America, there are so many flavors of pie, countless cultural and regional variations, and continual adaptations. Pie is a culinary exploration with infinite possibilities."

—Jacques Henry
CEO, Emile Henry
Marcigny, France

Put The Lime In The Coconut Custard Pie	162	Luscious Southern Coconut Pie	172
Grandma's Egg Custard Pie	164	Raisin Nut Custard Pie	174
Hawaiian Vanilla Custard Pie	166	Supreme Caramel–Chocolate Pie	176
Lemon Drop Custard Pie	168	Butterscotch Pecan Custard Pie	178
Linda's Luscious Raspberry Custard	170		

‹‹ *Put the Lime in the Coconut Custard Pie (recipe page 162)*

PUT THE LIME IN THE COCONUT CUSTARD PIE

Christine Fiedorowicz, Denver, CO
2010 APC Crisco National Pie Championships Amateur Division 1st Place Custard

CRUST
1 ½ cups flour
½ cup plus 1 tablespoon shortening
1 teaspoon salt
4 tablespoons water with 1 teaspoon
   vinegar

FILLING
14 oz. can condensed milk
9 oz. cream of coconut

1 cup heavy cream
1 teaspoon coconut extract
½ teaspoon vanilla extract
4 large eggs, beaten

TOPPING
4 oz. prepared, store-bought lime
   curd
½ cup shredded/flake coconut,
   sweetened

For the crust: Preheat oven to 425°F. Mix flour and salt together. Cut shortening into flour mixture, then add water/vinegar mixture. Form into one disc and refrigerate. Roll out and place in 9-inch pie pan. Prebake crust for 20 minutes. Use extra crust to cut out stars and place on top crust.

For the filling: Preheat oven to 300°F. Blend eggs with rest of ingredients and pour into prebaked crust. Bake on bottom 3rd rack for about 1 hour.

For the topping: Let pie cool completely. Spread lime curd over top and sprinkle toasted coconut over top. Chill in fridge for 2 hours.

Put The Lime In The Coconut Custard Pie

GRANDMA'S EGG CUSTARD PIE

Marles Reissland, Riverdale, NE
1999 APC Crisco National Pie Championships Amateur Division 1st Place Custard

CRUST
3 cups flour
1 teaspoon salt
1 teaspoon sugar
1 cup plus 1 tablespoon butter-
    flavored shortening, chilled
1/3 cup ice water
1 tablespoon vinegar
1 large egg, beaten

FILLING
3 eggs, well beaten
3/4 cup sugar

1/4 teaspoon salt
1 teaspoon vanilla
2 1/2 cups milk, scalded
1/4 teaspoon nutmeg

YELLOW FOOD COLORING (OPTIONAL)
1 egg white, for brushing crust

For the crust: Sift together flour, salt, and sugar into mixing bowl. Cut in shortening with a pastry blender until mixture resembles cornmeal. Combine water, vinegar, and egg. Add liquid one tablespoon at a time, sprinkling over flour mixture and tossing with a fork to form soft dough. Shape into three discs. Wrap with plastic wrap. Refrigerate 3 to 24 hours. Roll out dough for a bottom crust when ready. Extra pastry may be frozen for later use.

For the filling: Preheat oven to 400°F. Mix together eggs, sugar, salt, and vanilla. Stir well. Blend in the scalded milk. If more yellow color is desired, add few drops of food coloring. Line pie pan with pastry and brush inside bottom and sides of shell with egg white to help prevent a soggy crust. Pour custard mixture into pie crust. Sprinkle with nutmeg. Bake for 30 to 35 minutes or until knife inserted near center comes out clean. Cool pie on baking rack.

Grandma's Egg Custard Pie

HAWAIIAN VANILLA CUSTARD PIE

Stan C. Strom, Gilbert, AZ
2007 APC Crisco National Pie Championships Amateur Division 1st Place Custard

CRUST
2 cups all-purpose flour (slightly tossed with fork in bag, gently scooped and leveled, but not sifted)
1 cup Soft-as-Silk cake flour
½ teaspoon kosher salt
1 cup Crisco vegetable shortening (½ butter-flavored and ½ regular), chilled
2 tablespoons lemon juice or cider vinegar
1 large egg, beaten
⅓ cup ice water

FILLING
1 egg white, lightly beaten, plus 4 large eggs

1 cup milk
2 cups heavy cream
1 ¼ cups sugar
¼ teaspoon salt
¼ teaspoon freshly grated nutmeg
1½ teaspoon Hawaiian vanilla extract

TOPPING
1 fresh pineapple, cubed and chopped in processor for 30 seconds
1 cup sugar, divided
3 tablespoons coconut syrup
2 tablespoons tapioca or cornstarch
1 tablespoon lemon juice
½ teaspoon lemon zest
1 cup toasted fresh coconut, grated

For the crust: Preheat oven to 400°F. After measuring, sift flour, sugar, and salt; cut in shortening with pastry blender until coarse (pea-sized bits). Mix lemon juice, beaten egg, and ice water, then add liquid gradually to flour mixture. Form dough into ball by placing on a sheet of plastic wrap and folding inward from the outside corners. Chill for at least 30 minutes. Roll out between two layers of wide plastic wrap and fit into 9-inch (deep-dish) glass pie pan. Chill for 30 minutes or freeze for 15 minutes. Use extra pastry dough for cutouts (seasonal leaf designs, stars, or fruit shapes). Sprinkle cutouts with sugar and bake for 10 to 12 minutes. Cover with foil and bake for an additional 5 to 8 minutes. This recipe will make enough for one large 9-inch deep-dish pie with cutouts or one 9-inch double-crust pie.

For the filling: Preheat oven to 350°F. In a heavy saucepan, combine the milk and cream. Heat until mixture just comes to a simmer. Whisk the 4 large eggs, ¾ cup sugar, salt, nutmeg, and vanilla together to combine. Add the hot milk mixture to the egg-sugar mixture and whisk to blend. Transfer custard mixture to the pie shell and bake until the custard is set but still slightly wobbly in the center, 40 to 45 minutes. Transfer to a wire rack to cool. When cooled, transfer to the refrigerator to chill.

For the pineapple topping: While the pie is baking, make the pineapple topping. Combine the pineapple, ½ cup sugar, and coconut syrup in a heavy, non-reactive saucepan. Bring to a boil. In a small bowl, stir together the remaining ½ cup sugar, tapioca/cornstarch, lemon juice, and lemon zest. Stir the sugar-cornstarch mixture into the boiling pineapple and stir well to combine. Cook until thickened, stirring constantly, about 5 minutes. Remove from the heat and transfer to a small bowl. Place a piece of waxed paper or plastic wrap directly onto surface and chill, stirring occasionally, until completely cooled, about 2 hours.

When both the pie and the pineapple topping have cooled, top the pie with the topping. Serve immediately or continue to refrigerate, covered, for up to 1 day. If pie is refrigerated for more than 1 to 2 hours, allow to sit at room temperature a few minutes before serving.

LEMON DROP CUSTARD PIE

Johnna Poulson, Celebration, FL
2006 APC Crisco National Pie Championships Amateur Division 1ˢᵗ Place Custard

CRUST
1 ⅓ cups all-purpose flour
½ teaspoon salt
½ teaspoon sugar
½ cup shortening
3 to 4 tablespoons cold water

FILLING
2 cups half and half
5 egg yolks, slightly beaten

⅓ cup sugar
1 teaspoon vanilla
⅛ teaspoon salt
½ cup store-bought prepared lemon
   curd
1 cup whipping cream, whipped
Lemon drop candies for garnish

For the crust: Preheat oven to 450°F. Combine flour, sugar, and salt. Cut in shortening until mixture resembles coarse meal. Sprinkle cold water slowly over flour mixture. Mix with fingers until dry ingredients are moistened. Shape into a ball and chill. Roll dough to ⅛ inch thickness. Place in pie plate. Trim extra off edges. Dock bottom and sides of shell. Spray the bottom of another pie tin with cooking spray and place it on top of the pastry shell. Invert pans and bake upside-down at 450°F for 10 to12 minutes. Remove from oven and reduce heat to 350°F. Turn shell right-side up and let sit 2 to 3 minutes before removing top pie tin.

For the filling: Preheat oven to 350°F. In a heavy saucepan, heat half and half over medium heat until bubbly. Remove from heat and set aside. In a medium bowl, combine egg yolks, sugar, vanilla, and salt. Beat with a rotary beater until combined. Slowly whisk the hot half and half into the egg mixture.

Carefully pour filling into the partially baked pastry shell. Bake at for 40 minutes or until knife inserted near the center comes out clean. Cool on wire rack. Refrigerate overnight. The next day, spoon lemon curd over the top of the pie. Garnish edges with whipped cream and lemon drop candies.

LINDA'S LUSCIOUS RASPBERRY CUSTARD

Phyllis Bartholomew, Columbus, NE
2004 APC Crisco National Pie Championships Amateur Division 1st Place Custard

CRUST
2 cups flour
1 cup cake flour
1 cup Crisco shortening, butter-
    flavored
1 whole egg
1 tablespoon cider vinegar
½ teaspoon salt
⅓ cup ice water

FILLING
3 eggs
14 oz. can Eagle brand sweetened
    condensed milk
1 ¼ cups hot water
1 teaspoon pure vanilla extract
¼ teaspoon salt
⅛ teaspoon cinnamon
2 cups fresh or frozen raspberries

For the crust: Preheat oven to 425°F. Mix the flours and butter powder together. Cut in the shortening until it resembles coarse crumbs. Beat together the other ingredients and stir into the flour. Mix just until incorporated. Form dough into a disc and wrap in plastic wrap. Refrigerate to chill. Roll out about ⅓ of the dough between 2 sheets of plastic wrap. Place crust in a 9-inch pie dish. Bake for about 8 to 10 minutes. Let cool.

For the filling: Preheat oven to 400°F. Beat the eggs in a bowl. Add the water, milk, vanilla, salt, and cinnamon. Mix well. Fold in the raspberries very gently. Pour into the pie shell and arrange the raspberries evenly. Bake for 10 minutes at 400°F on the bottom rack and then reduce heat to 350°F and move the pie to the middle rack. Bake for 25 to 30 minutes more or until knife inserted near the center comes out clean. Cool before serving.

LUSCIOUS SOUTHERN COCONUT PIE

Shirley J. Myrsiades, Pinellas Park, FL
2005 APC Crisco National Pie Championships Amateur Division 3rd Place Custard

CRUST
1½ cups all-purpose flour
4 ½ tablespoons unsalted butter,
  cubed
½ teaspoon salt
4½ tablespoons ice water
4½ tablespoons Crisco butter-
  flavored shortening, cubed
1 egg white, for brushing pie
Egg wash

FILLING
2 large eggs plus 3 yolks, slightly
  beaten

1 cup sugar
½ cup butter, melted
½ cup cream of coconut
½ teaspoon salt
5 teaspoons lemon juice
1 ½ teaspoons vanilla extract
(2) 6.5 oz. packages of frozen
  coconut, thawed
½ cup shredded coconut

For the crust: Preheat oven to 350°F. Pre-chill bowl, flour, salt, cubed butter, cubed shortening, and pastry cutter. Combine flour and salt. Cut in fats with pastry cutter until fats are the size of small peas. Drizzle water, 1 tablespoon at a time, and blend with a fork. Continue adding water until dough forms into a ball. Do not over-handle pastry! Turn onto waxed paper and press into a 6-inch disc. Put in a plastic bag and let chill and rest for 1 hour. Roll out to an 11-inch circle and transfer to a pie tin. Trim edges and turn in and flute pastry. Prick bottom and sides of shell 20 times with a fork. Cover with foil and use pie weights or dry beans to ensure pie shell remains even. Prebake for 10 minutes. Let cool. Brush bottom and sides of shell with egg white. Brush top edge with egg wash, place on a foil-lined cookie sheet, shiny side down.

For the filling: Preheat oven to 350°F. Combine eggs, sugar, salt, butter, lemon juice, vanilla, and cream of coconut. Blend in the frozen and shredded coconut. Pour into pie shell. Bake for 40 to 50 minutes until top is golden and bubbly. Serve at room temperature.

Luscious Southern Coconut Pie

RAISIN NUT CUSTARD PIE

Karen Hall, Elm Creek, NE
2005 APC Crisco National Pie Championships Amateur Division 1st Place Custard

CRUST
2 cups all-purpose flour
½ teaspoon salt
¾ cup Crisco butter-flavored
    shortening
5 to 7 tablespoons cold water

FILLING
½ cup French vanilla-flavored liquid
    coffee creamer
1½ cups half and half
1 cup table cream
3 eggs
1 cup sugar

¼ teaspoon salt
1 teaspoon vanilla
2 tablespoons macadamia nuts,
    chopped
½ cup raisins
Fresh-ground nutmeg to sprinkle

GARNISH
Whipped topping (as desired)
¼ cup macadamia nuts, chopped
    (optional)
Berries (raspberries, blueberries, or
    berries of choice)

For the crust: Preheat oven to 375°F. Mix flour, salt, and butter powder in bowl. With pastry blender, cut in Crisco shortening until mixture resembles pea-sized chunks. Sprinkle cold water over mixture one tablespoon at a time, tossing with a fork until dough forms a ball. Divide dough into two equal parts; press between hands to form 5-inch pancake shapes. Wrap each pancake in plastic wrap. Refrigerate until needed. Makes one double-crust or two 9-inch single crusts. Line 9-inch pie dish with pastry.

For the filling: Preheat oven to 375°F. In saucepan over medium heat, combine coffee creamer, half and half, and table cream; scald mixture. In bowl, beat together eggs, sugar, salt, and vanilla. Add hot cream mixture; stir. Sprinkle 2 tablespoons macadamia nuts and ½ cup raisins in bottom of unbaked pie shell. Pour in custard. Sprinkle top of pie with fresh ground nutmeg. Cover edge of pie with foil to prevent excessive browning. Bake for 10 minutes. Reduce oven to 350°F degrees and bake an additional 25 to 30 minutes or until pie is set. Chill.

When ready to serve, garnish pie as desired with whipped topping and chopped macadamia nuts.

Raisin Nut Custard Pie

SUPREME CARAMEL–CHOCOLATE PIE

Katheryn Hanson, Orlando, FL
2008 APC Crisco National Pie Championships Amateur Division 2nd Place Custard

PECAN SHORTBREAD COOKIE CRUMB CRUST

1 ½ cups crushed pecan Sandies or
    pecan shortbread cookies
¼ cup butter, melted

FILLING

30 vanilla caramels
2 tablespoons butter
2 tablespoons water

½ cup chopped toasted pecans
8 oz. cream cheese
⅓ cup powdered sugar
4 oz. Hershey's milk chocolate bar
3 tablespoons hot water
1 teaspoon vanilla
2 cups heavy whipping cream
2 tablespoons powdered sugar
Chocolate shavings for garnish

For the crust: Preheat oven to 350°F. Combine ingredients. Press into 9-inch pie pan, and bake for 10 minutes.

For the filling: Over medium heat, melt the caramels, 2 tablespoons butter, and 2 tablespoons water, stirring frequently, until melted. Pour into the baked crust. Sprinkle the toasted pecans on top and chill for 1 hour. In medium mixing bowl, beat cream cheese and ⅓ cup powdered sugar until smooth. Spread over the chilled caramel base and place in the refrigerator.

Heat chocolate and 3 tablespoons hot water over low heat, stirring constantly until melted. Cool to room temperature. Stir in vanilla.

Beat the heavy whipping cream and 2 tablespoons powdered sugar until stiff. Reserve 1½ cups of whipped cream mixture. Fold chocolate mixture into the remaining whipped cream. Spread mixture over the cream cheese layer.

Garnish with the reserved whipped cream and chocolate shavings.

BUTTERSCOTCH PECAN CUSTARD PIE

By Carol Socier, Bay City, MI
2009 APC Crisco National Pie Championships Amateur Division 1st Place

CRUST
1½ cups all-purpose flour
½ cup butter-flavor Crisco
    shortening
3 to 4 tablespoons cold water
1 tablespoon vinegar

FILLING
1 cup packed brown sugar, divided
½ cup chopped pecans
¼ cup plus 1 tablespoon salted
    butter, divided
½ cup granulated sugar

3 tablespoons cornstarch
¼ teaspoon salt
3 egg yolks
2 cups half and half
½ cup butterscotch chips
1 teaspoon vanilla
2 cups whipping cream, whipped
½ cup Heath English Toffee bits

GARNISH
Pecan halves for garnish
Butterscotch ice cream topping

For the crust: Preheat oven to 400°F. In medium-size bowl, cut shortening into flour until coarse crumbs form. Combine water and vinegar. Sprinkle over flour, tossing with a fork until dough forms. Shape into a ball and cool for 15 minutes. Roll into a 12-inch circle on lightly floured board. Transfer to a 9-inch pie plate. Trim, flute, and prick bottom and sides with fork. Bake for 10 to 12 minutes or until golden brown.

For the filling: In small pan, heat ½ cup brown sugar, pecans, and ¼ cup butter. Cook and stir until butter is melted. Spread in baked pie shell and place in preheated oven for 5 minutes. Remove and cool.

Combine remaining sugars and cornstarch, mixing well. Add salt, egg yolks, half and half, and butterscotch chips. Cook over medium heat until very thick, stirring constantly. Remove from heat; add vanilla and 1 tablespoon of butter, stirring until butter is melted. Measure 1 cup of the custard mixture. Set aside to cool. Pour remaining mixture into pie shell. When the cup of custard is cooled, fold in half of the whipped cream. Spread on top of pie. Chill.

Garnish with remaining cream, toffee bits, and pecan halves. Drizzle with butterscotch topping. Keep refrigerated.

Butterscotch Pecan Custard Pie

FRUIT & BERRY

"Pie makes all things right with the world, and these fruit pies are the place to start. Rhubarb, raspberry, peach, blueberry. These pies have them all! If you're a pie lover like I am, this chapter will keep you happy."

—Gale Gand,
nationally acclaimed pastry chef,
restaurateur, cookbook author,
television personality,
root beer maker, James Beard Award winner, and mom.

Almond Cherry Pie	182	Fresh Blueberry Caramel Crumb Pie	196
Blueberry–Raspberry Pie	184	Fruity Fruit Pie	198
Blueberry–Cranberry Pie with Pecan Streusel Topping	186	Ginger, You're a Peach Pie	200
		Glazed Strawberry Cheesecake Pie	202
Bumbleberry Pie	188	Razzle Dazzle Berry Pie	204
Cherry Red Raspberry Pie	190	Rhubarb–Strawberry–Raspberry Pie	206
Classic Blueberry Pie	192	Blueberry & Basil Lime Pie	208
Four Seasons Strawberry–Rhubarb Pie	194		

‹‹ *Cherry Red Raspberry Pie (recipe page 190)*

ALMOND CHERRY PIE

Lola Nebel, Cambridge, MN
2003 APC Crisco National Pie Championships Amateur Division 1st Place Fruit/Berry

CRUST
5 cups flour
2 teaspoons salt
1 teaspoon baking powder
2 cups shortening
1 egg
1 teaspoon vinegar
Cold water

FILLING
1½ cups sugar, divided
4 tablespoons cornstarch

(2) 14.5 oz. cans pitted tart red cherries, packed in water, drained, and ¾ cup liquid reserved
1 tablespoon butter
½ teaspoon almond extract
¼ teaspoon red food coloring

TOPPING
2 tablespoons milk
2 tablespoons sugar
¼ cup sliced almonds

For the crust: In large bowl, stir together flour, salt, and baking powder. Cut in shortening. Break egg into a liquid measuring cup. Add vinegar and enough water to make 1 cup. Beat with fork to mix. Add liquid to dry ingredients, stirring lightly with fork until moistened. Divide into 5 equal parts. Shape into flat 6-inch discs and wrap in plastic. Refrigerate 2 discs; freeze the rest. After 30 minutes, roll out 1 refrigerated disc into a 10-inch round. Fit into 9-inch pie plate. Leave dough over edge of plate (do not trim off excess). Prepare a lattice top crust according to the directions below.

For the filling: In medium saucepan, combine ¾ cup sugar and cornstarch. Stir in reserved ¾ cup cherry liquid. Bring to a boil, stirring constantly with whisk. Cook 1 minute. Whisk in butter, almond extract, food coloring, and remaining sugar. Remove from heat. Fold in cherries. Set aside.

For the topping: In small saucepan, combine milk, sugar, and almonds for topping. Bring to boil, stirring and cooking 3 minutes.

For the lattice top: Preheat oven to 400°F. Roll dough disc into 10-inch round. Cut dough into ½ inch-wide strips. Pour filling into bottom crust. Weave strips in lattice design over filling. Trim strips even with bottom crust. Moisten strips with water, fold under with bottom crust, and pinch rim to make fluted edge. Brush strips with sugar almond topping. Bake at 400°F for 10 minutes, then reduce temperature to 350°F. Bake for 40 to 50 minutes at 350°F.

BLUEBERRY–RASPBERRY PIE

Raquel Hammond, St. Cloud, FL
2005 APC Crisco National Pie Championships Amateur Division 1st Place Fruit/Berry

CRUST

2 cups unbleached flour
1 cup cake flour
1½ tablespoons sugar
1 teaspoon salt
8 tablespoons (1 stick) frozen unsalted butter, cut up
½ cup plus 2 tablespoons frozen Crisco shortening, cut up
2 tablespoons vinegar
1 large egg yolk
4 to 5 tablespoons ice water, or as needed
¼ cup crushed cornflakes
Egg glaze: 1 large egg white with 1 tablespoon water added
¼ cup blueberry preserves

FILLING

2 cups fresh blueberries or (2) 15 oz. cans blueberries, drained (plump only)
2 cups frozen blueberries, partially thawed
4 cups frozen raspberries, partially thawed
¾ cup sugar
3½ tablespoons quick cooking tapioca
Big pinch of salt
¾ tablespoon cinnamon
¼ teaspoon nutmeg
1 tablespoon lemon juice
2 tablespoons unsalted butter, cut up

For the crust: Blend together dry ingredients in large bowl. Add the butter and shortening. Using a pastry blender, cut in fat until mixture resembles dry rice. Add egg yolk, vinegar, and a minimum amount of water. Lightly toss until mixture just begins to clump together. If dough looks too dry, sprinkle on a little more water. Dough should cling together and feel pliable, but not sticky.

Form dough into a cohesive ball on a piece of waxed paper by lifting opposite corners of paper and pressing them together. Flatten into 6-inch disk for single shell, or divide in half and make two discs for double-crust pie. Wrap dough in plastic wrap and refrigerate for at least 1 hour or even overnight (the longer the better). Soften dough at room temperature for a few minutes before rolling out. When ready, roll out bottom crust and line 9-inch pie plate. Roll out top crust. Refrigerate both for 15 minutes.

For the filling: Preheat oven to 425°F. In a large bowl, combine berries. In another bowl, combine sugar, tapioca, salt, cinnamon, and nutmeg. Sprinkle over berries, add lemon juice, and gently stir together. Brush egg glaze on bottom of pastry shell, then spread ¼ cup of blueberry preserves on bottom as well. Pour filling into pie shell and dot with butter. Attach top crust either as a whole or in pastry cutouts. If using a whole top crust, poke holes for steam to vent. Brush with egg glaze and sprinkle with sugar.

Bake at 425°F in lower third of oven for 15 minutes. Raise rack to center, lower temperature to 350°F, and then bake an additional 50 to 55 minutes. Cover half-way through with foil if browning too much.

Transfer to wire rack and cool for at least 2 hours or longer. Slice and serve. Refrigerate leftovers covered with loosely tented foil.

Blueberry–Raspberry Pie

BLUEBERRY–CRANBERRY PIE WITH PECAN STREUSEL TOPPING

Susan Asato, Aliso Viejo, CA
2011 APC Crisco National Pie Championships Amateur Division 1st Place Fruit/Berry

CRUST

- 8 tablespoons Earth Balance vegan butter, chilled (1 stick or 4 oz. by weight)
- 3 tablespoons Earth Balance vegan shortening, chilled (1.5 oz. by weight)
- 1 2/3 cups all-purpose flour (8 oz. by weight)
- 2 tablespoons organic sugar
- 1/4 teaspoon salt
- 3 to 6 tablespoons ice-cold water

FILLING

- 5 cups blueberries (24 oz. by weight)
- 2 1/2 cups cranberries (12 oz. by weight)
- 1 tablespoon lime juice (juice from from 1 to 2 limes)
- 1/2 cup sugar (4 oz. by weight, non-bone char processed)
- 1 tablespoon light brown sugar (non-bone char processed)
- 6 tablespoons tapioca flour (1.5 oz. by weight)
- 2 tablespoons all-purpose flour
- 1 teaspoon cinnamon
- 1/2 teaspoon salt

TOPPING

- 6 tablespoons Earth Balance vegan butter, melted (3/4 of a stick or 3 oz. by weight)
- 1 cup pecans, coarsely chopped (4 oz. by weight)
- 1/2 cup rolled oats (1.75 oz. by weight)
- 2/3 cup light brown sugar (4 oz. by weight, non-bone char processed)
- 2/3 cup all-purpose flour (3 oz. by weight)
- 1/2 teaspoon cinnamon

GLAZE

½ cup organic powdered sugar (2.5 oz. by weight, non-bone char processed)

2 to 3 tablespoons lime juice (juice from about 1 lime)

Blueberry–Cranberry Pie with Pecan Streusel Topping

For the crust: Preheat oven to 350°F. Combine flour, sugar, and salt in the bowl of a food processor. Cut the vegan butter stick and shortening into about ½ inch pieces. Pulse in food processor with flour, sugar, and salt about 10 times or until crumbly. Add 3 to 6 tablespoons ice water (amount will vary depending on kitchen temperature and humidity) and pulse about another 5 times or until mixture holds its shape when a small amount is squeezed in fist. Place dough in an airtight container and refrigerate for at least 1 hour. Roll out dough to about ⅛ inch thickness and press into a 9-inch deep-dish pie plate. Dock bottom with a fork, line with parchment paper, and fill with pie weights. Bake for 14 to 16 minutes or until very lightly browned.

For the filling: When crust has cooled, preheat oven to 375°F. Gently mix together all filling ingredients, then fill pie crust.

For the streusel topping: Mix together all ingredients well using a fork, then spoon evenly over the berry filling. Place pie on a cookie sheet and bake for 20 to 25 minutes, or until the topping and crust edges are browned. Loosely cover the entire pie with aluminum foil. Reduce the temperature to 350°F and bake for an additional 50 to 60 minutes or until the filling just begins to bubble around the edges. Allow to cool for at least 30 minutes.

For the glaze: Whisk together powdered sugar and 2 tablespoons lime juice. Gradually add additional lime juice, several drops at a time as needed until desired consistency is reached. Drizzle onto cooled pie.

BUMBLEBERRY PIE

Hunny Lee, Kokomo, IN
2010 APC Crisco National Pie Championships Amateur Division 1st Place Fruit/Berry

CRUST
1 cup butter-flavored shortening
3 tablespoons sugar
2 cups flour
½ cup cold water

FILLING
1 cup black raspberries
1 cup red raspberries

1 cup rhubarb
2 cups apples
⅓ cup flour
1 ⅓ cups sugar
4 tablespoons butter

For the crust: Mix shortening, flour, and sugar together until dough forms pea-size balls. Add water and gather dough into a ball (makes 2 single crusts). Roll out and place one crust in pie dish.

For the filling: Preheat oven to 350°F. Mix all fruit in a bowl. Add sugar and mix well. Then add flour to thicken. Add butter and mix again. Pour into pie crust. Roll out top crust. Cut dough into ½ inch wide strips. Weave strips in a lattice design over filling. Trim strips even with the bottom crust. Moisten strips with water and fold under with bottom crust. Crimp. Bake for 1 hour or until done.

Bumbleberry Pie

CHERRY RED RASPBERRY PIE

Phyllis Bartholomew, Columbus, NE
2004 APC Crisco National Pie Championships Amateur Division 1st Place Fruit/Berry and
Best of Show

CRUST
2 cups flour
1 cup cake flour
1 cup Crisco shortening, butter-flavored
1 whole egg
1 tablespoon cider vinegar
½ teaspoon salt
⅓ cup ice water

FILLING
10 oz. package frozen red raspberries
2 cups canned sour pitted cherries, drained
1 cup sugar
3 tablespoons cornstarch
2 tablespoons butter
¼ teaspoon salt
Milk and sugar (to top the crust)

For the crust: Mix the flours and butter powder and cut in the shortening until it resembles coarse crumbs. Beat together the other ingredients and stir into the flour. Mix just until it is incorporated. Form into a disc, wrap in plastic wrap, and chill. Roll out about ⅓ of the dough between 2 sheets of wax paper and line pie dish.

For the filling: Preheat oven to 350°F. Thaw frozen raspberries, saving the juice, and add enough of the juice from the cherries to make 1 cup liquid. In a saucepan, mix sugar, cornstarch, and salt. Stir in one cup of juice. Add cherries and cook over medium heat until thick and clear. Cook one more minute. Remove from heat and very gently fold in raspberries. Pour into pastry-lined pie dish. Add top crust. Seal edges, moisten top with hot milk, and sprinkle with sugar. Cut seam vents. Bake for about 45 minutes. This pie is extra pretty with a lattice top.

Cherry Red Raspberry Pie

CLASSIC BLUEBERRY PIE

Rick Johnson, Belleville, IL
2010 APC Crisco National Pie Championships Amateur Division Fruit/Berry

CRUST
3 cups all-purpose flour
1¼ cups butter
½ teaspoon salt
⅓ cup lard
½ cup cream cheese
½ teaspoon almond extract

FILLING
8 cups frozen blueberries
1½ cups sugar
1 teaspoon cinnamon
½ teaspoon salt
7 tablespoons Clearjel

For the crust: Combine all ingredients in a food processor and pulse until a ball forms. Chill dough overnight. When ready, roll out 2 crusts. Place one in a pie dish, and place the other to the side for a top crust.

For the filling: Preheat oven to 350°F. Combine blueberries and sugar in a saucepan, and cook on low until juice is released. Strain blueberry mixture, reserving the juice. Continue cooking juice until reduced by half, then add back the blueberries. Add the rest of the ingredients. Fill pie and apply top crust. Cut vents for steam. Bake for approximately 50 minutes.

Classic Blueberry Pie

FOUR SEASONS STRAWBERRY–RHUBARB PIE

Evette Rahman, Orlando, FL
2007 APC Crisco National Pie Championships Amateur Division Fruit/Berry

CRUST

2 cups flour
2 tablespoons sugar
¾ teaspoon salt
½ teaspoon baking powder
⅓ cup vegetable shortening
⅓ cup unsalted butter, very cold and cubed
1 tablespoon oil
1 tablespoon vinegar
⅓ cup heavy cream
1 egg white
Sugar for sprinkling

FILLING

16 oz. bag frozen whole strawberries: set out about 45 minutes to thaw slightly
16 oz. bag frozen sliced rhubarb: set out about 45 minutes to thaw slightly (cut into ½ inch pieces and discard any brown or pale-colored pieces)
½ teaspoon orange zest
¼ cup instant tapioca
1 ⅔ cups granulated white sugar
2 tablespoons cornstarch
1½ tablespoons salted butter, cubed

For the crust: Preheat oven to 375°F. Mix together flour, sugar, salt, and baking powder. Cut in shortening and butter. Stir together oil, vinegar, and cream. Add to flour. Form into two discs. Wrap in plastic. Refrigerate for 1 hour. Roll out 1 dough disc on lightly floured cold surface and place in deep-dish pie plate. Blind-bake for 15 minutes. Cool completely. Brush inside with some of the egg white and chill.

For the filling: Preheat oven to 400°F. Combine all filling ingredients, except butter. Cover and set aside for 15 minutes. Fill pie plate and top with butter. Roll out remaining dough into strips and create a lattice-design top crust over filling. (Strips should be made and refrigerated ahead of time.) Cut off excess dough and crimp edges. Mix remaining egg white with 1 teaspoon of water. Brush crust with egg wash and sprinkle with sugar. Put in freezer for 10 minutes. Place in large dark pan and bake at 400°F for 20 minutes, then reduce temperature to 375°F and bake for 1 hour or until bubbly and golden brown. Cover pie edges and top of pie with foil to prevent excess browning. Cool pie completely before cutting.

Four Seasons Strawberry–Rhubarb Pie

FRESH BLUEBERRY CARAMEL CRUMB PIE

Phyllis Szymanek, Toledo, OH
2010 APC Crisco National Pie Championships Amateur Division 2nd Place Fruit/Berry

CRUST
1 ⅓ cups flour
½ cup Crisco
½ teaspoon salt
3 tablespoons cold water

FILLING
5 cups fresh blueberries
1 cup sugar
1 teaspoon vanilla
3 tablespoons cornstarch
⅛ teaspoon nutmeg

⅛ teaspoon salt
1 tablespoon fresh lemon juice

TOPPING
1 cup light brown sugar
1 cup flour
½ cup chopped walnuts
½ cup quick oats
½ cup butter, cold
¼ cup Smucker's caramel ice cream
   topping

For the crust: Mix flour and salt in mixing bowl. Add Crisco. With pastry cutter, mix ingredients until mixture resembles coarse crumbs. Add water, one tablespoon at a time, until it forms into a ball. Roll out onto floured surface one inch larger than a 9-inch pie pan. Place into pie plate and flute edges.

For the filling: Combine sugar, cornstarch, nutmeg, and salt in mixing bowl. Add blueberries, vanilla, and lemon juice. Toss to coat. Pour into prepared pie crust.

For the topping: Preheat oven to 425°F. Combine brown sugar, flour, and oats. Cut in butter until crumbly. Add walnuts. Sprinkle over blueberries. Cover edges of crust loosely with foil. Bake at 425°F for 10 minutes, then at 375°F for 45 to 55 minutes. Remove foil the last 15 minutes. Cool on wire rack. Drizzle with Smucker's caramel topping before serving.

FRUITY FRUIT PIE

Caroline Imig, Oconto, WI
2011 APC Crisco National Pie Championships Professional Division 1st Place Fruit/Berry

CRUST
1½ cups flour
1 tablespoon sugar
½ tablespoon salt
½ cup cold Crisco shortening
¼ cup cold water

FILLING
1½ cups white chocolate chips
¼ cup evaporated milk

8 oz. package cream cheese,
   softened
1 tablespoon strawberry extract
2 drops red food coloring

FRUIT TOPPING
½ cup blueberries
3 cups sliced strawberries
4 sliced kiwis
1 cup raspberries
Whipped cream

For the crust: Preheat oven to 375°F. Combine dry ingredients. Cut cold shortening into flour mixture until particles are the size of small peas. Sprinkle in water, tossing with fork until all flour is moistened and pastry can be formed into ball. When ready, roll out pie crust and place in pie pan. Spread out foil on pie crust and fill with pie weights. Bake for 8 to 10 minutes or until golden brown.

For the filling: In microwave-safe bowl, place white chocolate chips and evaporated milk. Microwave 1 minute. Stir. If necessary, microwave an additional 15 seconds, stirring until chips are melted. Beat in cream cheese, strawberry extract, and red food coloring. Spread on bottom of baked pie shell.

For the topping: Arrange fruit in decorative pattern on top of filling. Garnish with whipped cream.

Fruity Fruit Pie

GINGER, YOU'RE A PEACH PIE

John Sunvold, Winter Springs, FL
2009 APC Crisco National Pie Championships Amateur Division Fruit/Berry

CRUST
1¼ cups ginger cookies/snaps crumbs, processed in food processor
¼ cup sugar
3 tablespoons butter, melted

CREAM LAYER
⅓ cup cream cheese, softened
⅓ cup powdered sugar
5 oz. Cool Whip

PEACH LAYER
4 to 6 fresh peaches (canned will work if no fresh peaches are available; allow 7 canned peach slices for each fresh peach)
½ cup water
¼ teaspoon cinnamon
⅔ cup brown sugar
3 tablespoons cornstarch
1 tablespoon butter
Whipped topping and ginger cookies (optional garnish)

For the crust: Preheat oven to 375°F. Mix all ingredients together and press mixture into a 9-inch pie plate. Bake for 8 to 10 minutes. Allow to cool to room temperature. Place in refrigerator to cool completely.

For the cream layer: Mix together softened cream and powdered sugar. Fold in thawed Cool Whip. Spread onto ginger crumb crust. Refrigerate for 2 hours.

For the peach layer: Peel peaches and remove stones. Slice peaches into around 6 to 8 slices per peach. Pat peaches dry and place on a drying rack. Take the four worst-looking slices and chop them into very small, marble-sized pieces. In small saucepan, mix water, brown sugar, cinnamon, cornstarch, and butter. Heat over medium heat and stir constantly. Bring to a boil, then add the chopped peach pieces. Simmer for up to 5 minutes or until thick. Cool.

Arrange fresh peach slices on top of cream layer so they cover top. Leave around ¼ inch of the cream layer showing all around. Pour the cooled brown sugar mixture over the peaches. Refrigerate 2 hours. Garnish with whipped topping and ginger cookies (optional).

GLAZED STRAWBERRY CHEESECAKE PIE

Valarie Enters, Sanford, FL
2010 APC Crisco National Pie Championships Professional Division
Honorable Mention Fruit/Berry

CRUST
2 cups cinnamon graham crackers,
    crushed
$\frac{1}{3}$ cup sugar
½ cup butter, melted

FILLING
3 packages cream cheese
½ cup sugar
¼ cup sour cream
1½ teaspoons vanilla
2 eggs

GLAZE
1 cup sugar
1 cup water
3 tablespoons Karo syrup
3 tablespoons cornstarch
3 tablespoons gelatin
Pinch salt
Red food color

TOPPING
2 quarts fresh strawberries
Whipped topping and graham cracker
    crumbs for garnish

For the crust: Preheat oven to 350°F. Mix ingredients together and press into the bottom and sides of a pie pan. Bake for 15 minutes, then let cool.

For the filling: Blend all ingredients together and pour into crust. Bake at 350°F until golden and set, about 30 minutes

For the glaze: Combine all ingredients in a saucepan. Bring to a boil over medium heat, then cool.

For the topping: Hull strawberries and rinse with water. Pat dry and set on paper towels. Dip strawberries in glaze and set on cheesecake. Garnish with whipped topping and graham cracker crumbs.

Glazed Strawberry Cheesecake Pie

RAZZLE DAZZLE BERRY PIE

John Michael Lerma, St. Paul, MN
2005 APC Crisco National Pie Championships Amateur Division 2nd Place Fruit/Berry

CRUST
3 cups all-purpose flour
1 tablespoon sugar
1 teaspoon kosher or Hawaiian salt
½ cup cold butter-flavored Crisco
 shortening, cut into small pieces
½ cup cold unsalted butter, cut into
 small pieces
½ cup cold water
1 egg yolk and 1 teaspoon water for
 egg wash

FILLING
1 cup sugar
Dash of kosher or Hawaiian salt

¼ cup cornstarch
½ teaspoon ground cinnamon
1 cup blueberries
1½ cups sliced strawberries
1 cup blackberries
1 cup red raspberries
½ cup water
2 tablespoons freshly squeezed lemon juice (about ½ a large lemon)
2 tablespoons unsalted butter
Egg wash and sugar for top crust

For the crust: All ingredients should be cold. Combine all the dry ingredients in a large mixing bowl. Add shortening and butter. Using a pastry blender, cut in the shortening and butter until the mixture resembles coarse meal. Drop by drop, add the cold water. Mix in with the fingertips, not hands, as the palms will warm the dough. Continue mixing water in until the dough begins to hold together without being sticky but not crumbly.

Divide dough into two pieces and place each in plastic wrap. Fold over plastic wrap and press down to form a disc. This will make rolling out easier after chilling. Finish wrapping in plastic and place in refrigerator for at least one hour. Lightly spray a 9-inch pie plate with butter or vegetable cooking spray. Roll out dough and place in pie plate. Return to refrigerator until filling is ready. Roll out top crust. Using a pastry cutter, cut strips for a lattice top. If using a full crust, cut slits in the top. Makes for 9-inch double-crust pie.

For the filling: Preheat oven to 350°F. In a heavy-bottom saucepan, combine sugar, salt, cornstarch, and cinnamon. Stir in berries. Add water and lemon juice. Cook over medium heat just to the boiling point. Stir filling gently so as not to crush the raspberries. Push with the back of a spoon or carefully swirl saucepan to shift the mixture to prevent scorching.

Pour into chilled pie shell; dot with butter and top with crust. Apply egg wash and sprinkle with sugar. Bake for about 45 minutes or until crust is golden.

Razzle Dazzle Berry Pie

RHUBARB–STRAWBERRY–RASPBERRY PIE

Susan Gills, Boulder, CO

1998 APC Crisco National Pie Championships Amateur Division 1st Place Fruit/Berry and Best of Show

CRUST
2/3 cup shortening
2 tablespoons butter
1 teaspoon salt
2 cups flour
4 tablespoons ice-cold water
Sugar for sprinkling

FILLING
1 cup strawberries, cut in half or in quarters

1 cup raspberries
2 cups rhubarb, cut into ½ inch pieces
¾ cup sugar
1/3 cup flour
1 tablespoon butter, melted
1 teaspoon lemon juice

For the crust: Mix flour and salt. Add shortening and butter, and mix until texture is like coarse cornmeal. Add water and form dough into a ball. Let sit at least 20 minutes before rolling out. Divide in half. Roll out bottom crust and place in pie pan.

For the filling: Mix sugar and flour. Add to fruits. Refrigerate overnight. Just before adding fruit to pastry-lined pie pan, add melted butter and lemon juice to fruit mixture.

Preheat oven to 400°F. Pour filling into pie shell. Roll out top crust and place on top. Crimp edges and sprinkle lightly with sugar. Bake at 400°F for 10 minutes, then turn the temperature down to 350°F. Bake for 40 to 50 minutes until crust is golden brown.

BLUEBERRY & BASIL LIME PIE

Linda Hundt, DeWitt, MI
2011 APC Crisco National Pie Championships Professional Division
Fruit/Berry Honorable Mention

CRUST
1 ½ cups flour
¼ teaspoon baking powder
½ teaspoon salt
1 teaspoon sugar
¼ cup cold butter, cut in small pieces
½ cup refrigerated Crisco shortening
Ice water

FILLING
5 cups frozen Michigan blueberries
1 cup sugar
¼ rounded cup cornstarch
3 teaspoons lime juice
½ teaspoon lime zest

6 large basil leaves in cheesecloth bag
2 ½ cups fresh Michigan blueberries,
   slightly mashed

CREAM MIXTURE
1 cup half and half
¼ cup sugar
1 egg
1 teaspoon real vanilla

CRUMB TOPPING
1½ cups flour
2 cups sugar
¼ teaspoon salt
1½ sticks butter, softened

For the crust: Mix all above ingredients except for the water in Kitchenaid style mixer on medium speed swiftly until dough texture appears "pea-like." Carefully sprinkle water in crust mix until it starts to become moistened and gathers together. Pat into a disc, wrap in plastic, and refrigerate for at least one half-hour. Roll out on to floured surface and place in pie pan. Crimp crust. Freeze until ready to use.

For the filling: Preheat oven to 400°F. Combine 5 cups frozen blueberries, sugar, and cornstarch in a saucepan over medium heat. When mixture begins boiling , add basil leaves bag and boil for 2 minutes, stirring constantly. Remove from heat. Add lime juice and lime zest. Pour 2½ cups of fresh blueberries on bottom of frozen pie crust. Top with blueberry filling.

For the cream mixture: Mix all ingredients well and carefully pour cream mixture on top of blueberry filling.

For the crumb topping: Mix together all crumb topping ingredients by hand or with a pastry blender until fine and crumbly. Top pie with crumb topping, spreading generously around edges.

Bake at 400 °F until filling bubbles over, about 45 minutes to one hour.

Blueberry & Basil Lime Pie

NUT

"Pies have come a long way in this millennium thanks to Crisco and the APC National Pie Championships. Both quality and creativity have pushed this American icon to new levels of consumption and on to future generations. It has been fun to have shared the experience with our family and many, many friends, and we hope to welcome many others in the coming years . . ."

—Rich Hoskins,
Director of Operations,
Colborne Foodbotics,
Chairman, Board of Directors,
American Pie Council

Cajun Pecan Pie	212	Maple-Kissed Butter Pecan		
Chocolate Chip Chipmunk Pie	214	Celebration Pie	224	
Macadamia Nut Chocolate Chunk Pie	216	Maple Peach Pecan Pie	226	
Chocolate Hazelnut Crunch Pie	218	White-Bottomed Caramel		
Deluxe Pecan Pie	220	Chocolate Pecan Pie	228	
Dream Date Pecan Pie	222			

‹‹ *Macadamia Nut Chocolate Chunk Pie (recipe page 216)*

CAJUN PECAN PIE

Diane Reeves, Jennings, LA
2009 APC Crisco National Pie Championships Amateur Division 2nd Place Nut

CRUST
1 ⅓ cups flour
½ teaspoon salt
½ cup butter-flavored shortening
3 to 4 tablespoons cold water

FILLING
1 cup sugar
¼ teaspoon salt
2 tablespoons flour
1 cup light corn syrup
½ teaspoon vanilla extract
3 tablespoons butter, melted
1½ cups chopped pecans
3 eggs, separated
Pecan halves for garnish

For the crust: Make a 9-inch pie crust by blending flour and salt together in a mixing bowl. Cut in shortening with a pastry blender or a large spoon until mixture is in small, uniform bits. Add water and mix until just blended. Form dough into a ball. Place ball of dough between sheets of waxed paper. Roll to about 1 inch larger than an inverted 9-inch pie dish. Place in pan, fold under excess crust, and flute the edge. Set aside.

For the filling: Preheat oven to 350°F. Mix sugar, salt, and flour in a bowl. Add corn syrup, vanilla extract, melted butter, and egg yolks. Mix well by hand. Put egg whites into another mixing bowl and beat until frothy. Add egg whites to filling mixture. Add chopped pecans and gently stir until just blended. Pour filling into unbaked pie crust. Top with pecan halves, covering entire mixture. Bake for 55 minutes (until center 3 to 4 inches can still move when gently shaken). Remove from oven, cool.

CHOCOLATE CHIP CHIPMUNK PIE

Naylet LaRochelle, Miami, FL
2008 APC Crisco National Pie Championships Amateur Division 3rd Place Nut

CRUST
1 ½ cups chocolate wafers, finely crushed
6 tablespoons butter or margarine, melted
¼ cup sugar

FILLING
1 envelope unflavored gelatin
½ cup heavy cream, cold
½ cup sugar
1 teaspoon pure vanilla extract
¼ teaspoon salt
½ cup semi-sweet chocolate chips, melted
2 tablespoons malted milk powder
1 cup heavy whipping cream

1½ cups mixed nuts, lightly salted, lightly toasted, (reserve ½ cup for nut brittle)

TOPPING
1½ cups whipped topping (Cool Whip)
1½ tablespoons malted milk powder
½ tablespoon meringue powder (dry egg whites)
Mini semi-sweet chocolate chips
Nut brittle (recipe follows)

NUT BRITTLE
½ cup lightly toasted, salted nuts
1¼ cups sugar

For the crust: Combine cookie crumbs, butter, and sugar. Press onto the bottom of a greased 9-inch pie pan. Refrigerate for 20 to 30 minutes.

For the filling: Sprinkle the gelatin into a small saucepan. Pour cream over gelatin, and let stand for about 1 minute. Add sugar, vanilla extract, and salt. Heat the mixture over medium-high heat for about 8 to 10 minutes or until sugar dissolves, stirring frequently. Reduce heat to low. Add melted chocolate and malted milk powder; stir until mixture has a smooth texture. Transfer to a large bowl; let cool for about 15 to 20 minutes.

In a medium bowl, beat whipping cream on medium to high speed until stiff consistency. Fold whipped cream into chocolate mixture. Add nuts.

Pour chocolate mixture into prepared crumb crust. Refrigerate for 30 minutes.

In a medium bowl, stir together whipped topping, malted milk powder, and meringue powder. Carefully spread over pie. Return to refrigerator and chill for 4 hours. Before serving, garnish with nut brittle and mini-chocolate chips.

For the nut brittle: Line a cookie sheet with non-stick aluminum foil; set aside. Heat 1¼ cups sugar in a heavy skillet. Cook until sugar is golden and syrupy. Mix in ½ cup of lightly toasted, lightly salted nuts. Spread mixture over prepared cookie sheet. Caramelized sugar will harden almost immediately. Break off pieces to create nut brittle. Sprinkle pieces over pie before serving.

Chocolate Chip Chipmunk Pie

MACADAMIA NUT CHOCOLATE CHUNK PIE

Emily Lewis, Mt. Dora, FL
2004 APC Crisco National Pie Championships Amateur Division 1ˢᵗ Place Nut

CRUST
1 cup Crisco shortening, cut up
6 tablespoons butter, cut up
6 tablespoons ice water
1½ teaspoon salt
3 cups all-purpose flour

FILLING
3 eggs
1 cup dark brown sugar
1 cup light corn syrup

1 oz. unsweetened chocolate, melted
5 tablespoons browned butter,
   melted
2 teaspoons vanilla extract
½ teaspoon salt
2 cups chopped macadamia nuts,
   toasted
½ cup chocolate bar, roughly
   chopped
1 oz. chocolate for top decoration
   (optional)

For the crust: Put flour and salt into work bowl of processor. Pulse. Add Crisco and pulse 6 times. Add butter and pulse 6 times. Add water 1 tablespoon at a time, pulsing after each addition. Pour out of bowl onto plastic wrap. Divide into 2 parts. Create two discs and flatten. Refrigerate. At this point, save one disc in a freezer bag for another use. It can be stored in the freezer for weeks. After about 15 minutes in the refrigerator, remove the disc you are using. Place a piece of plastic wrap or parchment paper on the counter. Flour it. Cover your disc with another piece of plastic wrap or parchment. Roll out from the center until disc is about 11 inches in diameter. Remove top wrap, flour the surface lightly and drape crust over rolling pin. Center over pie plate and put it in. Smooth into pan. Remove wrap. Trim crust edge about ½ inch around outside of pan. Fold edge under and flute using thumb and forefingers to make a stand-up edge. Refrigerate until ready to fill.

For the filling: Preheat oven to 350°F. Toast macadamia nuts on a cookie sheet for about 5 minutes. In a large bowl, beat eggs lightly. Stir in sugar, corn syrup, melted chocolate, butter, vanilla, and salt. Into prepared crust, place a layer of the chopped chocolate bar, then sprinkle nuts on top. Slowly pour egg mixture over nuts. Bake for 15 minutes at 350°F. Remove from oven and cover edge with foil. Return to oven. Bake for another 40 minutes or until toothpick inserted in center comes out clean. When pie has cooled, melt chocolate in a small sandwich baggie for 15 seconds. Cut a small corner off the bag and squiggle melted chocolate over top to decorate.

CHOCOLATE HAZELNUT CRUNCH PIE

Alberta Dunbar, San Diego, CA
2011 APC Crisco National Pie Championships Amateur Division 1st Place Nut

CRUST
1 ⅓ cups all-purpose flour
½ teaspoon salt
½ stick Crisco all vegetable shortening
3 to 6 tablespoons ice water

FILLING
12 oz. cream cheese, softened
3 tablespoons heavy cream
4 oz. milk chocolate
4 oz. semi-sweet chocolate
4 oz. dark chocolate

1½ cups ground toasted hazelnuts
¾ cups toffee baking bits
1 cup heavy cream whipped with 1½ teaspoons hazelnut extract

TOPPING
2 cups heavy cream
¼ cup powdered sugar
¾ teaspoon hazelnut extract

GARNISH
Chocolate hazelnuts
Chocolate leaves (optional)

For the crust: Preheat oven to 400°F. Spoon flour into measuring cup and level. Mix flour and salt in a medium bowl. Cut in shortening using pastry blender or 2 knives until flour is blended and forms pea-size chunks. Sprinkle with 1 tablespoon of water at a time. Toss lightly with a fork until dough forms a ball. Roll on lightly floured board to fit a 9-inch pie plate with ½ inch overlap. Turn into pie plate and flute edges. Prick bottom and sides with fork. Bake for 10 minutes or until golden brown. Cool on rack completely before filling.

For the filling: Place cream cheese and cream in a large bowl, then beat on high until smooth. In a medium microwave-safe bowl, place all 3 kinds of chocolate and melt at 50% power at 15-second intervals until melted. Cool chocolate.

Beat cooled chocolate into cream cheese mixture until combined using a wooden spoon. With the spoon, carefully fold in nuts and toffee bits. Fold in whipped cream with hazelnut extract. Pour into cooled shell, spread evenly, and smooth top. Chill for 30 to 40 minutes.

For the topping: Combine all ingredients in medium bowl. Beat on high until stiff. Put 2 cups in pastry bag with rosette tip. Frost pie with topping, reserving ⅓ of topping. With remaining ⅓ of topping, pipe large rosettes around outer edge and in center of pie.

For the garnish: Place a chocolate hazelnut on each rosette. Surround center rosette with chocolate leaves (optional).

Chocolate Hazelnut Crunch Pie

DELUXE PECAN PIE

Evette Rahman, Orlando, FL
2007 APC Crisco National Pie Championships Amateur Division 1st Place Nut

CRUST
1 cup flour
1 tablespoon sugar
½ teaspoon salt
¼ teaspoon baking powder
3 tablespoons vegetable shortening
3 tablespoons unsalted butter
3 tablespoons heavy cream
½ tablespoon vinegar
½ tablespoon oil
1 egg, separated
Sugar for sprinkling

FILLING
⅓ cup unsalted butter, softened
½ cup dark brown sugar

¼ cup granulated white sugar
3 large eggs, slightly beaten
2 teaspoons pure vanilla extract
¼ teaspoon salt
½ teaspoon grand cinnamon
¼ teaspoon ground ginger
½ cup light corn syrup
½ cup maple syrup
½ cup chopped pecans
¾ cup pecan halves
Whipped cream (optional)

For the crust: Mix flour, sugar, salt, and baking powder. Cut in shortening and butter. Stir together oil, vinegar, and cream. Add to flour. Form dough into disc. Wrap in plastic. Refrigerate for 1 hour. Roll out dough on lightly floured, cold surface and place in deep-dish pie plate. Crimp edges. Brush inside with some of the egg white. Mix 1 teaspoon water with remaining egg. Brush edges with egg wash, sprinkle with sugar, and chill in freezer.

For the filling: Preheat oven to 400°F. Cream butter and sugars. Beat in eggs slowly, mixing until well combined. Beat in vanilla, salt, and spices. Mix in syrups and chopped pecans. Pour into prepared pie shell and arrange pecan halves on top. Bake for 20 minutes, then reduce oven to 350°F. Bake for 30 minutes or until pie is almost completely set. Cool completely. Serve with whipped cream if desired.

DREAM DATE PECAN PIE

Marles Riessland, Riverdale, NE
2006 APC Crisco National Pie Championships Amateur Division 1st Place Nut

CRUST
1 cup pastry flour
2 cups all-purpose flour
1 teaspoon salt
1 teaspoon sugar
½ teaspoon baking powder
1 cup plus 1 tablespoon butter-
   flavored Crisco, chilled
⅓ cup water (ice-cold)
1 tablespoon vinegar
1 egg, beaten

FILLING
4 eggs, well-beaten
¾ cup sugar

⅓ cup pure maple syrup
½ cup light corn syrup
½ cup dark corn syrup
2½ teaspoons vanilla
¼ teaspoon salt
⅓ cup dates, cut into small pieces
1 cup pecans, broken
⅓ cup butter, melted
Additional pecan halves, as desired

GLAZE
2 tablespoons maple syrup

For the crust: In large bowl, combine the flours, salt, sugar, and baking powder. Cut in shortening with a pastry blender until the mixture resembles cornmeal. In small bowl, mix water and vinegar with the beaten egg. Add the liquid mixture, one tablespoon at a time, to the flour mixture, tossing with a fork to form a soft dough. Shape into three discs. Wrap in plastic wrap and chill in refrigerator. Use one disc for this recipe. Roll out a single pastry and line a 9-inch pie dish; flute edge.

For the filling: Preheat oven to 375°F. In medium bowl. combine sugar, syrups, vanilla, and salt with beaten eggs; stir until blended. Stir in dates, pecans, and melted butter. Pour filling into pie shell. Place pecan halves on top, as desired. Protect edge of pie with foil to prevent excessive browning. Bake 20 minutes. Reduce oven temperature to 350°F and bake 30 to 35 minutes or until center is set.

For the glaze: Brush hot pie with 2 tablespoons maple syrup. Cool and store in refrigerator.

MAPLE-KISSED BUTTER PECAN CELEBRATION PIE

Sandi Klinger, Fitzpatrick, AL
2004 APC Crisco National Pie Championships Amateur Division 2nd Place Nut

CRUST
2 cups flour
1 teaspoon salt
¾ cup butter-flavor Crisco
¼ cup finely chopped pecans
3 tablespoons ice water

FILLING
1 stick butter
1 cup light Karo syrup
1 cup sugar
3 large eggs

2 tablespoons real maple syrup
1 teaspoon vanilla
Dash of salt
1 cup chopped pecans

TOPPING
⅓ cup firmly packed brown sugar
3 tablespoons honey
3 tablespoons butter
1 tablespoon real maple syrup
1½ cups pecan halves

For the crust: Combine flour, salt, and pecans. Cut in shortening until coarse crumbs form. Sprinkle ice water over crumbs 1 tablespoon at a time. Toss with a fork. Form a ball and roll to fit 9-inch pie pan. Use leftovers to make decorations.

For the filling: Preheat oven to 425°F. Brown butter in saucepan until it is golden brown. Do not burn. Let cool. In a separate bowl, add ingredients in order listed; stir. Blend in browned butter well. Pour in unbaked pie shell. Bake at 425°F for 10 minutes, then lower to 350°F for 30 to 40 minutes. Pie should be well-browned and set in the center.

For the topping: Combine sugar, butter, maple syrup, and honey in a saucepan. Bring to a boil. Cook about 2 minutes, stirring constantly. Add nuts and stir until coated. Spoon evenly on top of the pie. Bake 10 minutes more until bubbly. Cool pie to room temperature.

Decorate with pastry leaves if desired.

MAPLE PEACH PECAN PIE

Charlie Campbell, Belleville, WI
2006 APC Crisco National Pie Championships Amateur Division 2nd Place Nut

CRUST
⅓ cup and 1 tablespoon shortening
    or lard
1 cup all-purpose flour
½ teaspoon salt
1 to 3 tablespoons cold water

FILLING
3 eggs
⅔ cup brown sugar
½ teaspoon salt
⅓ cup butter or margarine
⅔ cup pure maple syrup
⅓ cup peach preserves
1 cup pecans

For the crust: Cut shortening into the flour and salt until the particles are the size of small peas. Sprinkle in water, 1 tablespoon at a time, tossing with fork until all the flour is moistened and pastry almost cleans the side of the bowl. Form dough into a ball. When ready to use, roll out and place in a 9-inch pie pan.

For the filling: Preheat oven to 375°F. Beat together the eggs, sugar, salt, butter, maple syrup, and peach preserves just until smooth. Put the cup of pecans onto the bottom unbaked pie crust. Pour the filling into the pie crust over the pecans. Bake for about 45 to 55 minutes.

WHITE-BOTTOMED CARAMEL CHOCOLATE PECAN PIE

Lisa Sparks, Atlanta, IN
2011 APC Crisco National Pie Championships Professional Division 1st Place Nut

CRUST
3/4 cup butter–flavored Crisco
2 cups all-purpose flour
1 teaspoon sugar
5 tablespoons cold water
Cream Cheese Layer
1 package cream cheese, softened
1/3 cup sugar
1 egg

FILLING
1/2 cup sugar
1 cup light corn syrup
1 tablespoon flour
3 tablespoons butter
1 tablespoon vanilla
3 eggs
1 cup whole pecans
1/3 cup caramel syrup
1/2 cup Ghirardelli semi-sweet
    chocolate, shaved

For the crust: Cut Crisco, flour, and sugar together. Add cold water and toss until dough forms ball. Refrigerate overnight. When ready, roll out on a floured surface and place in a pie plate.

For the cream cheese layer: Combine ingredients and beat until smooth. Spread cream cheese mixture in bottom of unbaked pie shell.

For the filling: Preheat oven to 350°F. Mix together sugar and flour. Add corn syrup and mix well. Add butter and vanilla and mix. Add eggs and mix until completely incorporated. Stir in pecans. Add layer of caramel syrup over the cream cheese layer. Then sprinkle the shaved Ghirardelli semi-sweet chocolate over the caramel syrup layer. Carefully add pecan mixture. Bake approximately 20 minutes. Dome pie and bake 1 hour or until slight crust forms on top of filling.

White-Bottomed Caramel Chocolate Pecan Pie

OPEN

"Pie, The Universal Dessert. Pie to Celebrate, Pie for Comfort, for every occasion, for everyone."

—Chef Kim R Montello, CMB
Johnson and Wales University

Ambrosia Pie	232	Lovin My Latte Pie	244
Back to the Islands Pie	234	Peaches and Creamy Cranberry Pie	246
Chocolate-Covered Strawberry Pie	236	Strawberry Thin Mint Pie	248
Classic Italian Tiramisu Pie	238	Chocolate Toffee Pie	250
Coffee Cup Chocolate Pie	240	Raspberry Chocolate Mint Ribbon Pie	252
Deep-Dish Deluxe Banana Split Pie	242		

‹‹ Lovin My Latte Pie (recipe page 244)

AMBROSIA PIE

Melanie Stein, Groveland, FL
2006 APC Crisco National Pie Championships Amateur Division 1st Place Open

CRUST
1 cup vanilla wafer crumbs (about 20 cookies)
1 cup toasted coconut
4 tablespoons butter
2 tablespoons sugar

FILLING
1 box coconut cream instant pudding mix (4 serving size)
16 oz. can crushed pineapple in juice, drained, reserving juice

8 oz. package cream cheese, room temperature
8 oz. container Cool Whip, softened
½ cup shredded sweetened coconut
¼ cup cream of coconut

TOPPING
1 cup heavy cream
1 teaspoon vanilla
1 tablespoon sugar
Toasted coconut and pineapple pieces for garnish

For the crust: Preheat oven to 350°F. Combine all ingredients in a food processor until well blended. Press into bottom and up sides of 9-inch pie dish. Bake 10 minutes until crust is set. Allow to cool completely.

For the filling: In a bowl, use a whisk to blend together reserved pineapple juice, cream of coconut, and pudding. With a mixer, beat cream cheese for 1 minute in a separate bowl. Add pudding mixture, beat well. Add pineapple and shredded coconut. Beat until blended. Fold in Cool Whip. Pour into cooled crust. Refrigerate 2 hours before serving.

For the topping: Beat ingredients together, then spread over top of pie. Garnish with toasted coconut and small pieces of pineapple.

BACK TO THE ISLANDS PIE

Janet Ropp, Edgewater, FL
2008 APC Crisco National Pie Championships Amateur Division 1st Place Open

CRUST
2 cups graham cracker crumbs
½ cup butter, melted
3 tablespoons sugar
2 tablespoons vanilla flavoring

FILLING
8 oz. package cream cheese, softened
3.4 oz. package instant vanilla pudding
2½ cups milk

⅔ cup coconut
Fruit Layer
2 bananas, sliced
1 cup chopped mango, fresh or frozen
8 oz. can crushed pineapple, drained

TOPPING
8 oz. frozen whipped topping, thawed
¼ teaspoon coconut flavoring
⅓ cup chopped macadamia nuts

For the crust: Preheat oven to 350°F. Melt butter and add to rest of crust ingredients. Press into 9 ½-inch glass pie plate and bake for 10 minutes. Let crust cool before adding filling.

For the filling: Beat together cream cheese and milk. Add instant vanilla pudding and beat well for about 2 minutes. Add coconut and blend well.

For the fruit layer: Place sliced bananas over crust. Cover with pudding mixture. Drain pineapple and mix with chopped mango. Sprinkle mango and pineapple over pudding mixture.

For the topping: Mix together frozen whipped topping and coconut flavoring. Spread over pie. Sprinkle with chopped macadamia nuts. Chill. Serve pie chilled.

Back to the Islands Pie

CHOCOLATE-COVERED STRAWBERRY PIE

Phyllis Szymanek, Toledo, OH
2010 APC Crisco National Pie Championships Amateur Division 1st Place Open

CRUST
1 1/3 cups Pillsbury all-purpose flour
1/4 cup butter, cold
1/2 teaspoon salt
1/4 cup Crisco shortening (chilled)
3 to 4 tablespoons cold water
1 tablespoon sugar

FILLING AND GLAZE
7.25 oz. bottle Smucker's Magic
   Shell Chocolate Fudge

1 cup sugar
1 cup 7UP
2 tablespoons cornstarch
Pinch of salt
3 oz. box strawberry Jell-O
1 quart fresh strawberries (wash,
   dry, and cut off stems)
Cool Whip for garnish (optional)

For the crust: Preheat oven to 425°F. Mix flour, salt, and sugar. Cut in Crisco and butter with a pastry cutter until pea-sized pieces form. Add water, one tablespoon at a time, until dough forms into a ball. Wrap in plastic wrap and chill for 1 to 2 hours or overnight. Roll out on floured surface until pastry is 1 inch larger than 9-inch pie pan. Place into pie pan and flute edges. Prick bottom and sides of pie crust. Bake for 12 to 15 minutes. Remove from oven and cool on wire rack. Chill in refrigerator until ready to fill.

For the filling and glaze: Pour ½ bottle of Magic Shell Chocolate Fudge into bottom of chilled pie crust; refrigerate until set. In a small saucepan over medium heat, combine sugar, cornstarch, and salt. Gradually add 7UP. Cook until thick and clear. Remove from heat. Add Jell-O. Mix well. Let cool until almost set. Dip each strawberry into glaze and set into pie crust. Chill pie. Thirty minutes before serving, drizzle pie with remaining Magic Shell Chocolate Fudge. Roll 2 to 3 strawberries in Magic Shell and place in center of pie. Return to refrigerator until ready to serve. Top with Cool Whip if desired.

CLASSIC ITALIAN TIRAMISU PIE

Michele Stuart, Norwalk, CT
2010 APC Crisco National Pie Championships Professional Division 1st Place Open

CRUST
2 cups flour
1 teaspoon salt
¾ cup Crisco
5 tablespoons very cold water
Cream to brush on pie crust edge

FILLING
3 cups strong coffee, brewed
32 ladyfingers (see recipe below)
10 egg yolks
10 tablespoons sugar
1 pound mascarpone cheese

Kahlúa flavoring to taste
2 cups heavy cream

LADY FINGERS
4 eggs, separated
⅛ teaspoon salt
10 tablespoons sugar
2 teaspoons vanilla extract
⅓ cup sifted flour

GARNISH
2 cups whipped cream
Cocoa powder

For the crust: Preheat oven to 425°F. Combine flour and salt in a mixing bowl. Cut Crisco into the flour mixture until coarse crumbs form. Add water 1 tablespoon at a time, mixing gently until incorporated and dough can form a ball. Wrap dough in plastic and refrigerate for at least 30 minutes. Divide dough in half. Use only half the dough for this recipe. Roll out and place pastry in a 9-inch pan. Brush the edge of pie crust with cream. Bake for 15–20 minutes or until golden brown. Let the crust cool completely before filling.

For the filling: Whisk the egg yolks and sugar in a large mixing bowl until they are smooth and frothy. Add the mascarpone and Kahlúa flavoring, then whisk until blended and smooth. In another bowl, beat the cream until stiff. Fold the cream into the mascarpone mixture until well-blended and smooth. Layer the bottom of the pie-crust lightly with about ⅓ of the cream mixture, reserving some to layer on top of the ladyfingers. Pour the coffee into a baking dish to cool.

For the ladyfingers: Preheat oven to 350°F. Line baking sheets with parchment paper. Beat the egg whites and salt until foamy. Add 2 tablespoons of the sugar and beat until soft peaks form. Set aside. In another bowl, beat the egg yolks until thickened. Then gradually beat in the remaining sugar and the vanilla. Beat until very thick and lemon-colored. Sprinkle the flour over the egg yolk mixture. Then fold in the flour carefully. Fold the egg yolk mixture into the egg

Classic Italian Tiramisu Pie

whites. Using a pastry tube, make 3-inch long finger shapes of batter two inches apart on the prepared baking sheets. Bake for 5 minutes or until deep golden brown. Cool 2–3 minutes. Once cool, carefully remove the ladyfingers from the paper with a sharp knife. Dip the ladyfingers quickly into the coffee. Place the ladyfingers on top of the cream layer in the pie crust, covering the entire area. Spread ⅓ of the cream mixture on top of the ladyfingers. Dip the remaining ladyfingers quickly into the coffee and arrange them over the second cream layer. Spread the remaining cream mixture over the ladyfingers.

Refrigerate pie for at least 6 hours. When ready to serve, pipe whipped cream decoratively on top of pie. Sprinkle the cocoa powder over pie. Serve cold.

COFFEE CUP CHOCOLATE PIE

Ted Cano, Athens, GA
2008 APC Crisco National Pie Championships Amateur Division 3rd Place Open

CRUST
6 tablespoons butter, melted
24 graham crackers
¼ cup sugar

FILLING
1 cup semi-sweet chocolate chips
⅓ cup whipping cream
1 tablespoon vanilla extract
Dash salt

½ cup pecans
4 oz. cream cheese, softened
1½ cups milk
2 tablespoons brewed coffee
(2) ¾ oz. packages instant vanilla pudding mix
2 tablespoons instant coffee granules
1 large container frozen whipped topping, thawed and divided

For the crust: Preheat oven to 350°F. Melt butter and combine with crumbs and sugar. Press into a pie plate and bake for 8 to 10 minutes.

For the filling: In a saucepan, melt chocolate chips, cream, vanilla, and salt over low heat, stirring until smooth. Spoon into the crust. Sprinkle with pecans. In a large mixing bowl, beat cream cheese until smooth. Gradually add milk and brewed coffee, then mix well. Add pudding mixes and instant coffee, beating until smooth. Fold in 1½ cups whipped topping. Spoon over pecans. Spread remaining whipped topping over filling. Refrigerate for at least 3 hours before serving.

Coffee Cup Chocolate Pie

DEEP-DISH DELUXE BANANA SPLIT PIE

Carol Socier, Bay City, MI
2011 APC Crisco National Pie Championships Amateur Division 1st Place Open

CRUST
1½ cups all-purpose flour
⅓ cup crushed vanilla wafers
1 teaspoon sugar
½ cup Crisco shortening
5 to 6 tablespoons cold water

FILLING
½ cup chocolate fudge ice cream
   topping
¼ cup plus 2 tablespoons sugar
2 tablespoons cornstarch
¼ teaspoon salt
¾ cup water
½ 3 oz. package strawberry Jell-O

10 oz. package frozen strawberries
3 large bananas
3 oz. package French vanilla instant
   pudding
1 ¾ cups half and half
1 cup whipped cream
1½ cups miniature marshmallows

GARNISH
Whipped cream
Maraschino cherries
Chopped peanuts
Chocolate Magic Shell ice cream
   topping

For the crust: Preheat oven to 400°F. Combine flour, wafers, and sugar in large bowl. Cut in shortening with pastry blender until pea-size pieces form. Add water, 1 tablespoon at a time, tossing with a fork until dough forms a ball. On lightly floured surface, roll out dough to fit 9-inch deep-dish pie plate. Flute edges, and prick bottom and sides with a fork. Bake for 12 to 15 minutes or until golden brown. Cool for at least 1 hour before filling.

For the filling: Drizzle chocolate fudge ice cream topping on bottom pie crust and refrigerate. Combine sugar, cornstarch, salt, and water in a saucepan. Cook over medium heat until thick and clear. Add strawberry Jell-O, stirring until dissolved. Add frozen strawberries. Place in refrigerator until cool and thick. Assemble pie by slicing bananas over fudge topping. Gently spoon strawberry mixture over bananas. Put in refrigerator until set. Meanwhile, prepare instant French vanilla pudding according to package directions, using half and half. Fold in whipped cream and marshmallows. Spread over strawberry layer.

Garnish with more whipped cream, cherries, and chopped peanuts. Drizzle with Magic Shell. Keep refrigerated.

Deep-Dish Deluxe Banana Split Pie

LOVIN MY LATTE PIE

Diane E. Selich, Vassar, MI
2010 APC Crisco National Pie Championships Professional Division
Honorable Mention Open

CRUST
1¼ cups graham cracker crumbs
¼ cup sugar
⅓ cup cocoa powder
½ cup butter, melted

FILLING
(2) 8 oz. packages cream cheese, softened
¼ cup sugar

½ cup French vanilla instant coffee mix
2 eggs, slightly beaten
¼ cup French vanilla liquid creamer
¼ teaspoon clear vanilla

GARNISH
¾ cup chocolate chips
2 cups whipped cream

For the crust: Combine all ingredients. Press mixture into bottom and sides of pie plate. Set aside until ready to fill.

For the filling: Preheat oven to 350°F. Cream together the cheese, eggs, and vanilla. Add the coffee mix, sugar, and creamer. Mix well. Pour into pie shell and bake for 35 to 40 minutes. Cool.

For the garnish: Melt ¾ cup chocolate chips in a double boiler. Drizzle chocolate over the pie. Garnish the edges with 2 cups of whipped cream.

PEACHES AND CREAMY CRANBERRY PIE

Lisa Schiessl, Fond du Lac, WI
2009 APC Crisco National Pie Championships Amateur Division 3rd Place Open

CRUST
¾ cup all-purpose flour
½ tablespoon sugar
Pinch salt
½ cup Crisco
¼ cup cake flour
1 tablespoon liquid egg substitute
½ tablespoon vinegar
Water (to equal ¼ cup liquid)

FILLING
½ cup sour cream
½ cup mascarpone cheese
8 oz. cream cheese
1 egg
2 tablespoons flour

1 teaspoon vanilla
2 tablespoons peach jam
¾ cup sugar
1 teaspoon cinnamon
1 teaspoon nutmeg
2 cups diced peaches (frozen or fresh)
1 cup whole cranberries
1 cup crushed cranberries

TOPPING
¾ cup crushed coconut macaroons
¼ cup brown sugar
½ teaspoon cinnamon
1 tablespoon flour
¼ cup butter (melted)

For the crust: In medium-sized bowl, whisk together all-purpose flour, sugar, and salt. With a pastry blender, cut in Crisco until pieces of dough resemble coarse crumbs. Sift cake flour over crumbs and mix lightly with fork. In separate small bowl, whisk together liquid egg, vinegar, and enough water to equal ¼ cup liquid. Stir egg mixture into flour mixture just until moistened. Roll dough into large ball. On a lightly floured board, roll out ball of dough to fit a 9-inch pie plate. Transfer prepared dough to pie plate; trim and flute.

For the filling: Preheat oven to 400°F. In large mixing bowl, cream together sour cream, mascarpone cheese, cream cheese, egg, flour, vanilla, peach jam, sugar, cinnamon, and nutmeg. Mix until well blended. Add diced peaches, whole cranberries, and crushed cranberries. Stir to coat. Pour into prepared bottom pie crust. Bake pie for 10 minutes, then reduce oven to 350°F and bake for 25 to 30 minutes.

For the topping: While pie is baking, in small mixing bowl combine crushed coconut macaroons, brown sugar, cinnamon, and flour. Pour melted butter evenly over combined topping ingredients. Set aside for 5 minutes, then using your fingertips break the mixture into ¼- to ½-inch crumbs. Top pie with coconut macaroon topping and bake 10 to 15 more minutes at 350°F.

STRAWBERRY THIN MINT PIE

Raine Gottess, Coconut Creek, FL
2007 APC Crisco National Pie Championships Amateur Division 1ˢᵗ Place Open

CRUST
¾ package Keebler mint chocolate-
    covered cookies
5 tablespoons butter, melted
1 tablespoon sugar

LAYER ONE
8 oz. cream cheese, softened
1 ½ cups powdered sugar
1 tablespoon milk
1 teaspoon vanilla
8 oz. Cool Whip

FILLING
1 cup Smucker's strawberry jam

LAYER TWO
8 oz. Strawberry Jammin'
    Philadelphia Cream Cheese
1 tablespoon milk
1 teaspoon vanilla
1½ cups powdered sugar
8 oz. creamy Cool Whip

OPTIONAL TOPPING
Strawberries, strawberry glaze, Cool
    Whip

For the crust: Crush cookies. Add sugar and butter, mixing until moist. Press with the back of a spoon into a 10-inch deep-dish pie pan. Freeze.

For layer 1: With a mixer, beat together cream cheese, vanilla, and milk until well combined. Add in powdered sugar and Cool Whip. Spread ½ the mixture over the cookie crust and freeze for about 10 minutes. Set aside the remainder of the mixture.

For filling: Spread jam over layer 1 and freeze.

For layer 2: In a mixing bowl, beat well the cream cheese, milk, and vanilla. Add powdered sugar and Cool Whip. Add the remaining batter from layer 1 and mix well. Spread over the jam.

Top pie with strawberries drizzled with strawberry glaze. Decorate edges with Strawberry Cool Whip. Refrigerate overnight to firm.

Strawberry Thin Mint Pie

CHOCOLATE TOFFEE PIE

Diane Kretschmer, Clermont, FL
2005 APC Crisco National Pie Championships Amateur Division 2nd Place Open

CRUST
1½ cups crushed vanilla wafers
½ cup ground almonds
6 tablespoons butter

FILLING
⅔ cup butter, softened
1½ cups confectioner's sugar, sifted
2 egg yolks

2 cups semi-sweet chocolate pieces, melted
1 cup chopped almonds
1 teaspoon vanilla
2 egg whites, stiffly beaten (use pasteurized eggs)

GARNISH
Whipped cream
1 toffee candy bar (crushed)

For the crust: Preheat oven to 350°F. Mix ingredients together. Pat into pie plate. Bake for 10 minutes. Cool.

For the filling: Cream butter and sugar together. Stir in yolks, chocolate, almonds, and vanilla.

Fold in beaten egg whites. Pour mixture into cooled pie shell. Chill.

Garnish with whipped cream and crushed toffee bar and serve.

RASPBERRY CHOCOLATE MINT RIBBON PIE

Beth Campbell, Belleville, WI
2003 APC Crisco National Pie Championships Amateur Division 1st Place Open

CRUST
1 cup flour
½ cup Crisco shortening
¼ cup cold water
Pinch of salt

CHOCOLATE FILLING
1½ sticks butter
1½ cups powdered sugar
5 egg yolks
½ teaspoon peppermint flavoring
3 squares baking chocolate, melted and cooled
5 egg whites, stiffly beaten

CREAM CHEESE FILLING
3 oz. cream cheese, softened
⅓ cup sifted powdered sugar
1 teaspoon vanilla
1 cup heavy whipped cream

RASPBERRY FILLING
(you can substitute 1 cup of seedless raspberry jam)
1½ tablespoons sugar
1 cup frozen raspberries
½ tablespoon cornstarch

For the crust: Preheat oven to 475°F . Cut shortening into salt and flour until pea-sized pieces form. Add cold water slowly until mixture forms a ball. Refrigerate several hours or overnight. Roll out on a floured board. Put in pie pan. Prick crust on bottom of pan with a fork. Bake for 8 to 10 minutes until light brown. Cool.

For the chocolate filling: Cream together butter and powdered sugar. Add egg yolks one yolk at a time. Add peppermint flavoring and melted chocolate. Fold in egg whites.

For the cream cheese filling: Mix together powdered sugar, vanilla, and cream cheese. Fold in whipped cream until smooth.

For the raspberry filling: Cook raspberries in a saucepan over medium-low heat until they are partially cooked. Run raspberries through a cheesecloth or sieve to remove the seeds. Return to heat and add cornstarch. Boil over medium heat. Allow to cool and then spread half of the raspberry filling into baked pie shell gently. Spread half of the chocolate filling over that and chill. Spread half the cream cheese filling over the chocolate filling. Repeat the layers. Refrigerate until ready to serve.

PEANUT BUTTER

"I first met the members of the American Pie Council in 2005 when I participated in the National Pie Championship--I was shaking like a leaf. Immediately I was included into the family of pie bakers and haven't been the same since. I liken it to spending time with the family you have always wanted or wished for. But what would one expect from the best pie bakers in the United States."

—John Michael Lerma
APC Crisco National Pie Championships, Blue Ribbon Winner
Food Network Challenge, Minnesota State Fair and other contests.
Author, Garden County Pie, Owner, Garden County Cooking
St. Paul, MN

Category Five Peanut Butter Pie 256

Flutter Nutter Peanut Butter
Candy Bar Pie 258

It's All About the Peanut Butter Pie 260

Oreo Peanut Butter Mousse Pie 262

William's Peanut Butter Paradise Pie 264

Peanut Butter Proposal Pie 266

Peanut Butter -n- Strawberry
Explosion Pie 268

Premier Peanut Butter Pie 270

The Ultimate Peanut Butter Pie 272

‹‹ It's All About the Peanut Butter Pie (recipe page 260)

CATEGORY FIVE PEANUT BUTTER PIE

Phyllis Szymanek, Toledo, OH
2009 APC Crisco National Pie Championships Amateur Division 1st Place Peanut Butter and Best of Show

CRUST
1 ⅓ cups finely crushed vanilla wafers
2 tablespoons sugar
½ teaspoon vanilla
⅓ cup melted butter, unsalted

FILLING 1
¾ cup powdered sugar
⅓ cup Jif creamy peanut butter
3 tablespoons softened butter (unsalted)
¼ cup chopped peanuts (save small amount for garnish)

FILLING 2
⅔ cup sugar
3 tablespoons cornstarch
1 tablespoon Pillsbury all-purpose flour
½ teaspoon salt
3 cups milk
3 egg yolks, lightly beaten
¾ cup Jif peanut butter
1½ teaspoons vanilla extract
6 small (.55 oz.) frozen peanut butter cups, chopped

For the crust: Preheat oven to 350°F. Mix all the ingredients in a bowl until blended; pour into a 9-inch pie dish sprayed with Crisco spray. Press into the bottom and sides. Bake for 8 to 12 minutes or until lightly browned. Let cool.

For filling 1: Mix sugar, peanut butter, and butter in a small bowl. Spread into bottom of cooled pie shell and sprinkle with peanuts.

For filling 2: In medium saucepan combine sugar, cornstarch, flour, and salt over medium heat. Gradually stir in milk until smooth. Bring to a boil. Cook and stir for 2 minutes. Remove from heat. Gradually stir one cup of hot filling into egg yolks. Return all to saucepan, stirring constantly. Return to a boil. Cook and stir for 2 minutes. Remove from heat. Add vanilla and peanut butter. Let cool. Fold in 5 chopped peanut butter cups. Pour into cooled pie shell. Garnish with Cool Whip and remaining chopped peanut butter cups and chopped peanuts.

Category Five Peanut Butter Pie

FLUTTER NUTTER PEANUT BUTTER CANDY BAR PIE

Melanie Adams
2010 APC Crisco National Pie Championships Amateur Division 1st Place Peanut Butter

CRUST
12 peanut butter sandwich crème
   cookies, such as Nutter Butters
¼ cup granulated sugar
6 tablespoons butter, melted
Candy Bar Layer
½ cup chocolate hazelnut spread,
   such as Nutella
8 miniature peanut butter cups,
   coarsely chopped

FILLING
8 oz. package cream cheese

7 oz. jar marshmallow cream
¾ cup creamy peanut butter
8 oz. container frozen whipped
   topping, thawed

GARNISH
2 coarsely chopped peanut butter
   sandwich crème cookies, such as
   Nutter Butters
3 coarsely chopped miniature peanut
   butter cups

For the crust: Process the peanut butter sandwich crème cookies in a food processor until fine crumbs are formed. Add in melted butter and sugar and process until blended, about 30 seconds. The mixture will resemble wet sand. Press mixture into a 9-inch pie plate that has been sprayed with non-stick cooking spray.

For the candy bar layer: Spread chocolate hazelnut spread on top of the crust and sprinkle with the coarsely chopped miniature peanut butter cups.

For the filling: Blend the cream cheese, marshmallow cream, and peanut butter with an electric mixer until smooth. Add in the whipped topping and mix with an electric mixer until blended. Spoon the filling on top of the candy bar mixture and smooth out so that it is evenly distributed.

Garnish by sprinkling coarsely chopped peanut butter sandwich crème cookies and miniature peanut butter cups over pie. Chill for a minimum of 2 hours.

IT'S ALL ABOUT THE PEANUT BUTTER PIE

Patricia Lapiezo, La Mesa, CA
2010 APC Crisco National Pie Championships Amateur Division 3rd Place Peanut Butter

CRUST
12 Nutter Butter cookies
4 Nature Valley peanut butter granola
  bars
1/3 cup butter, melted

FILLING
2 8 oz. packages cream cheese,
  softened
1 1/3 cups powdered sugar
2 teaspoons vanilla
4 oz. semi-sweet chocolate, melted

3/4 cup creamy peanut butter
2½ cups heavy whipping cream,
  stiffly beaten
2/3 cup chopped miniature peanut
  butter cups
2.1 oz. Butterfinger candy bar,
  chopped
Peanut Butter Ganache
½ cup semi-sweet chocolate chips
1/3 cup heavy whipping cream
3 to 4 tablespoons creamy peanut
  butter

For the crust: In a food processor, finely grind the cookies and granola bars. Pulse in butter until blended. Press onto bottom and up sides of a 9-inch pie dish. Freeze at least 10 minutes while preparing filling.

For the filling: In a large bowl, combine the cream cheese, powdered sugar, and vanilla and beat until fluffy. Divide in half. To the first half, beat in the melted chocolate until combined. Fold in half of the whipped cream and chopped peanut butter cups. To the other half, beat in the peanut butter until combined and then fold in remaining whipped cream and chopped Butterfinger bar. Spread the chocolate layer in the prepared pie crust, then top with the peanut butter layer, smoothing top.

For the peanut butter ganache: In a small saucepan over low heat, heat the chocolate chips and whipping cream until melted. Stir in 2 tablespoons peanut butter. Pour over top of pie to within ½ inch of edge. Heat the remaining peanut butter until of pouring consistency and place in a pastry bag or Ziploc bag fitted with a fine tip. Pipe parallel lines about ½ inch apart on top of ganache. With a sharp knife or toothpick, draw lines crosswise through these lines, alternating direction each time. Decorate edge of pie with a border of sweetened whipped cream. Chill pie 2 hours, or until firm.

OREO PEANUT BUTTER MOUSSE PIE

Steve Delph, Lakeland, FL
2011 APC Crisco National Pie Championships Amateur Division 2nd Place Peanut Butter

CRUST
16.6 oz. package Oreo Double Stuff
    cookies
1½ sticks (12 tablespoons) salted
    butter
1 tablespoon sugar

PEANUT BUTTER MOUSSE FILLING
¾ cup creamy or chunky peanut
    butter
8 oz. mascarpone cheese, softened
¾ cup sugar
1 ½ cups heavy cream
¼ cup confectioner's sugar
1 teaspoon vanilla extract or vanilla
    powder

WHIPPED PIE TOPPING
1 cup heavy cream
¼ cup confectioner's sugar
1 teaspoon vanilla extract or vanilla
    powder

For the crust: Preheat oven to 350°F. Open the package of Oreo cookies. Separate the double stuff filling from each cookie and place the filling in a separate container for use in the peanut butter mousse. This should leave you with approximately 4 cups of Oreo cookies. Put the 4 cups of cookies into a food processor and do a rough chop. Melt the 1½ sticks of butter and add this plus the 1 tablespoon of sugar to the chopped cookies. Pulse several times to mix the butter and sugar into the cookies to a point where the cookies look like crumbs. Be careful to not over-chop the cookies. Once complete, reserve ¾ cups of the crumbs for topping. Put these crumbs in an oven-safe container. These crumbs will be used later as a garnish for the whipped topping. Press the remainder of the crumbs into a pie pan. Put the pie pan and remaining crumbs in the oven and bake for 10 minutes. Once done, let the pie crust and crumbs cool.

For the peanut butter mousse filling: Put the peanut butter into the mixer bowl. Using a stand mixer with a whisk attachment, begin to mix with the whisk. Add the mascarpone cheese and ¾ cups of sugar and mix thoroughly on medium-high. As this mixes, begin to add all of the double-stuff cream into the mixture a little at a time. Continue mixing until all ingredients are thoroughly mixed. You may need to stop the mixer and scrape the bowl several times during this process. In a separate bowl, and with a clean whisk attachment, begin to whip 1 ½ cups of heavy cream. Add ¼ cup of confectioner's

Oreo Peanut Butter Mousse Pie

sugar and 1 teaspoon vanilla. Whisk to the stiff peak stage. Gently fold this whipped cream into the peanut butter mixture. Once done, pour the peanut butter mixture into the prepared Oreo pie crust.

For the whipped pie topping: In a clean mixing bowl, and with a clean whisk, begin whipping the 1 cup of heavy cream. Add ¼ cup of confectioner's sugar and 1 teaspoon vanilla. (For additional flavor you can add 2 teaspoons maple sugar and/or 1 teaspoon maple syrup.) Whisk to the stiff peak stage. Once at the stiff peak stage, remove the bowl from the mixer. Stir the ¾ cup of reserved Oreo cookie crumbs into the whipped cream. Spoon this mixture onto the peanut butter mousse and smooth to finish. Put the pie in the refrigerator and let cool prior to serving.

WILLIAM'S PEANUT BUTTER PARADISE PIE

Dionna Hurt, Longwood, FL
2011 APC Crisco National Pie Championships Professional Division
Peanut Butter Honorable Mention

CRUST
12 peanut butter sandwich crème
  cookies
¼ cup granulated sugar
6 tablespoons butter, melted

FILLING
½ cup chocolate hazelnut spread

¼ cup honey-roasted peanuts,
  chopped
8 oz. cream cheese
Small jar Marshmallow Fluff
1 cup peanut butter
2 cups whipped cream

For the crust: Process the peanut butter sandwich crème cookies in a food processor until fine crumbs are formed. Add in melted butter and sugar and process until blended. The mixture will resemble wet sand. Press mixture into a 9-inch pie plate that has been sprayed with non-stick cooking spray.

For the filling: Blend the cream cheese, marshmallow cream, and peanut butter with an electric mixer until smooth. Add in the whipped cream and mix with an electric mixer until blended.

Place ½ of filling in crust. Spread chocolate spread over filling and sprinkle with chopped honey-roasted peanuts. Spread remaining filling over chocolate spread and nuts.

Garnish with additional chopped nuts, chocolate spread, and whipped cream.

William's Peanut Butter Paradise Pie

PEANUT BUTTER PROPOSAL PIE

Raine Gottess, Coconut Creek, FL
2006 APC Crisco National Pie Championships Amateur Division 1st Place Peanut Butter

CRUST
18 Nutter Butter cookies, finely
   crushed
3 ½ tablespoons butter, melted

LAYER 1
12 oz. cream cheese, softened
1½ cups powdered sugar
1 tablespoon milk
1 teaspoon vanilla
8 oz. creamy Cool Whip

FILLING
4 Reese's Peanut Butter Cups

LAYER 2
¼ cup brown sugar
1 cup creamy peanut butter
6 oz. Cool Whip

GARNISH
Cool Whip
Crushed peanuts
Reese's Peanut Butter Cups

For the crust: Mix ingredients together in a bowl until moist and press into 9- or 10-inch deep-dish pie pan. Freeze 10 minutes to firm.

For layer 1: In a mixer, beat all ingredients together well until blended and spread ½ of the mixture over the crust.

For the filling: Chop Reese's Peanut Butter Cups and place over Layer 1, then freeze pie about 5 minutes. Then take remaining half of layer 1 and spread over peanut butter cups.

For layer 2: In a mixer, blend all the ingredients together thoroughly. Spread over filling.

To garnish: Decorate with Cool Whip over entire pie. Add a sprinkle of crushed peanuts and 4 chopped Reese's Peanut Butter Cups. Refrigerate 8 hours.

Peanut Butter Proposal Pie

PEANUT BUTTER -N- STRAWBERRY EXPLOSION PIE

Erika Werkheiser, Orlando, FL
2008 APC Crisco National Pie Championships Amateur Division 3rd Place Peanut Butter

CRUST
30 vanilla wafers, crushed
¼ tablespoon butter, melted
½ cup strawberry jelly

FILLING
8 oz. package (⅓ less fat) cream
  cheese

¾ cup sugar
1¾ cups peanut butter
8 oz. tub frozen whipped topping,
  thawed

GARNISH
Fresh strawberries
Strawberry jelly

For the crust: Mix vanilla wafers and melted butter together and spread evenly on bottom and sides of pie plate. Chill in refrigerator for 15 to 20 minutes. Spread strawberry jelly evenly on bottom crust. Cover, refrigerate.

For the filling: Beat cream cheese in bowl until smooth. Slowly beat in sugar. Stir in peanut butter and whipped topping until blended. Spoon mixture onto crust over strawberry jelly. Cover. Refrigerate at least 8 hours.

For the garnish: Put fresh strawberries or peanut butter chips on top of pie. Fill a candy decorating bag with strawberry jelly. Decorate pie with the jelly and make swirls in the jelly with a toothpick.

PREMIER PEANUT BUTTER PIE

June Daley, Cincinnati, OH
2007 APC Crisco National Pie Championships Amateur Division 2nd Place Peanut Butter

CRUST
2½ cups graham crackers, crushed
½ cup chopped peanuts
2 tablespoons sugar
1 stick (½ cup) butter, melted

PEANUT BUTTER LAYER
4 oz. cream cheese
1 cup powdered sugar
1 cup peanut butter
4 oz. Cool Whip
1 teaspoon vanilla
6 regular-size peanut butter cups,
  chopped

FUDGE LAYER
½ cup hot fudge sauce

TOPPING
8 oz. Cool Whip
4 oz. cream cheese
½ cup powdered sugar

GARNISH
Peanut butter cups
Chopped peanuts

For the crust: Preheat oven to 350°F. Mix crust ingredients together. Press into plate. Bake for 10 minutes. Cool completely.

For the peanut butter layer: Mix cream cheese and powdered sugar. Add Cool Whip, peanut butter, and vanilla to mixture. Fold in chopped peanut butter cups. Place mixture in cooled graham cracker crust.

For the fudge layer: Microwave hot fudge for 45 seconds. Smooth a thin layer of hot fudge over the peanut butter layer. Put in refrigerator to firm slightly.

For the topping: Mix topping ingredients. Spoon topping over hot fudge layer.

Garnish pie with 3 chopped regular-size peanut butter cups and 2 tablespoons chopped peanuts.

Refrigerate for at least 6 hours.

THE ULTIMATE PEANUT BUTTER PIE

Laura Francese, Gerry, NY
2007 APC Crisco National Pie Championships Amateur Division 1st Place Peanut Butter

CRUST
10 Nutter Butter cookies, crushed
2 tablespoons brown sugar
1 cup quick oats
¼ cup flour
6 tablespoons butter, melted

BOTTOM AND TOP LAYERS
¼ cup heavy cream
¾ cup semi-sweet chocolate chips
½ cup chopped peanuts

PEANUT BUTTER FILLING
8 oz. package cream cheese, room
  temperature
1 cup creamy peanut butter
1 cup powdered sugar
1 teaspoon vanilla extract
12 oz. whipped topping

For the crust: Preheat oven to 350°F. Combine all crust ingredients and press into a deep-dish 9-inch pie pan. Bake for 7 minutes. Remove from oven and let cool to room temperature.

For the bottom and top layers: Microwave cream and chocolate chips in a microwave-safe bowl 30 seconds at a time until smooth and creamy. Do not overheat. Sprinkle ¼ cup of the chopped peanuts on the bottom cooled crust. Drizzle half the melted chocolate mixture on top of the peanuts in pie crust, extending mixture up the sides of the crust. Refrigerate for 30 minutes. Save the remaining chocolate and peanuts for the pie top layer.

For the peanut butter filling: Cream the peanut butter and cream cheese together until thoroughly combined. Slowly add sugar and vanilla to mixture. Fold in whipped topping. Pour this mixture over the chocolate-covered peanut layer. Sprinkle the remaining peanuts and melted chocolate on top of the pie filling. Refrigerate at least 2 hours before serving.

PUMPKIN

Sears Hometown Stores and our local owners have been happy to support the APC Crisco National Pie Championships. After all, it takes a winning oven like Kenmore to bake a championship pie.

—Jackie Schauer, Sears Hometown Stores

Farm-Fresh Pumpkin Pie
  with Pecan Topping ... 276
Grandma's Pumpkin Pie ... 278
Harvest Pumpkin Pie ... 280
Honey Crunch Pumpkin Pie ... 282
Pecan Maple Streusel Pumpkin Pie ... 284

Octoberfest Pie ... 286
Old-Fashioned Pumpkin Pie ... 288
Real Pumpkin Pie ... 290
Tasty Pumpkin Pie ... 292
Walnut Crunch Pumpkin Pie ... 294

‹‹ *Tasty Pumpkin Pie (recipe page 292)*

FARM-FRESH PUMPKIN PIE WITH PECAN TOPPING

Tricia Largay, Brewer, ME
2011 APC Crisco National Pie Championships Amateur Division 3rd Place Pumpkin

CRUST
⅓ cup plus 2 tablespoons Crisco
    butter-flavored shortening
1 cup all-purpose flour
¼ teaspoon salt
Pinch of sugar
6 to 7 tablespoons ice-cold water

FILLING
2 cans pure pumpkin (fresh pump-
    kins when in season cooked fork
    tender)
4 tablespoons melted butter
½ cup sugar

1 tablespoon brown sugar
½ teaspoon pumpkin pie spice
1 tablespoon molasses
2 large farm-fresh eggs
Pinch of ground cloves
⅓ cup evaporated milk

TOPPING
¾ cup brown sugar
⅓ cup flour
3 tablespoons butter, melted
½ cup chopped pecans

For the crust: Mix flour, salt, and sugar. Cut in shortening with fingers or fork until mixture resembles small peas. Add just enough water to allow entire mixture to stick together. Roll out on floured waxed paper. Press into 9-inch pie plate.

For the filling: Preheat oven to 350°F. Put pumpkin in large mixing bowl. Blend with spices. Mix by hand until completely blended. Add eggs, sugars, molasses, butter, and evapo-rated milk. Mix until smooth. Pour into prepared pie shell.

For the topping: Put brown sugar and flour in bowl and mix. Add chopped pecans and melted butter. Spread over pumpkin pie.

Bake for 50 to 60 minutes or until topping is golden brown. Serve warm or chilled.

Farm-Fresh Pumpkin Pie with Pecan Topping

GRANDMA'S PUMPKIN PIE

Vicky Hart, Kokomo, IN
2007 APC Crisco National Pie Championships Amateur Division 2nd Place Pumpkin

CRUST
1 cup Crisco shortening
3 tablespoons sugar
2 cups Wondra flour
½ cup cold water

FILLING
16 oz. pumpkin

¾ cup sugar
1 teaspoon cinnamon
1 teaspoon pumpkin spice
6 oz. evaporated milk
7 oz. sweetened condensed milk
2 eggs
1 tablespoon Wondra flour

For the crust: Combine Wondra flour, sugar, and Crisco using a pastry blender until crumbly. Add water and mix with pastry blender until able to form a ball. Cover and refrigerate for at least 2 hours. When cold, roll out onto a floured surface until ⅛ inch thick. Place into a 9-inch pie pan and prick bottom with fork. Fold edges under and decorate with desired cutouts.

For the filling: Preheat oven to 350°F. Mix pumpkin, sugar, flour, and spices until blended. Add sweetened condensed milk and mix until blended. Slowly blend in evaporated milk. Add eggs and mix until blended. Put in a prepared pie shell. Bake for approximately 1 hour and 15 minutes or until knife inserted in center comes out clean.

HARVEST PUMPKIN PIE

Amy Freeze, Sebring, FL
2011 APC Crisco National Pie Championships Amateur Division 2nd Place Pumpkin

CRUST
¼ cup butter
¼ cup shortening
1¼ cups all-purpose flour
1 tablespoon sugar
¼ teaspoon salt
1 egg yolk
2 tablespoons ice water
½ teaspoon vinegar

FILLING
15 oz. can pumpkin
14 oz. can sweetened condensed milk
4 eggs
1 cup apple butter

1 teaspoon cinnamon
½ teaspoon ground ginger
½ teaspoon nutmeg
½ teaspoon salt
1 teaspoon vanilla extract
1 cup chopped candied pecans

TOPPING
8 oz. Cool Whip
⅛ teaspoon nutmeg
¼ teaspoon ground ginger
½ teaspoon cinnamon
1 teaspoon clear vanilla

For the crust: Beat together butter and shortening until smooth and creamy. Chill until firm. Sift together flour, sugar, and salt in medium bowl. Using fork, cut butter and shortening into dry ingredients until mixture has a coarse crumb texture. Mix egg yolk, ice water, and vinegar into dough, then form into ball and refrigerate at least 1 hour. Roll out on floured surface, place in pan, crimp edges, and fill.

For the filling: Preheat oven to 425°F. In a large bowl, whisk pumpkin, condensed milk, eggs, apple butter, spices, vanilla, and salt until smooth. Pour into prepared crust. Bake at 425°F for 10 minutes. Reduce heat and bake at 350°F for 20 minutes. Sprinkle with chopped pecans and continue baking for 15 minutes or until knife inserted in center comes out clean. Cool completely before refrigerating.

For the topping: Gently fold together all ingredients. Pipe rosettes around edge of pie before serving.

Harvest Pumpkin Pie

HONEY CRUNCH PUMPKIN PIE

Phyllis Bartholomew, Columbus, NE
2003 APC Crisco National Pie Championships Amateur Division 2nd Place Pumpkin

CRUST
2 cups flour
1 cup cake flour
1 cup Crisco shortening
2 tablespoons powdered butter flavoring
½ teaspoon salt
½ to 1 teaspoon pumpkin pie spice
1 egg
1 tablespoon cider vinegar
⅓ cup ice water

FILLING
1 cup brown sugar
1 tablespoon cornstarch
2 teaspoons cinnamon
¾ teaspoon ground ginger
¼ teaspoon salt

(1) 16 oz. can of solid-packed pumpkin
¾ cup whipping cream
½ cup sour cream
3 large eggs, beaten

HONEY CRUNCH TOPPING
¼ cup packed brown sugar
2 tablespoons honey
2 tablespoons butter
¾ cup chopped nuts (pecans are best)

WHIPPED CREAM TOPPING
1 cup heavy whipping cream
3 tablespoons powdered sugar
1 teaspoon unflavored gelatin
2 tablespoons cold water

For the crust: Mix all the dry ingredients together and cut in the shortening to resemble coarse crumbs. Beat the rest of the ingredients together and add to flour. Stir only until incorporated. Wrap in plastic and chill for several hours. Roll out and line pie dish.

For the filling: Preheat oven to 400°F. Mix together brown sugar, cornstarch, cinnamon, ground ginger, and salt so there are no lumps. Then add the rest of the ingredients. Stir well to blend. Pour into a 9- or 10-inch pastry-lined pie dish and bake at 400°F on the bottom rack for 10 minutes. Reduce the temperature to 350°F, move to the middle rack, and bake for an additional

50 minutes, just until set in the middle. Remove from the oven and cool on a rack.

For the honey crunch topping: Cook sugar, honey, and butter in a small pan until the sugar is dissolved, about 2 minutes. Add the nuts and let cool. When cool, add to the middle two thirds of the pie. For the whipped cream topping: Sprinkle gelatin over the water and let set for several minutes. Set over low heat until melted. Whip the cream to soft peaks and add the gelatin and sugar. Beat to stiff peaks. Pipe a decorative ribbon of whipped cream around the pie between the crust and the nut mixture.

Honey Crunch Pumpkin Pie

PECAN MAPLE STREUSEL PUMPKIN PIE

Jennifer Nystrom, Morrow, OH
2008 APC Crisco National Pie Championships Amateur Division 2nd Place Pumpkin

CRUST
2 ¾ cups all-purpose flour
1 teaspoon table salt
¾ cup vegetable shortening
½ cup butter (not margarine)
1 egg, slightly beaten
⅓ cup cold buttermilk

FILLING
2 eggs, slightly beaten
15 oz. canned pumpkin
14 oz. canned sweetened condensed
    milk
1 teaspoon cinnamon
½ teaspoon ground ginger

½ teaspoon ground nutmeg
⅛ teaspoon ground cloves

TOPPING
¼ cup packed light brown sugar
3 tablespoons flour
½ teaspoon cinnamon
2 tablespoons cold butter
½ cup chopped pecans

MAPLE DRIZZLE GARNISH
1 cup confectioner's sugar
3 tablespoons whipping cream
½ teaspoon Mapleine

For the crust: In a large bowl, mix together the flour and the salt. With a pastry blender, cut in shortening until flour resembles cornmeal. Cut in butter until it resembles small peas. In a small bowl, beat egg with a fork. Beat in buttermilk. Mixture will look almost gelatinous. Quickly mix buttermilk mixture in with the flour until flour just begins to hold together. Separate flour mixture into halves and form each half into a disc. Wrap each disc tightly with plastic wrap and refrigerate for at least an hour and up to two days.

After the dough has chilled, preheat oven to 375°F and remove one disc from refrigerator (save second disc for another use). On a lightly floured surface, roll out disc to fit a 9-inch pie pan. Place a piece of parchment paper inside pie pan over the crust and fill with pie weights. Bake for 20 minutes or until almost done and just beginning to turn lightly brown. Remove from oven and remove parchment paper and pie weights. Set aside to cool slightly.

For the filling: While crust is cooling, preheat oven to 425°F. In a medium bowl that allows for easy pouring, slightly beat eggs. Whisk in pumpkin and sweetened condensed milk. Whisk in cinnamon, ginger, nutmeg, and cloves until well combined. Set aside.

To make the streusel topping: In a medium-sized bowl, mix brown sugar, flour, and cinnamon. Cut in butter until it resembles small peas. Mix in pecans.

Pour pumpkin mixture into baked crust. Top evenly with streusel mixture, making sure to put it on very lightly so as not to mix it in with the pumpkin. Bake in a 425°F oven for 15 minutes. Reduce heat to 350°F and bake for an additional 45 minutes or until a knife inserted in the center comes out clean. Place foil around the edges so as not to burn the crust.

Remove the pie from the oven and let cool completely. When completely cooled, make maple drizzle by thoroughly mixing the confectioner's sugar, whipping cream, and Mapleine in a small bowl with a spoon. Drizzle glaze over cooled pie. Refrigerate at least two hours before serving.

OCTOBERFEST PIE

Raine Gottess, Coconut Creek, FL
2008 APC Crisco National Pie Championships Amateur Division 1st Place Pumpkin

CRUST
18 whole Keebler cinnamon graham crackers
½ cup butter
4 tablespoons sugar

FILLING—LAYER ONE
8 oz. package Philadelphia Cream Cheese, softened
⅛ cup sour cream
1 small egg
¼ cup sugar
½ teaspoon vanilla
1 tablespoon flour

FILLING—LAYER TWO
8 oz. package Philadelphia Cream Cheese, softened

1 teaspoon vanilla
1½ cups powdered sugar
½ cup canned plain pumpkin
¼ teaspoon cinnamon
¼ teaspoon ginger
⅛ teaspoon cloves
8 oz. Cool Whip topping

FILLING—LAYER THREE
4 oz. Jell-O cheesecake flavored pudding mix
½ cup milk
¾ cup plain canned pumpkin
¼ teaspoon ginger
¼ teaspoon cinnamon
⅛ teaspoon nutmeg
⅛ teaspoon cloves
1 cup Cool Whip topping

For the crust: Using a food processor, finely crumble the graham crackers. Add sugar, and then place in a bowl. Toss in melted butter until moistened. Using the back of a large spoon, press mixture into a 10-inch deep-dish pie pan to form a crust. Freeze.

For layer 1: Preheat oven to 450°F. Using a mixer, beat well the softened cream cheese, sugar, and egg. Add in sour cream, flour, and vanilla. Pour into graham cracker crust. Cover the edges with foil. Bake as follows without opening the oven door: In a 450°F oven, bake for 8 minutes. Decrease oven temperature to 250°F and continue baking for another 20 minutes. Turn off oven, and leave in oven for 15 minutes. Cool on a wire rack.

For layer 2: Using a mixer, beat softened cream cheese with vanilla. Add powdered sugar. Mix in pumpkin and spices. Fold in Cool Whip. Spread over cooled pie. Freeze.

For layer 3: In a bowl, using a wire whisk, toss pudding and milk until thickened. Add in pumpkin and spices. Fold in Cool Whip. Spread over layer 2. Refrigerate about 6 hours until firm.

Octoberfest Pie

OLD-FASHIONED PUMPKIN PIE

Pat Legler
2003 APC Crisco National Pie Championships Amateur Division 2nd Place Pumpkin

CRUST
2 cups flour
¼ teaspoon salt
1 cup shortening (¾ lard and ¼ Crisco)
½ cup cold water

FILLING
1¾ cups pumpkin
½ teaspoon salt

1¾ cups evaporated milk
3 eggs
⅔ cup packed brown sugar
2 tablespoons white sugar
1¼ teaspoons cinnamon
½ teaspoon ginger
½ teaspoon nutmeg
¼ teaspoon cloves
3 tablespoons molasses

For the crust: Mix dry ingredients together and cut in shortening with pastry blender until pieces are pea-sized. Then add cold water and mix until dough forms a ball. Try not to handle with hands a lot. Keep ingredients cold. Roll out and put in pie pan.

For the filling: Preheat oven to 425°F. Beat all ingredients together until well mixed. Pour into pie shell. Bake 45 to 55 minutes. Cool. Top with whipped cream.

REAL PUMPKIN PIE

Jill Jones, Palm Bay, FL
2009 APC Crisco National Pie Championships Amateur Division 1st Place Pumpkin

CRUST
1 cup flour
½ teaspoon salt
¼ tablespoon sugar
½ cup shortening
1 egg
1 ½ tablespoons water (ice-cold)
¼ tablespoon vinegar

FILLING
1 small cooking pumpkin (4 to 6 inches)

¾ cup sugar
½ teaspoon salt
1 teaspoon cinnamon
¾ teaspoon pumpkin pie spice
1 smidgen fresh ground nutmeg
¼ teaspoon pure vanilla
2 eggs
14 oz. can sweetened condensed milk

For the crust: Mix flour, salt, and sugar, then cut in shortening with fork or pastry cutter until crumbly. Add egg, water, and vinegar. Scrape out of bowl onto floured surface. Roll into ball, wrap in plastic wrap, and refrigerate ½ to 1 hour. Roll dough out on a floured surface and place in pie pan.

For the filling: Preheat oven to 425°F. Cut pumpkin in half, and scrape out seeds and string membranes of pumpkin. Quarter pumpkin. In a double steamer, steam pumpkin until soft and skin peels off by touch (45 minutes to 1 hour). Mash with potato masher, then squeeze water out of mashed pumpkin through cheesecloth. Combine pumpkin, sugar, salt, cinnamon, pumpkin pie spice, nutmeg, and vanilla, and mix well. Add eggs and milk. Mix well. Pour into unbaked pie crust. Bake for 15 minutes. Reduce heat to 350°F and cover crust edge. Bake for 40 to 50 minutes. Let cool 3 hours before serving. Refrigerate.

TASTY PUMPKIN PIE

Sarah Spaugh, Winston-Salem, NC
2005 APC Crisco National Pie Championships Amateur Division 3rd Place Pumpkin

CRUST
2 cups flour
1 teaspoon salt
2/3 cup Crisco shortening
5 to 6 tablespoons cold water
1 tablespoon vinegar

FILLING
3 large eggs
2 cups fresh pumpkin, mashed, or 15-oz. can solid-packed pumpkin
1/2 cup granulated sugar
1/4 cup firmly packed dark brown sugar
1/4 cup 100% amber maple syrup

1 teaspoon allspice
1/2 teaspoon cinnamon
1/8 teaspoon ground cloves
1/2 cup milk
1/4 cup light cream

MAPLE LEAVES TOPPING
Cut out maple leaves or small pumpkins from crust scraps

WHIPPED CREAM TOPPING (OPTIONAL)
1 cup whipping cream
4 tablespoons pulverized sugar
1/2 teaspoon vanilla

For the crust: Combine the flour and the salt. Cut the shortening into the flour. Then combine the water and vinegar. Gradually add the vinegar mixture into the flour until dough just holds together. Form into a ball, roll out, and place into a 9-inch pie pan.

For the filling: Preheat oven to 350°F. Beat the eggs lightly with a whisk in a large bowl. Stir in the pumpkin. Combine the sugar and spices. Stir in the maple syrup. Slowly stir in the milk and cream. Pour into a 9-inch pie shell. Bake for about 45 minutes or until the center is set.

For the maple leaves topping: Cut out maple leaves or small pumpkins from crust scraps. Bake 10–12 minutes or until golden brown and place on pie before serving.

For the optional whipped cream topping: Combine ingredients and whip until stiff. Put on top of pie before serving.

Tasty Pumpkin Pie

WALNUT CRUNCH PUMPKIN PIE

Christine Montalvo, Windsor Heights, IA
2005 APC Crisco National Pie Championships Amateur Division 1st Place Pumpkin

CRUST
2 ½ cups all-purpose flour
½ teaspoon salt
1 ½ sticks (¾ cup) cold unsalted butter
¼ cup cold Crisco shortening
4 to 6 tablespoons ice water

FILLING
⅔ cup golden brown sugar, packed
½ cup sugar
2 tablespoons all-purpose flour
½ teaspoon salt
½ teaspoon ground cinnamon
⅛ teaspoon ground allspice
⅛ teaspoon ground cloves
⅛ teaspoon ground ginger
1½ cups canned solid-packed pumpkin
2 tablespoons mild-flavored (light) molasses
3 large eggs
1 cup whipping cream

TOPPING
4 tablespoons butter
1 cup chopped walnuts
¾ cup packed brown sugar
1 cup whipping cream plus 3 tablespoons powdered sugar

For the crust: In a food processor, add flour and salt. Pulse to mix. Add cold butter and Crisco, which have been cut into small pieces. Pulse 6 to 8 times until mixture resembles coarse meal with some small pea-size butter lumps. Drizzle 4 tablespoons ice water evenly over mixture and pulse 3 to 4 times more until dough holds together. Add more water, 1 tablespoon at a time, until dough holds together. Form into 2 balls, and then flatten each into a disc. Wrap discs separately in plastic wrap and refrigerate at least 1 hour.

Divide dough into 2 pieces. On a lightly floured surface with a lightly floured rolling pin, roll out one piece of dough into a 10-inch round (about 1/8 inch thick). Fit a 9-inch pie plate with one piece of dough and flute edges. Reserve 2nd piece of dough for another time. Refrigerate (or freeze) while preparing filling.

For the filling: Place baking sheet in oven and preheat to 450°F. Whisk brown sugar, sugar, flour, salt, cinnamon, allspice, cloves, and ginger together in large bowl to blend. Whisk in pumpkin, molasses, eggs, and whipping cream. Pour mixture into frozen crust. Place pie on preheated baking sheet in oven. Bake 10 minutes. Reduce heat to 325°F and bake until sides puff and

Walnut Crunch Pumpkin Pie

center is just set, about 40 minutes. Cool completely. Preheat broiler. Prepare Walnut Crunch topping.

For the walnut crunch topping: In a small saucepan, over low heat, melt butter. Stir in walnuts and brown sugar and mix until thoroughly combined. Spoon evenly over pie. Broil pie 3 minutes, 5 to 7 inches from broiler, or until topping is golden and sugar dissolves. Cool pie again on wire rack.

In a small bowl, beat heavy whipping cream and powdered sugar with electric mixer until stiff peaks form. Pipe around edge of cooled pie.

RAISIN

"Enjoy a slice of American heritage with California Raisin pie! California raisins are the perfect ingredient for pie whether you are looking for a traditional raisin pie, a Dutch apple pie, or a more contemporary version, such as chocolate raisin walnut pie, a blue-ribbon winner. The depth of flavor that 100-percent natural, antioxidant rich California raisins lends to any pie is limited only by your imagination!"

—Larry Blagg
Senior Vice President of Marketing,
California Raisin Marketing Board

Californese Raisin and Nut Pie	298	"Lovin' Spoonful" Cinnamon	
California Raisin Harvest Pie	300	Roll Raisin Custard Pie	310
California Sunshine Raisin Pie	302	California Raisin Maple Crunch Pie	312
Chocolate Raisin Walnut Pie	304	Old-World Sour Cream Pie	314
Golden Nugget Raisin Pie	306	Raisin Pie Delight	316
Helen's Apple Cider Raisin Pie	308		

« *Golden Nugget Raisin Pie (recipe page 306)*

CALIFORNESE RAISIN AND NUT PIE

John Michael Lerma, St. Paul, MN
2011 APC Crisco National Pie Championships Professional Division Honorable Mention
California Raisin

Crust

1½ cups all-purpose flour

½ tablespoon white granulated sugar

½ teaspoon sea salt

¼ cup Crisco butter-flavored shortening, chilled and cut into small pieces

¼ cup cold unsalted butter, cut into small pieces

¼ cup cold water

1 egg yolk and 1 teaspoon water for egg wash

Cooking spray

FILLING

3 large eggs, beaten

⅓ cup unsalted butter, melted

1 cup white granulated sugar

1 teaspoon pure vanilla extract or vanilla bean paste

1 tablespoon distilled white vinegar

⅓ cup chopped pecans

⅓ cup shredded coconut

1 cup raisins

For the crust: All ingredients should be cold. Combine all the dry ingredients in a large mixing bowl. Add shortening and butter. Using a pastry blender, cut in the shortening and butter until the mixture resembles coarse meal. Drop by drop, add the cold water. Mix in with the fingertips, not hands, as the palms will warm the dough. Continue mixing water in until the dough begins to hold together without being sticky but not crumbly.

Place dough in plastic wrap. Fold over plastic wrap and press down to form a disc. This will make rolling out easier after chilling. Finish wrapping in plastic and place in the refrigerator for at least ½ hour. Lightly spray a 9-inch pie plate with cooking spray. Roll out dough and place in pie plate. Remove excess dough and crimp. Brush bottom and sides of crust with egg wash. Return to the refrigerator until filling is ready. Makes pastry for one 9-inch single-crust pie.

For the filling: Preheat oven to 350°F. In a medium mixing bowl, combine eggs, butter, sugar, vanilla extract, and vinegar. Beat until smooth. Stir in pecans, coconut, and raisins. Pour mixture into pastry shell. Bake for 40 minutes. Cool before serving.

Californese Raisin and Nut Pie

CALIFORNIA RAISIN HARVEST PIE

Andrea Spring, Bradenton, FL
2011 APC Crisco National Pie Championships Professional Division 1st Place
California Raisin

CRUST
½ cup hazelnuts, toasted and finely ground
1¼ cups graham cracker crumbs
¼ cup plus 1 tablespoon butter, melted
4 tablespoons light brown sugar

FILLING 1
1 egg
½ cup light brown sugar
¼ cup butter, melted
¼ cup dark corn syrup
½ cup hazelnuts, chopped
½ cup dark raisins

FILLING 2
4 oz. cream cheese, room temperature
½ cup sugar
1 cup pumpkin puree
½ cup golden raisins
⅛ teaspoon ground ginger
⅛ teaspoon ground nutmeg
½ teaspoon ground cinnamon
8 oz. whipped topping
Sweetened whipped cream, chopped hazelnuts, and raisins for garnish

For the crust: Preheat oven to 325°F. Press crumbs into a sprayed 10-inch pie pan. Bake for 5 minutes. Remove and cool.

For filling 1: Mix ingredients and pour into pie shell. Bake for 20 to 25 minutes or until slightly set. Chill.

For filling 2: Whip cream cheese and sugar well. Add pumpkin, mix well. Add raisins and spices. Mix well. Add whipped topping and fold in until blended. Spoon on top of cooled dark raisin layer. Chill well. Garnish with sweetened whipped cream, chopped hazelnuts, and raisins.

California Raisin Harvest Pie

CALIFORNIA SUNSHINE RAISIN PIE

Patricia Lapiezo, LaMesa, CA
2011 APC Crisco National Pie Championships Amateur Division 1st Place California Raisin

CRUST
3 cups all-purpose flour
1 teaspoon salt
1 cup plus 2 tablespoons Crisco
   shortening
1 egg, lightly beaten
5 tablespoons ice water
1 tablespoon vinegar

FILLING
2 cups seedless golden raisins
½ cup boiling water
¼ teaspoon salt
2 tablespoons cornstarch
⅓ cup fresh orange juice

2 teaspoons grated orange rind
1 teaspoon grated lemon rind
2 tablespoons butter

TOPPING
(2) 8 oz. packages cream cheese,
   softened
½ cup granulated sugar
1 teaspoon vanilla
¼ cup sour cream
2 large eggs
¼ cup whipping cream
1 teaspoon lemon juice
½ teaspoon grated lemon rind
¼ teaspoon cinnamon

For the crust: Preheat oven to 400°F. Combine flour and salt in medium bowl. Cut in shortening. Mix the water, egg, and vinegar. Gradually stir into flour until moistened and dough comes together. Divide in half and form into two discs. Chill at least 30 minutes. On a floured surface, roll out one disc to fit a 10-inch-deep pie pan. Place in pan and flute edges. Prick bottom and sides with a fork and place pie weights in pie pan. Bake blind for 15 minutes. Remove weights and bake an additional 10 minutes or until crust is light golden brown. Cool while preparing filling. Decrease oven temperature to 350°F.

For the filling: Place raisins in a medium saucepan with water, sugar, and salt. Heat to boiling. Mix cornstarch and orange juice. Stir into raisin mixture and cook over low heat, stirring constantly until thick. Remove from heat, then add orange and lemon rind and butter. Stir well and set aside.

For the topping: In a large mixing bowl, beat cream cheese until light and fluffy. Beat in sugar until well blended. Blend in vanilla and sour cream. Add eggs, one at a time, beating lightly after each addition. Stir in whipping cream.

California Sunshine Raisin Pie

Measure out 2 tablespoons butter in a small cup and stir in cinnamon until well blended. Place this in a small pastry bag with a small writing tip.

Spread raisin mixture into bottom of pie crust. Pour cheese topping over raisins. With the pastry bag filling, pipe graduating concentric circles from center to within 1-inch of edge of crust. With a sharp knife or toothpick, draw 8 lines from center to edge of crust, alternating directions. Bake for 35 to 40 minutes or until topping is set and edges are light golden brown. Remove and cool for ½ hour. Refrigerate at least 2 hours.

CHOCOLATE RAISIN WALNUT PIE

Andrea Spring, Bradenton, FL
2010 APC Crisco National Pie Championships Professional Division 1st Place and
Best of Show California Raisin

CRUST
1½ cups Crisco shortening
1 teaspoon white vinegar
2 tablespoons milk
½ cup hot water
4 cups all-purpose flour
2 teaspoons salt
1 tablespoon cornstarch

FILLING
3 eggs
⅔ cup granulated white sugar
¼ teaspoon cinnamon
1 teaspoon vanilla extract
⅓ cup butter, melted
1 cup dark corn syrup
¾ cup milk chocolate chips
1 cup dark raisins
¾ cup chopped walnuts

For the crust: Combine shortening, vinegar, and milk. Pour in hot water. Mix well. In separate bowl, mix together flour, salt, and cornstarch. Combine flour mixture with shortening mixture until dough forms. Separate into four equal balls. Wrap in plastic wrap and refrigerate 1 portion for at least one hour before rolling out. Freeze remainder for future use. Roll out one portion of pie dough. Place in 10-inch pie pan.

For the filling: Preheat oven to 400°F. Sprinkle raisins over bottom of pie shell. Mix eggs, vanilla extract, sugar, cinnamon, butter, and corn syrup until well blended. Add chocolate chips and walnuts. Mix well. Set aside. Carefully pour filling over raisins. Bake for 10 minutes at 400°F. Lower temperature to 350°F and bake for 30 minutes or until center of pie is just set. Garnish with whipped cream and chocolate-covered raisins if desired.

Chocolate Raisin Walnut Pie

GOLDEN NUGGET RAISIN PIE

Carol Socier, Bay City, MI
2009 APC Crisco National Pie Championships Amateur Division 2nd Place
California Raisin

CRUST
1¼ cups flour
1 teaspoon sugar
½ teaspoon salt
¼ cup butter-flavored Crisco
   shortening, cold
¼ cup unsalted butter, cold
1 egg yolk
3 to 4 tablespoons cold milk

FILLING
8 oz. can crushed pineapple in its
   own juice
1 cup golden raisins
3 large eggs
¼ cup sugar

1 teaspoon vanilla
¼ cup butter, melted
1 cup white chocolate chips
1 cup coarsely chopped walnuts

TOPPING
(2) 8 oz. packages Philadelphia Pineapple Cream Cheese Spread
1 cup powdered sugar
1 tablespoon pineapple juice
½ cup golden raisins

GARNISH
1 cup whipping cream, whipped and
   sweetened
Walnut halves

For the crust: Preheat oven to 450°F. In medium-sized bowl, combine flour, sugar, and salt. Add cold shortening and butter, cutting with a fork or pastry blender until coarse pieces form. Beat egg yolk, then add to cold milk. Add egg mixture to flour mixture small amounts at a time until dough holds. Shape into a disc. Roll to fit a 9-inch deep-dish pie pan. Flute edges, trimming excess dough and chill 30 minutes. Prick all over with a fork or line with foil, add pie weights, and bake for 8 minutes.

For the filling: Preheat oven to 375°F. Combine pineapple and raisins. Let stand for 30 minutes.

In a separate bowl, beat eggs until frothy. Add sugar, vanilla, and melted butter. Stir in pineapple and raisins, white chocolate chips, and walnuts. Pour into prepared pie crust. Bake for about 45 minutes or until center is almost set. Cool on wire rack for 2 to 3 hours.

For the topping: Blend cream cheese spread, powdered sugar, and pineapple juice. Gently fold in raisins. Spread on top of cooled pie. Garnish with whipped cream and walnut halves.

Golden Nugget Raisin Pie

HELEN'S APPLE CIDER RAISIN PIE

Bryan Ehrenholm, Modesto, CA
2010 APC Crisco National Pie Championships Professional Division
Honorable Mention California Raisin

CRUST
2 cups all-purpose flour
1 teaspoon salt
1 cup Crisco shortening, chilled
½ cup ice water

FILLING
1 cup raisins
2 cups apple cider (store bottled is
　　fine)

1 cup canned milk
1 cup sugar
1 tablespoon flour
½ teaspoon cinnamon
¼ teaspoon nutmeg
¼ teaspoon cloves
2 eggs, beaten

For the crust: Place dry ingredients in a mixing bowl and mix together (you can use an electric mixer). Slowly add in chilled shortening and mix until mixture resembles coarse crumbs. Slowly add in ice water until dough forms (you may not use all the water). Place dough on floured surface and roll out into crust about 1/16 inch in thickness. Do not overwork dough. Dough may be refrigerated overnight. You may prepare crust, place in pie dish, and freeze until ready to use. Recipe makes enough dough for 2 single-use crusts or 1 double-crust pie. Preheat oven to 400°F.

Lightly poke the dough with the tip of a fork all over to prevent pie crust from bubbling up. Place tin foil or parchment paper over crust and fill with dried beans or pie weights and bake for 15 to 20 minutes until crust is set. Remove the foil/parchment paper with beans and bake crust for another 15 minutes, until crust is lightly browned. Remove from oven and let cool.

For the filling: Place raisins and apple cider in saucepan and bring to a boil. Gently boil until raisins plump up and are tender. Drain raisins in colander, return them to pan, add canned milk, sugar, flour, and spices. Cook 5 minutes until mixture starts to boil. Add beaten eggs and continually stir until mixture thickens. Pour into pre-baked pie crust. Cool completely and top with your favorite whipped topping. Garnish the top with a sprinkle of cinnamon or raisins.

"LOVIN' SPOONFUL" CINNAMON ROLL RAISIN CUSTARD PIE

Karen Hall, Elm Creek, NE
2011 APC Crisco National Pie Championships Amateur Division 2nd Place
California Raisin

CRUST

3 cups unbleached flour
1 cup plus 1 tablespoon butter-flavored Crisco, cold
½ teaspoon baking powder
1 egg
1 teaspoon sea salt
¼ cup plus 1 tablespoon ice-cold water
1 tablespoon sugar
1 tablespoon rice vinegar

CINNAMON ROLLS

1 container crescent rolls, butter-flavor or original
1 tablespoon butter, melted
2 teaspoons cinnamon sugar

RAISIN CUSTARD FILLING

1 cup California raisins
2½ cups whole milk
3 eggs, beaten
¾ cup sugar
1 tablespoon flour
¼ teaspoon cinnamon
2 teaspoons vanilla extract
2 to 3 drops yellow food color, optional

CINNAMON ROLL ICING

2 oz. cream cheese, softened
1 cup powdered sugar
1 tablespoon milk
1 tablespoon butter, softened

For the crust: In a large bowl, combine flour, baking powder, salt, and sugar. With a pastry blender, cut in Crisco until mixture resembles coarse crumbs. In a small bowl, beat egg, water, and vinegar together. Add egg mixture slowly while tossing with fork until mixture is moistened (do not overmix). Divide dough and shape into 3 balls. Flatten each to form disc. Wrap each disc with plastic wrap and refrigerate at least 30 minutes before using. Makes three 9-inch single crusts. Use one disc for this recipe.

For the cinnamon rolls: Preheat oven to 375°F. Unroll crescent rolls from container. Leave in a rectangle shape. Brush top side with butter; sprinkle with cinnamon sugar. Roll into a log lengthwise; pinch seams. Cut log into 20 miniature cinnamon rolls. Place on ungreased cookie sheet. Bake for 8 to 10 minutes or until golden. Set aside.

For the filling: Preheat oven to 425°F. Prepare and roll out pastry for one 9-inch single-crust pie. Line pie dish with pastry. Crimp edge. Arrange raisins into bottom of pie shell. In a medium saucepan, heat milk over medium heat until hot (do not boil), whisking constantly. Remove from heat. In a medium mixing bowl, combine beaten eggs, sugar, flour, cinnamon, vanilla, and yellow food color (optional). Mix until ingredients are well blended. Slowly pour and whisk mixture

Lovin' Spoonful Cinnamon Roll Raisin Custard Pie

into hot milk. Blend well. Carefully pour custard into pie shell. Place miniature cinnamon rolls onto custard filling, distributing evenly. Bake at 425°F for 8 minutes. Reduce oven to 350°F. Protect edge of pie with foil to prevent overbrowning. Bake at 350°F for 30 to 35 minutes, or until center is set. Chill pie.

For the cinnamon roll icing: In a small bowl, combine softened cream cheese, powdered sugar, milk, and butter. Stir until smooth. Before serving, pipe icing in a swirling pattern onto each cinnamon roll on top of chilled pie.

CALIFORNIA RAISIN MAPLE CRUNCH PIE

Patricia Lapiezo, La Mesa, CA
2009 APC Crisco National Pie Championships Amateur Division 1st Place
California Raisin

CRUST
1¼ cups all-purpose flour
¼ cup powdered sugar
¼ cup plus 2 tablespoons finely
    chopped pecans
⅛ teaspoon salt
½ cup Crisco butter-flavored
    shortening
3 tablespoons ice water

FILLING
½ cup butter, melted
½ cup light brown sugar, packed

½ cup light corn syrup
¼ cup maple syrup
⅛ teaspoon salt
½ teaspoon vanilla flavoring
3 large eggs, lightly beaten
4 crunchy granola bars, crushed
    (yields about ¾ cup)
½ cup chopped pecans
¼ cup mini maple or butterscotch
    chips
1 cup California raisins

For the crust: Combine flour, powdered sugar, finely chopped pecans, and salt. Cut in shortening until flour is blended to form pea-size chunks. Sprinkle mixture with water, 1 tablespoon at a time. Toss lightly with fork until dough forms a ball. Form a disc. Roll and press crust into a 9-inch pie plate. Set aside while preparing filling.

For the filling: Preheat oven to 350°F. In a large bowl, combine the butter, brown sugar, corn syrup, and maple syrup until blended. Beat in salt, vanilla flavoring, and eggs. Stir in crushed granola bars, pecans, maple chips, and raisins. Bake 40 to 50 minutes, or until filling is set and crust is golden. Cool, then refrigerate. Decorate with sweetened whipped cream, if desired.

California Raisin Maple Crunch Pie

OLD-WORLD SOUR CREAM PIE

Liza Ludwig, Curlew, IA
2010 APC Crisco National Pie Championships Amateur Division 2nd Place
California Raisin

CRUST
3 cups flour
2 tablespoons sugar
½ tablespoon salt
4 tablespoons milk
1 cup lard
Some cinnamon and sugar for
   sprinkling on crust

FILLING
2 cups California raisins
1 cup sugar
¼ cup water
1½ cups sour cream
¼ cup sugar
2 tablespoons cinnamon

For the crust: Combine dry ingredients. Cut in lard. Add milk. Form dough into 2 discs and refrigerate for ½ hour. Roll out first disc and place in 9-inch pie dish. Roll out remaining disc for top crust.

For the filling: Preheat oven to 375°F. Combine first raisins, sugar, and water in a saucepan and cook over medium heat until softened. Let cool.

While cooling, combine the rest of the ingredients and set aside. Pour the cooled raisins into the sour cream mixture. Fold together. Pour the mixture into 9-inch pie shell, smoothing out evenly. Place the 9-inch top crust on the pie. Seal edges. Sprinkle with some cinnamon and sugar. Bake for 50 to 60 minutes. The crust should be a nice light brown color. Cool before cutting.

RAISIN PIE DELIGHT

Carolyn Blakemore, Fairmont, WV
2010 APC Crisco National Pie Championships Amateur Division 1st Place
California Raisin

CRUST
2 cups flour, sifted
1 teaspoon salt
1 tablespoon sugar
½ cup butter-flavored Crisco
¼ cup margarine
1 tablespoon vinegar
3 tablespoons cold water

FILLING
2½ cups mixed California raisins

½ cup dried cranberries
½ cup sugar
½ cup orange juice
2 tablespoons cornstarch
1 teaspoon grated lemon peel
3 tablespoons lemon juice
½ cup chopped walnuts
1 tablespoon butter

For the crust: In a bowl, sift together flour, salt, and sugar. With pastry blender, cut in Crisco and margarine. Combine vinegar and water. Sprinkle on flour by tablespoons, then stir with a fork to form a ball. Wrap in wax paper and chill until ready to roll out. You will need a top and bottom crust.

For the filling: Preheat oven to 375°F. In a saucepan, bring orange juice to a boil and re-move from heat. Add raisins, cover, and set aside to plump raisins. Add cranberries. Mix. Combine sugar and cornstarch, stir into raisins, and return to heat. Add lemon zest and lemon juice. Cook, stirring until thickened. Cool. Roll out crust to fit pie pan, sprinkle on walnuts, and add filling. Dot top with butter and cover with a top crust. Flute edges. Cover crust rim with foil strips to bake. Bake for 35 minutes until browned. Cool.

Raisin Pie Delight

SPECIAL CATEGORIES

Each year at the APC Crisco National Pie Championships we add in a new category. Sometimes the category is holiday-oriented, sometimes it's date-oriented, and sometimes it's just plain fun. The recipes in this chapter are from those categories.

Sticky Toffee Pudding Apple Pie	320
My Big Fat Italian Strawberry–Basil Wedding Pie	322
Vanilla Bean Brûlée Pie	324
Holiday Cranberry Mince Pie	326
The Engagement Ring	328
Royal Sapphire Blueberry Pie	330
Brandy Apple Pie	332
Celebration Cheese Pie	334
Celebration of Liberty Chocolate Pie	336
KP's Berry Pie	338
Sunshine Pie	340

‹‹ Celebration Cheese Pie (recipe page 334)

STICKY TOFFEE PUDDING APPLE PIE

Linda Hundt, DeWitt, MI
2011 APC Crisco National Pie Championships Professional Division 1st Place
Crisco Innovation and Best of Show

CRUST

1½ cups flour
¼ teaspoon baking powder
½ teaspoon salt
1 teaspoon sugar
¼ cup cold butter cut in small pieces
½ cup of refrigerated Crisco shortening

STICKY TOFFEE PUDDING FILLING

½ cup praline pecans
1 stick of butter, softened
½ cup brown sugar
2 tablespoons heavy cream
1 tablespoon lemon juice
1 egg, beaten
½ cup self-rising flour

APPLE FILLING

5 medium-to-large Michigan Cortland, Ida Red apples, peeled, thinly sliced, diced
1 cup brown sugar
3 tablespoons flour
4 tablespoons melted butter
2 teaspoons cinnamon
1 teaspoon lemon juice
¼ teaspoon salt

HOMEMADE CARAMEL

14 oz. can sweetened condensed milk
1 cup light corn syrup
1 cup sugar
½ cup brown sugar
½ stick butter
1 tablespoon real vanilla extract

CRUMB TOPPING
¾ cup flour
1 cup sugar
¼ teaspoon salt
1 stick butter, softened

PRALINE PECAN GARNISH
1 cup chopped pecans
2 tablespoons butter
2 tablespoons brown sugar

Sticky Toffee Pudding Apple Pie

For the crust: Mix all above ingredients in KitchenAid-style mixer on medium speed swiftly until crust appears "pea-like." Carefully sprinkle water in crust mix until it starts to become moistened and gathers together. Pat into a disc. Wrap and refrigerate for at least one half hour. Roll out on to floured surface and make and crimp crust.

For sticky toffee pudding layer: Mix ingredients just until blended. Spread on bottom of pie crust.

For apple filling: Cook ingredients in large pan on medium heat until cooked half-way.

For homemade caramel: In heavy 3-quart saucepan, combine all ingredients but vanilla. Cook over medium heat, stirring constantly, covering all parts of bottom of pan with wire whisk to avoid scorching. Stir until mixture comes to a boil. Reduce heat to low and cook, constantly stirring, until mixture comes to a boil. Reduce heat to low and continue stirring until caramel reaches 244°F on a candy thermometer, or firmball stage. Pour in glass container. Cool to use.

Stir in ¾ cup homemade caramel into the apple filling mixture until melted. Pour apple mixture onto the sticky toffee pudding in pie shell.

For crumb topping: Mix together all crumb topping ingredients by hand or a pastry blender until fine and crumbly. Sprinkle pie with crumb topping.

Preheat oven to 400°F. Bake pie for one hour or until knife easily slides into center of pie with no resistance. If pie becomes too brown before done, turn down oven to 350°F to finish baking. Cover with foil completely.

For praline pecan garnish: Melt butter in small pan on medium-low heat until melted. Add pecans and sugar and stir ingredients until you start smelling the nuts roasting. Take off heat and cool. Crumble. Top pie with a generous amount of homemade caramel sauce, praline pecans, and powdered sugar (if desired).

MY BIG FAT ITALIAN STRAWBERRY–BASIL WEDDING PIE

Naylet LaRochelle, Miami, FL

2011 APC Crisco National Pie Championships Amateur Division 1st Place Crisco Innovation

CRUST

2½ cups flour
1 tablespoon sugar
1 teaspoon salt
½ cup (1 stick) unsalted butter, cold
½ cup Crisco butter-flavored shortening, cold
½ cup finely ground pine nuts
⅓ cup ice water
2 teaspoons white wine vinegar
1 egg
1 tablespoon water

FILLING

1 envelope unflavored gelatin
¼ cup whipping cream, plus ½ cup whipping cream
10 oz. jar Smucker's strawberry spreadable fruit

8 oz. container mascarpone cheese
1 teaspoon pure vanilla extract
Pinch of salt
1 teaspoon grated lemon peel
1½ cups fresh strawberries, crushed
2 tablespoons finely chopped fresh basil leaves

VANILLA BEAN-WHITE CHOCO-LATE MOUSSE TOPPING

¾ cup white chocolate chips
½ cup heavy whipping cream, plus 2 tablespoons
1½ teaspoons vanilla paste
White chocolate curls, for garnish
White fondant flowers, for garnish, if desired

For the crust: Preheat oven to 425°F. In a large bowl, combine the flour, sugar, and salt. Using a pastry cutter, cut in the butter and shortening. Add the pine nuts. Drizzle the water and vinegar into the flour mixture and combine with hands until a ball of dough is formed. Divide dough in half and shape each half into a flat disc. Refrigerate for about 1 hour to chill dough. On a lightly floured surface, roll out one disc to fit a 9-inch pie plate. Ease pie dough into pie plate; trim pastry edges. Do not prick pastry. Line the pastry with foil; fill with pie weights. Bake 10–12 minutes or until golden brown.

For the filling: In a small microwavable bowl, combine gelatin and ¼ cup whipping cream. Set aside for 5 minutes. Microwave in 30-second intervals, until gelatin is completely dissolved. Let cool 10 minutes. In a large bowl, stir together strawberry spreadable fruit, mascarpone, vanilla extract, salt, lemon peel, and dissolved gelatin mixture until well combined. Add strawberries and basil; stir until combined. In a medium bowl, using an electric mixer, beat on high remaining ½ cup whipping cream until stiff peaks form. Fold into the strawberry mixture. Pour filling into prebaked pie shell. Refrigerate 2 hours, or until filling is set.

My Big Fat Italian Strawberry-Basil Wedding Pie

For the topping: In a small saucepan, melt white chocolate chips and 2 tablespoons cream, stirring often, over low heat. When chocolate is completely melted, remove from heat. Stir in vanilla paste. Let chocolate cool (but not harden). In a medium bowl, using an electric mixer, beat ½ cup whipping cream until stiff peaks form. Fold whipped cream into cooled white chocolate mixture. Spread over top of pie, or pipe in a decorative manner. Return pie to refrigerator for 2 to 3 hours, or until topping is set. Garnish pie with white chocolate curls

VANILLA BEAN BRÛLÉE PIE

Dionna Hurt, Longwood, FL
2011 APC Crisco National Pie Championships Professional Division 1ˢᵗ Honorable Mention Crisco Innovation

CRUST
2 ½ cups flour
½ teaspoon salt
3 tablespoons sugar
½ cup Crisco
½ cup butter, ice-cold
1 egg
1 teaspoon vanilla bean paste
1 tablespoon vinegar
2 to 4 tablespoons cold water

FILLING
3 tablespoons cornstarch
1 ⅔ cups heavy cream
14 oz. can sweetened condensed milk
3 egg yolks, beaten
1 tablespoon butter
1 tablespoon vanilla extract
1 tablespoon vanilla bean paste
¼ to ⅓ cup sugar
Sweetened whipped cream, to
    garnish

For the crust: Combine flour, salt, and sugar in a large mixing bowl. Cut Crisco and ice-cold butter into flour mixture until it resembles coarse crumbs. In a measuring cup, combine egg, vanilla paste, vinegar, and water. Pour egg mixture into flour mixture a little at a time, fluffing with a fork after each addition. After all egg mixture has been incorporated into flour, turn it out onto a piece of wax paper. Using wax paper, press dough into a ball and wrap it up. Place ball in refrigerator for at least one hour and up to overnight. When ready, preheat oven to 375°F. Roll dough into a circle at least ¼ inch thick. Place into pie dish. Bake for 10 minutes, or until golden brown.

For the filling: In a heavy saucepan, dissolve the cornstarch in the cream. Stir in sweetened condensed milk and egg yolks. Cook and stir until thick and bubbly. Remove from heat, then add butter, vanilla extract, and vanilla paste. Pour into pastry shell and chill for 2 or more hours. Top with sugar and brown under the broiler. Garnish with sweetened whipped cream around the edge. Refrigerate leftovers.

Vanilla Bean Brûlée Pie

HOLIDAY CRANBERRY MINCE PIE

Carolyn Blakemore, Fairmont, WV
2007 APC Crisco National Pie Championships Amateur Division 2nd Place Holiday Pie

DOUBLE CRUST
2 cups flour, sifted
½ teaspoon salt
1 tablespoon sugar
½ cup butter-flavored Crisco
¼ cup butter
1 tablespoon lemon juice
3 tablespoons ice water

FILLING
2 cups Jared mince filling
¾ cup whole berry cranberry sauce

1½ cups diced apple
¼ teaspoon lemon zest
1 tablespoon lemon juice
⅓ cup brown sugar
⅓ cup chopped walnuts

TOPPING
⅓ cup brown sugar
¼ cup flour
2 tablespoons butter
¼ cup chopped walnuts

For the crust: In a bowl, sift together flour, salt, and sugar. With pastry blender, cut in Crisco and butter until crumbly. Mix juice and water, sprinkling on by tablespoon, and mix with a fork until mixture forms a ball. Wrap in wax paper. Chill until ready to roll out. When ready, roll dough out to fit a 9-inch pan.

For the filling: Preheat oven to 375°F. In a bowl, mix together mince filling, cranberry sauce, apples, lemon zest, juice, sugar, and walnuts. Pour into a 9-inch pastry-lined pie pan.

For the topping: In a small dish, combine sugar, flour, butter, and walnuts. Mix until crumbly. Sprinkle over mince filling. Cover with a top crust. Flute edge. Cover crust rim with foil strips and bake for 35 minutes. Cool completely.

Holiday Cranberry Mince Pie

THE ENGAGEMENT RING

Bryan Ehrenholm, Modesto, CA

2011 APC Crisco National Pie Championships Professional Division 1st Place Royal Wedding and Best of Show

The engagement ring worn by Kate Middleton is rich with history and grace, symbolizing the eternal love of Diana for her son William, and William for his future Queen. So this pie is rich with the history of English walnuts and dates, graced by a meringue crust, topped the deep color of blueberries, and encircled with the lightness of whipped cream and diamond dust.

This pie does not have a traditional crust. The meringue will form the crust.

MERINGUE
4 egg whites
1 cup sugar
1 cup vanilla wafers (crushed with rolling pin)
1 teaspoon baking powder
1 cup dried English dates (chopped)
1 cup English walnuts (chopped)

TOPPING
2 pints fresh blueberries
1 cup sugar

1/3 cup cornstarch
1/2 cup water

GARNISH
Whipped cream
Diamond dust (from Michael's Crafts) or large kids' "diamond" rings

For the meringue: Preheat oven to 300°F. Beat egg whites until fluffy. Gradually beat in sugar, fold in wafers, baking powder, dates and walnuts. Pour into a greased pie pan. Bake for 30 minutes. Cool completely. Center will slightly cave, which is normal.

For the topping: Place 1½ cups of water, 1 cup of sugar, and ⅓ cup of corn starch in a small pan. Bring to a boil until thick syrup forms. Cool to room temperature. Mixture should be like a glaze. Toss mixture with blueberries and heap on top of pie, leaving about ½ inch around the edge.

Instructions for the Sparkle: Sprinkle with Diamond Dust or Sparkle Flakes, available at most cake and candy supply stores.

(I purchase from Edwards Cake and Candy Supply at 209-522-2414. They will ship.)

Large candy diamonds are made from a product called Isomalt, which is an inedible sugar product you heat up and put into silicon molds to create the diamonds. Isomalt and molds are available at local cake and candy supply stores and at www.sugarcraft.com. If you don't want to make the diamonds, Sugarcraft sells the actual diamonds pre-made.

Finish pie with whipped topping around edge and garnish with sprinkles. This pie is like eating divinity with blueberries and whipped cream.

The Engagement Ring

ROYAL SAPPHIRE BLUEBERRY PIE

Susan Boyle, DeBary, FL
2011 APC Crisco National Pie Championships Professional Division Honorable
Mention Royal Wedding

VANILLA WAFER CRUMB CRUST
2½ cups of vanilla wafer crumbs, finely crushed
½ cup of butter-flavored Crisco

CREAM FILLING
8 oz. package cream cheese, softened
1/3 cup confectionary sugar
1 teaspoon pure vanilla extract
1/8 teaspoon salt
1 cup whipped topping

BLUEBERRY FILLING
5 cups fresh blueberries
¾ cup water

¾ cup sugar
1/8 teaspoon salt
1/8 teaspoon cinnamon
3 tablespoons flour
1 tablespoon cornstarch
½ tablespoon lemon juice

WHIPPED TOPPING
1 cup heavy whipping cream
½ cup milk
1 tablespoon sugar

For the crust: Heat oven to 350°F. Combine ingredients until well-blended. Press into pie plate and bake for 10 minutes. Chill until ready to fill.

For the filling: Beat cream cheese, sugar, salt, and vanilla on medium speed until smooth. Add 1 cup of whipped topping. Continue to whip until very thick and smooth.

To bottom chilled vanilla wafer cookie crust, add a layer of cream filling and put back in refrigerator to set while preparing blueberry filling.

For the blueberry filling: In heavy saucepan on medium heat, mix water, cornstarch, flour, sugar, salt, and cinnamon, and stir until mixture starts to thicken. Add lemon juice and continue to stir, adding blueberries to the hot thick mixture. Remove from heat and allow to cool. When cool, spoon on top of cream cheese layer. Pile high for added appeal.

For the whipped topping: Whip ingredients on medium speed in a cold mixing bowl until stiff. Set aside. Garnish pie with whipped topping and blueberries. Optional: Vanilla wafer cookie crumbs or frosted sugar blueberries can be added to the edges or top for that royal look of diamonds and sapphires. Chill several hours before slicing.

Royal Sapphire Blueberry Pie

BRANDY APPLE PIE

Beverly Grey, Celebration, FL
2005 APC Crisco National Pie Championships Amateur Division 1st Place Celebration

CRUST
2 to 2¼ cups flour
1 teaspoon salt
²/₃ cup plus 2 tablespoons shortening
5 to 6 tablespoons cold water

FILLING
6 tablespoons butter
6 to 7 Granny Smith apples (3 lbs. for a big pie plate), peeled, cored, and thinly sliced

½ cup brown sugar
1 cup sugar
2 tablespoons flour or 3 tablespoons cornstarch blended with ¼ cup cold water
1 ½ to 2 teaspoons cinnamon
½ teaspoon nutmeg
¼ teaspoon salt
1 tablespoon whiskey
1 to 2 tablespoons lemon juice

For the crust: Combine flour and salt in bowl. Cut in shortening until blended and consistency resembles peas. Sprinkle water over surface. Stir with a fork until moistened. Shape into a ball with hands and work until soft (not very long). Roll into two circles. Line pie pan with single crust and fill with apple mixture. Top with single pie crust. Flute edges, cut five slits, and bake as stated below.

For the filling: Preheat oven to 375°F. Place ½ the apples in large skillet with ½ the melted butter and sprinkle with ½ the lemon juice and ½ of the sugars. Cook until tender, stirring often, about seven minutes. Transfer to a large pan. Repeat with rest of butter, apples, lemon juice, and sugars. Add seasonings and flour. Transfer to 10-inch pie plate with a bottom crust. Cover filling with top crust and flute the edges. Cut slits in the top. Brush the top with lightly beaten egg yolk, 2 teaspoons of heavy cream or water. Sprinkle cinnamon and sugar over top. Bake on middle rack on a baking sheet for 40 to 50 minutes or until top is golden. Cool on wire rack for 30 minutes.

Brandy Apple Pie

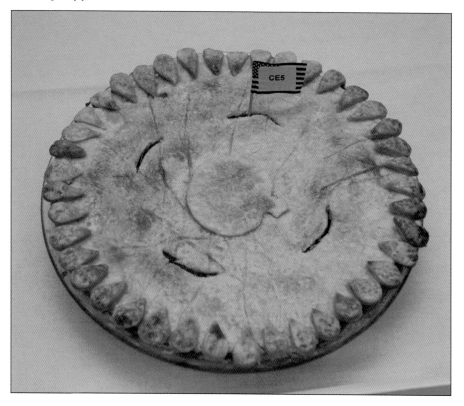

CELEBRATION CHEESE PIE

Raine Gottess, Coconut Creek, FL
2003 APC Crisco National Pie Championships Amateur Division 1st Place Celebration

CRUST
15 to 18 Keebler pecan Sandie
   cookies, crushed
¼ cup butter, melted

LAYER #1
2 oz. Philadelphia Cream Cheese,
   softened
2 cups Cool Whip
1 tablespoon sugar
¼ cup confectioner's sugar

LAYER #2
2 oz. Philadelphia Cream Cheese,
   softened

⅓ cup confectioner's sugar
2 cups Cool Whip
¾ cup peanut butter

LAYER #3
2 oz. Philadelphia Cream Cheese,
   softened
⅓ cup confectioners' sugar
2 cups Cool Whip
2 oz. Baker's German Sweet Chocolate Baking Squares, melted

For the crust: Stir butter into finely crushed cookies with fork. Press into 9-inch pie pan to form crust. Freeze to firm.

For layer 1: Beat all ingredients in mixer until blended. Spread onto crust and freeze while making the other layers.

For layer 2: Beat cream cheese, confectioner's sugar, and Cool Whip together until blended. Divide into two bowls, setting one bowl aside. Add peanut butter to one bowl of cream cheese mixture and combine well. Mix with remaining mixture in second bowl and spread on top of pie. Freeze.

For layer 3: Beat cream cheese, sugar, and Cool Whip together until blended. Add the melted Baker's German Sweet Chocolate Baking Squares to the bowl, beat, and spread on top of pie. Freeze.

Decorate with Cool Whip. Can be kept frozen and cut to serve.

Celebration Cheese Pie

CELEBRATION OF LIBERTY CHOCOLATE PIE

Diane Finney, Celebration, FL
2002 APC Crisco National Pie Championships Amateur Division 1st Place Celebration

CRUST
1½ cups unsalted butter
6 cups semi-sweet chocolate chips
 (36 oz.)
8 eggs

CHOCOLATE GLAZE
3 tablespoons unsalted butter
1½ tablespoons dark rum

1 tablespoon plus 1 teaspoon light
 corn syrup
Pinch salt
3 oz. white chocolate (½ cup chips)
Raspberries, blueberries, or strawberries for garnish

For the crust: Preheat oven to 350°F. Butter a pie tin. In a saucepan, melt the butter. In another saucepan, melt the chocolate chips slowly. While chocolate is melting, vigorously beat 8 eggs in a bowl for 5 minutes. Add melted butter to the melted chocolate and blend well. In three parts, add the chocolate mixture to the eggs and blend well. Pour mixture into the buttered pie tin. Bake for 15 to 20 minutes. It might look a little loose, but it will firm up as it cools. Refrigerate for 8 hours. It can also be frozen to set.

For the chocolate glaze: Stir butter, rum, corn syrup, and salt in a small heavy saucepan over low heat until butter is melted. Increase heat to medium and bring mixture to a boil, stirring constantly for one minute. Remove from heat. Stir in white chocolate chips until completely melted. Cool at room temperature until mixture coats a spoon but does not drip off the edge. About 5 minutes cooling is sufficient. Use at once. Spread glaze on crust in pie dish and garnish chocolate pie with raspberries, blueberries, or strawberries.

KP'S BERRY PIE

Karen Panosian, Celebration, FL
2005 APC Crisco National Pie Championships Amateur Division 2nd Place Celebration

CRUST
2 cups all-purpose flour
½ teaspoon salt
⅔ cup Crisco shortening
1 teaspoon vanilla extract
6 tablespoons cold water

LAYER 1
1¼ cups crushed graham crackers
   and chopped walnuts, mixed
⅓ cup butter
¼ cup sugar

FILLING
1¼ cups fresh blueberries
1¼ cups fresh raspberries
1¼ cups fresh blackberries
1¼ cups fresh strawberries
¾ cup sugar
⅓ cup all-purpose flour
⅛ teaspoon cinnamon
⅛ teaspoon ginger
⅛ teaspoon nutmeg
⅛ teaspoon allspice
½ cup coconut
Butter for dotting

GLAZE
¼ cup milk
Sugar for sprinkling

For the crust: Combine flour and salt. Cut in shortening until texture resembles coarse meal. Mix water and vanilla. Add water mixture 1 tablespoon at a time until crust comes together. Form into a ball. Divide in two. Roll out one half to line the bottom of a 9-inch pie dish. Roll out the other for a top crust.

For layer 1: Preheat oven to 375°F. Combine ingredients and press into the bottom crust.

For the filling: Combine fruit, sugar, flour, spices, and coconut in a large bowl. Coat well. Pour into pie crust. Dot the fruit filling with butter.

For the glaze: Place top crust on pie. Brush the crust with milk and sprinkle with sugar. Cut vents as appropriate. Bake pie at 375°F for 50 minutes.

KP's Berry Pie

SUNSHINE PIE

Melissa Mace, Celebration, FL
2002 APC Crisco National Pie Championships Amateur Division 2nd Place Celebration

CRUST

1¾ cups flour
1 teaspoon salt
10 tablespoons butter
2 tablespoons Crisco
5 tablespoons ice water

FILLING

2 Florida oranges
1 Florida lemon
2 cups sugar
¼ teaspoon salt
2 tablespoons cornstarch
4 eggs
4 tablespoons melted butter

For the crust: Combine flour and salt. Cut butter and Crisco into flour and salt until it looks like coarse meal. Add up to 5 tablespoons water. Form into a loose ball. Knead several times on a lightly floured surface. Divide into two balls and refrigerate for 30 minutes. Roll crusts out between two lightly floured pieces of plastic wrap.

For the filling: Preheat oven to 425°F. Grate orange and lemon zest into a bowl. Thinly slice oranges into quarter rounds. Discard ends and seeds. Gently toss with zest. Add sugar and salt. Cover and leave at room temperature for 24 hours. Juice lemon. Dissolve cornstarch in lemon juice and lemon pulp. Whisk eggs until frothy. Add lemon juice mixture and butter. Stir in oranges.

Place bottom crust in pie plate. Pour in orange mixture. Cover with top crust. Fold and crimp edges. Brush with water and sprinkle with sugar. Cut vent holes in top crust. Bake for 25 minutes. Turn oven down to 350°F and bake for an additional 25 to 30 minutes.

SPECIAL DIETARY

We have added some special categories that might help with some dietary restrictions, such as gluten-free and no sugar added. This chapter includes some of those recipes.

Freedom Pie	344	Razzle Dazzle Splenda Pie	354
Momma's Mud Puddle Pie	346	Splenda-Did Peanut Butter Pie	356
Second Chance Pie	348	Splendid Pineapple Pie	358
Caramel Toffee Turtle	350	Strawberry Smoothie Splenda Pie	360
Fantastico Neapolitan Pie	352		

‹‹ *Second Chance Pie (recipe page 348)*

FREEDOM PIE

John Sunvold, Winter Springs, FL
2011 APC Crisco National Pie Championships Amateur Division 2nd Place Gluten-Free

CRUST
1½ cups Kinnikinnick graham-style
   cracker crumbs
¼ cup sugar
6 tablespoons butter, melted

LIME FILLING
14 oz. can sweetened condensed milk
½ cup lime juice
1 egg

LAYER 1
1 can Oregon brand blueberries (not
   pie filling)

LEMON FILLING
14 oz. can sweetened condensed milk
½ cup lemon juice
1 egg

LAYER 2
1 small jar red raspberry preserves

TOPPING
2½ cups heavy cream
6 oz. gluten-free white chocolate
   broken into small pieces

For the crust: Preheat oven to 375°F. Mix all ingredients together and press mixture into a 9-inch pie plate. Chill in freezer for 15 minutes. Bake for 8 minutes. Allow to cool down to room temperature.

For the lime filling: Mix together condensed milk, lime juice, and egg. Pour into cooled crust.

For layer 1: Drain blueberries. Sprinkle all of the blueberries on the lime mixture.

For lemon filling: Preheat oven to 375°F. Mix together condensed milk, juice, and egg. Gently ladle the lime filling over the blueberries, making sure to cover each berry. Bake for 20 to 25 minutes or until center is set. Remove from oven and cool on a cooling rack. Chill.

For layer 2: Cover the pie with a ¼ inch layer of red raspberry preserves.

For the topping: Bring one cup of cream to a boil over medium heat. Add white chocolate and stir constantly until the chocolate is melted and thoroughly combined. Remove from heat and let cool to room temperature. Refrigerate for at least four hours. In a large bowl, beat the rest of the cream with an electric mixer set on high speed. Beat until soft peaks form. Slowly add the white chocolate mixture and continue to beat until stiff. Cover and refrigerate for 2 hours.

Spread over red raspberry preserves. Keeping with the red, white, and blue look of the pie, you may garnish the pie in a variety of ways, if desired. For example, patriotic decorations.

Freedom Pie

MOMMA'S MUD PUDDLE PIE

Liza Ludwig, Curlew, IA
2011 APC Crisco National Pie Championships Amateur Division 1st Place Gluten Free

CRUST
1 cup rice flour
¼ teaspoon salt
¼ cup sugar
8 tablespoons butter
2 eggs
¼ cup chocolate syrup

FILLING
2 large eggs
½ cup brown sugar
2 tablespoons dark molasses
1 cup cream
¼ cup brownie batter from crust
2 tablespoons Mexican cocoa powder

1 tablespoon Mexican vanilla
⅛ cup chopped nuts
¼ cup butterscotch chips
½ cup mini-marshmallows

GANACHE LAYER
2 tablespoons butter
2 tablespoons cocoa powder
4 tablespoons cream
4 oz. semi-sweet chocolate, high
   quality

GARNISH
1 Skor candy bar, crushed
Whipped cream

For the crust: Preheat oven to 375°F. Mix together all ingredients. Pour half into your pie pan. Reserve other half of batter for later use. Bake for 10 minutes.

For the filling: Mix eggs, brown sugar, dark molasses, cream, brownie batter, cocoa powder, and vanilla at medium speed. Pour into the hot brownie layer in pie pan. Mix the remaining items together and allow them to settle to the bottom of filling. Return to oven and continue to bake for another 20 to 30 minutes.

The marshmallows will turn dark brown. Cool completely.

For the ganache layer: In a heavy-bottomed saucepan, heat the cream and butter just to the point of scalding. Remove from heat. Add the chocolate and cocoa powder. Stir until smooth. Let cool until it starts to thicken. Pour on top of cooled pie. Let set overnight.

Top with whipped cream and the crushed Skor candy bar.

Momma's Mud Puddle Pie

SECOND CHANCE PIE

Judy Sunvold, Chicago, IL
2011 APC Crisco National Pie Championships Amateur Division 3rd Place Gluten Free

CRUST
2½ cups finely chopped raw almonds
3 tablespoons sugar
2 tablespoons unsweetened cocoa powder
4 tablespoons butter, melted

FILLING
13.5 oz. can of coconut milk
3 oz. half and half
2 eggs

½ cup sugar
3 tablespoons cornstarch
1½ cups shredded coconut
1 teaspoon vanilla

TOPPING
1 cup milk chocolate candy, processed into small pieces, or hot fudge sauce
1 cup salted roasted almonds, chopped

For the crust: Preheat oven to 350°F. Put all ingredients in food processor and pulsate until all ingredients are mixed thoroughly. Pour mixture into pie plate and press into pie plate, forming crust on bottom and sides. Bake for 10 minutes. Let pie crust cool.

For the filling: Put shredded coconut in food processor and chop until fine pieces. Cook coconut milk, half and half, eggs, sugar and cornstarch in a heavy saucepan over medium-low heat until boiling, stirring frequently. Add coconut and vanilla and mix until completely incorporated. Pour into prepared almond crust pie shell. Refrigerate for 2 to 3 hours or until set.

Garnish and decorate as desired.

Second Chance Pie

CARAMEL TOFFEE TURTLE

Patricia Lapiezo, La Mesa, CA
2011 APC Crisco National Pie Championships Amateur Division 1st Place
No Sugar Added

CRUST
3 cups all-purpose flour
1 teaspoon salt
1¼ cups Crisco butter-flavored
   shortening
5 tablespoons ice water
1 tablespoon vinegar
1 egg, lightly beaten

CHOCOLATE TURTLE LAYER (TOP AND BOTTOM)
4 oz. sugar-free chocolate
½ cup heavy whipping cream
1 cup Russell Stover pecan delights,
   chopped
2 tablespoons Smucker's sugar-free
   caramel topping

CARAMEL TOFFEE FILLING
8 oz. package cream cheese,
   softened
1 cup Smucker's sugar-free caramel
   topping
1 tablespoon Torini sugar-free
   caramel syrup
½ cup finely chopped sugar-free
   toffee
1 cup heavy whipping cream

TOPPING
Whipped cream
1 tablespoon Splenda
Shaved sugar-free chocolate

For the crust: Preheat oven to 400°F. Combine flour and salt in large bowl. Cut in shortening. In a small bowl, combine water, vinegar, and egg. Stir into flour mixture until dough comes together. Shape dough into two discs. Wrap in plastic wrap and refrigerate at least 1 hour. Roll 1 disc out onto floured surface to fit a 9 inch-deep pie dish. Prick bottom and sides with fork. Bake blind for 15 minutes. Remove pie weights and bake another 10 minutes, or until light golden brown. Remove from oven and cool while preparing filling.

For chocolate turtle layer: For bottom layer, melt chocolate and ½ cup cream, stirring until chocolate melts. Pour ½ into bottom of prepared pie crust. Sprinkle with ½ cup chopped pecan delights and drizzle with 1 tablespoon caramel topping.

For the caramel toffee filling: Beat the cream cheese in a large bowl until light and fluffy. Blend in the caramel syrup and caramel topping until well blended. Fold in whipped cream and chopped toffee. Spread onto chocolate turtle layer and smooth top.

Spread the remaining chocolate turtle layer over top of pie and sprinkle with remaining ½ cup chopped pecan delights and drizzle with 1 tablespoon caramel topping.

Decorate edge of pie with whipped cream sweetened with Splenda and sprinkle with shaved sugar-free chocolate.

Caramel Toffee Turtle

FANTASTICO NEAPOLITAN PIE

Alberta Dunbar, San Diego, CA
2011 APC Crisco National Pie Championships Amateur Division 2nd Place
No Sugar Added

CRUST
2 cups sugar-free shortbread cookie crumbs
6 tablespoons butter, melted

LAYER 1
4 oz. cream cheese, softened
4 oz. sugar-free dark chocolate, melted and cooled
¾ cup milk
1 oz. package sugar-free vanilla instant pudding
1 teaspoon Kona coffee extract
¾ cup heavy cream, whipped

LAYER 2
4 oz. cream cheese, softened
4 oz. sugar-free white chocolate, melted and cooled
¾ cup milk

1 oz. package sugar-free vanilla instant pudding
1 teaspoon strawberry extract
1 drop red food coloring
¾ cup heavy cream, whipped
1 cup strawberries, diced large

LAYER 3
4 oz. cream cheese, softened
4 oz. sugar-free white chocolate, melted
¾ cup milk
1 oz. package sugar-free instant vanilla pudding
1 teaspoon rum extract
1 drop green food coloring
¾ cup heavy cream, whipped
½ cup ground toasted pistachios (no salt)

TOPPING
2 cups heavy cream
2 tablespoons Splenda
1 teaspoon rum extract

GARNISH
Shredded sugar-free chocolate

Fantastico Neapolitan Pie

For the crust: Mix ingredients in a small bowl with a fork until well mixed. Press on bottom and sides of 9-inch pie plate. Freeze until ready to use.

For layer 1: Place cream cheese and milk in medium bowl. Beat until well blended and smooth. Beat in cooled chocolate. Add pudding and extract. Beat well with wooden spoon and fold in whipped cream. Carefully spread in pie shell. Smooth top and refrigerate.

For layer 2: Repeat directions for layer 1 with first 7 ingredients. Carefully fold in strawberries and spread over first layer.

For layer 3: Repeat above instructions for the first two layers with first 7 ingredients for layer 3. Fold in pistachios. Spread over second layer. Smooth top and chill until set.

For topping: Place ingredients in medium bowl and beat on high until stiff. Fill pastry bag with medium strips and pipe all over pie. Sprinkle with shredded chocolate if so desired.

RAZZLE DAZZLE SPLENDA PIE

Martha Campbell, Richmond, VA
2008 APC Crisco National Pie Championships Amateur Division 1st Place Splenda

CRUST
1½ cups all-purpose flour
½ teaspoon salt
½ cup Crisco shortening
2 tablespoons unsalted butter, melted
3½ to 4 tablespoons ice water
1 egg beaten with 2 tablespoons
   water for egg wash
Optional for baking empty crust:
   16 oz. dry beans, parchment paper

FILLING
8 oz. Philadelphia cream cheese,
   softened

½ cup plus 2 tablespoons Splenda
   No Calorie sweetener, granular
(2) 1 oz. package sugar-free white
   chocolate instant pudding mix
1 tablespoon cornstarch
2 cups whole milk
1 vanilla bean, split lengthwise
1 cup Smucker's sugar-free red
   raspberry preserves
1 cup heavy cream
Fresh raspberries for garnish

For the crust: Combine flour and salt. Cut in Crisco with a pastry blender. Add melted butter and mix just until combined. Add ice water a little at a time. Form a ball, wrap in plastic wrap and chill for about 30 minutes. When chilled, preheat oven to 350°F. Roll out on a pastry cloth and lay crust in lightly greased pie dish, fitting the crust into the corners. Trim excess dough. Crimp edges with fingers, or use excess dough to make crust design with small cookie cutters. Prick bottom and sides with fork. Brush top edge (not bottom and side) of crust with egg wash. Place parchment paper on dough and fill with dry beans (spray paper lightly first with cooking spray on side touching crust). Bake for 25 minutes. Remove from oven and take out beans and parchment paper. Return crust to oven to bake another 10 minutes. Remove and let cool completely.

For the filling: Place split vanilla bean in a bowl with 2 cups milk. Let stand a while. Combine dry pudding mix, ½ cup Splenda, and cornstarch in a bowl and set aside. In another bowl, beat softened Philadelphia brand cream cheese. To the cream cheese, add dry mixture alternately with vanilla-infused milk until everything is added and mixture is smooth. Discard vanilla bean. Pour into cooled pie crust. Chill pie until filling begins to set up. Top with 1 cup Smucker's sugar-free red raspberry preserves. Chill several hours. Before serving, add 2 tablespoons Splenda to 1 cup heavy cream and beat until there are stiff peaks. Pipe cream onto pie with a pastry bag and then garnish with fresh raspberries.

SPLENDA-DID PEANUT BUTTER PIE

Laura Francese, Gerry, NY
2009 APC Crisco National Pie Championships Amateur Division 1st Place Splenda

CRUST
½ cup instant oatmeal
10 Nutter Butter cookies, crushed
2 packages instant oatmeal cereal
6 tablespoons butter, melted
Pinch of salt

CHOCOLATE CREAM MIXTURE
1 cup chocolate chips
¼ cup heavy cream
½ cup chopped peanuts

PEANUT BUTTER FILLING
(1) 8 oz. package cream cheese
½ cup Splenda
¼ cup vanilla frosting
1 cup creamy peanut butter
12 oz. tub whipped topping, reserving
    1 cup for decorating

For the crust: Preheat oven to 350°F. Combine ingredients and press into a pie plate. Bake for 7 minutes. Set aside to cool.

For the chocolate cream: Heat cream in a saucepan and add chocolate chips, stirring until smooth. Drizzle half chocolate mixture on cooled crust. Sprinkle half of chopped nuts over chocolate mixture. Cool 15 minutes.

For the peanut butter filling: Mix ingredients until smooth, then set aside. Spoon peanut butter filling over chocolate mixture. Drizzle with remaining chocolate cream mixture. Sprinkle remaining nuts over top of pie and decorate with whipped topping. Refrigerate for 1 hour or overnight.

SPLENDID PINEAPPLE PIE

Jeanne Ely, Mulberry, FL
2007 APC Crisco National Pie Championships Amateur Division 3rd Place Splenda

CRUST
3 cups flour
1 teaspoon salt
1 cup butter-flavored Crisco shortening
¼ cup shortening
1 egg
5 tablespoons cold water
1 tablespoon vinegar
½ teaspoon almond extract

FILLING
1¾ cups milk
3 eggs, beaten
1 teaspoon vanilla
20 oz. can unsweetened pineapple (undrained)
1 cup Splenda
3 tablespoons flour
Pinch of salt
2 tablespoons butter

MERINGUE
3 egg whites
½ teaspoon cream of tartar
⅓ cup Splenda
½ teaspoon vanilla

For the crust: Preheat oven to 350°F. Cut together flour, salt, and shortening until oatmeal-like in consistency. Beat egg in cup; add water, vinegar, and almond flavoring. Beat all and pour into flour mixture. Blend well. Roll out pie crust and bake for 20 minutes.

For the filling: Heat milk in a saucepan. Add Splenda, pinch of salt, and flour. Cook until slightly thickened. Add well-beaten egg yolks, butter, and vanilla. Return to heat, then add pineapple. Cook until thickened. Pour into 9-inch baked pie shell from above recipe.

For the meringue: Preheat oven to 400°F. Beat egg whites and cream of tartar until foamy. Beat in Splenda and vanilla. Beat until stiff and glossy. Put on top of pineapple filling. Bake about 10 minutes or until delicate brown.

STRAWBERRY SMOOTHIE SPLENDA PIE

Terri Beaver, Olalla, WA

2009 APC Crisco National Pie Championships Amateur Division 3rd Place Splenda

CRUST (makes two 9-inch pie crusts)

2¾ cups flour, plus extra for rolling
1 teaspoon salt
2 tablespoons Splenda sweetener
10 tablespoons butter-flavored Crisco
6 tablespoons Crisco shortening
½ cup ice water
1 tablespoon apple cider vinegar
1 ice cube

FILLING

16 oz. bag whole frozen strawberries (unsweetened), thawed
1 cup Splenda sweetener
½ cup sugar-free strawberry jam
2 envelopes unflavored gelatin
½ cup cold water
4 oz. cream cheese, room temperature
½ cup plain yogurt
½ cup heavy cream
1 teaspoon vanilla

GLAZE TOPPING

½ cup Splenda sweetener
1 tablespoon potato starch or cornstarch
Reserved strawberry juice
Water
2 drops red food coloring (if desired)
1 pint fresh strawberries, cleaned, hulled, and halved

For the crust: Combine flour, salt, and Splenda in a large bowl. Cut in both shortenings until texture is about the size of small peas. Mix water and vinegar in a small bowl. Add ice cube. (You will not use all of this). One tablespoon at a time, add 6 to 8 tablespoons of water mixture to flour mixture until doughy. Divide into two discs and wrap in plastic wrap. Chill thoroughly, at least 2 hours. You will use one disc for this recipe.

Take one disc and roll out on floured surface. Carefully place in pie plate and flute edges. Put in freezer or refrigerate for at least 30 minutes. Preheat oven to 400°F. Line pie shell with parchment paper and bake with pie weights for 15 minutes. Remove pie weights and lower oven temperature to 375°F. Bake for 12 to 15 minutes. Cover edges with foil or a pie guard if needed. Let cool.

For the filling: Drain strawberries and reserve juice for glaze. Take one half the berries and coarsely chop. Set aside. In a saucepan, sprinkle gelatin over cold water. Let sit for 1 minute. Over medium heat, stir until completely dissolved. Add jam and heat until liquid. Let cool about 10 minutes. Place remaining berries in a blender with the Splenda and puree. Add cream cheese, yogurt, vanilla, and cream. Blend well. Add the jam mixture and blend. Stir in the strawberry pieces. Pour into prepared pie crust. Chill in refrigerator.

For the glaze topping: Mix Splenda and potato starch in a saucepan. Add enough water to the reserved strawberry juice to make 1 cup. Pour into saucepan. Whisk over medium heat until it just comes to a boil. Add red food coloring if desired. Cool to room temperature. Place berries cut side-down on chilled pie. Pour glaze over the top and chill thoroughly before serving.

SWEET POTATO

"Having the most mouthwatering pie recipes at my fingertips is just amazing. Each category is filled with an array of different ingredients. I can't wait to bake them all!"

—The Longest Time Judge,
Gary Solomon, www.recipeexchange.com

Fall Splendor—Sweet Potato Pie
   in a Gingerbread Crust — 364
Maple Pecan Sweet Potato Pie — 366
Maple Sweet Potato Surprise Pie — 368
Sweet Potato Praline Pie
   with Marshmallow Meringue — 370
Streusel-Topped Sweet Potato Pie — 372
Sweet Potato Pie — 374
Sweet Potato Pie with Pecan Topping — 376
Sweet Potato Praline Cloud Pie — 378
Sweet Potato Pie with
   Pecan Topping — 380

‹‹ *Streusel Topped Sweet Potato Pie (recipe page 372)*

FALL SPLENDOR—SWEET POTATO PIE IN A GINGERBREAD CRUST

Kathleen Harter, Hancock, MI
2011 APC Crisco National Pie Championships Amateur Division 1st Place Sweet Potato

CRUST

1½ cups unbleached King Arthur flour
½ cup brown sugar
1 teaspoon cinnamon
¼ teaspoon nutmeg
1 teaspoon ginger
1 teaspoon baking powder
½ teaspoon salt
2 teaspoons buttermilk powder
½ teaspoon lemon juice
½ cup toasted and finely chopped pecans
½ cup European-style butter, cold
1 tablespoon unsulfured organic molasses
3 tablespoons cold water
1 small egg white, lightly beaten (used on crust after baking)

FILLING

4 sweet potatoes
¼ cup European-style butter, melted
1 cup sugar
½ cup whole milk
2 eggs
½ teaspoon cinnamon
½ teaspoon nutmeg
½ teaspoon ginger
¼ teaspoon salt
1 teaspoon lemon extract

TOPPING

½ cup cream cheese, softened
¼ cup cooked sweet potato
⅛ teaspoon cinnamon
Dash nutmeg

For the crust: Mix all dry ingredients including the chopped pecans. Add molasses, lemon juice, and butter and mix just until the mixture resembles cornmeal. Add cold water and mix by hand until incorporated. Don't overmix. Once blended, form into a ball, flatten slightly, wrap in plastic wrap and place in refrigerator for ½ hour to 1 hour. Remove from refrigerator and place on lightly floured surface. Roll dough into a circle that fits the pie plate. Place rolled crust into the pie plate, pressing into bottom edge and on fluted edges of pie plate. Use any remaining dough as a decorative element on top of assembled pie.

Use a fork to poke the bottom of pie plate before placing in freezer. Place crust in pie plate in freezer for ½ hour. Preheat oven to 350°F. Remove pie plate from freezer and pre-bake in heated oven for 10 minutes. Once cooled, brush entire crust with lightly beaten egg white (helps to prevent fruit juices from soaking into crust).

For the filling: Preheat oven to 350°F. Peel and slice sweet potatoes into one-inch cubes.

Place in large saucepan, cover with water, and cook on medium heat until soft.

Drain water and place sweet potatoes in a large mixing bowl (reserving ¼ cup for topping). Using

Fall Splendor—Sweet Potato Pie in a Gingerbread Crust

a paddle attachment of a stand mixer, add one egg at a time and then add spices, lemon extract, melted butter, and milk. Pour sweet potato filling into cooled crust. Bake pie for about 55 to 60 minutes, until a toothpick inserted in the middle comes out clean. Set aside and cool.

For the topping: Place all ingredients in a mixer and mix until well incorporated. Put topping in a piping bag, and use a star point tip. Pipe topping in a pleasing design and decorate with additional pecans if desired.

MAPLE PECAN SWEET POTATO PIE

Jill Jones, Palm Bay, FL
2011 APC Crisco National Pie Championships Amateur Division 3rd Place Sweet Potato

CRUST
1 cup flour
½ teaspoon salt
¼ tablespoon sugar
½ cup shortening
1 egg
1½ tablespoons ice water
¼ tablespoon vinegar

FILLING
1 cup brown sugar
1 teaspoon cinnamon

2 tablespoons flour
2½ cups mashed sweet potatoes (3 potatoes)
2 eggs, slightly beaten
¼ teaspoon salt
1 teaspoon nutmeg, fresh
5 oz. can evaporated milk
1 teaspoon pure vanilla
¼ teaspoon pumpkin pie spice
1 cup chopped pecans
2 tablespoons maple syrup

For the crust: Mix flour, sugar, and salt. Cut in shortening with fork or pastry cutter until mix is crumbly. Add egg, vinegar, and water. Mix until it comes together and is slightly sticky. Scrape out of bowl and place on a floured surface. Roll into a ball and wrap in plastic wrap. Refrigerate for 1 hour. Roll out on a floured surface.

For the filling: Preheat oven to 450°F. Mix sugar, cinnamon, flour, salt, nutmeg, and pumpkin pie spice with mashed sweet potatoes. Mix milk, eggs, and vanilla into sweet potato mixture. Pour into unbaked pie shell. Mix pecans and syrup together and spread on top of pie before baking. Bake at 450°F for 15 minutes, then reduce temperature to 325°F for 30 to 45 minutes longer or until done.

Maple Pecan Sweet Potato Pie

MAPLE SWEET POTATO SURPRISE PIE

Karen Hall, Elm Creek, NE
2007 APC Crisco National Pie Championships Amateur Division 1st Place Sweet Potato

CRUST
3 cups unbleached flour
1 tablespoon buttermilk powder
½ teaspoon baking powder
1 teaspoon salt
1 cup plus 1 tablespoon butter-
    flavored Crisco cut into
    ¼-inch parts
1 egg
⅓ cup cold water
1 tablespoon vinegar

CREAM CHEESE LAYER
4 oz. cream cheese, softened
¼ cup sugar
1 egg white
2 tablespoons walnuts, chopped

FILLING
2 cups cooked mashed sweet potato

3 eggs, plus 1 egg yolk, beaten
½ cup light brown sugar, packed
½ cup maple syrup
½ cup evaporated milk
½ teaspoon cinnamon
⅛ teaspoon cloves
⅛ teaspoon ginger
⅛ teaspoon sea salt

CREAM CHEESE ICING
2 oz. cream cheese, softened
½ cup powdered sugar
1 tablespoon milk

GARNISH
8 oz. frozen whipped topping, thawed
¼ cup walnuts, chopped
Pastry cutouts

For the crust: In a large bowl, combine flour, buttermilk powder, baking powder, and salt. With a pastry blender cut in Crisco until mixture resembles coarse crumbs. In a small bowl, beat egg, water, and vinegar together. With a pastry fork, add egg mixture slowly while tossing with fork until mixture is moistened (do not overmix). Divide dough and shape into 3 balls. Flatten each to form disc. Wrap each disc with plastic wrap and refrigerate at least 30 minutes before using. Makes 3 single crusts. Use one disc for this recipe. Roll out a single pastry and line a 9-inch pie dish. Crimp edge.

For the cream cheese layer: In a small mixing bowl, blend together cream cheese, sugar, and egg white until smooth. Sprinkle walnuts into bottom of unbaked pie shell and press into pastry gently. Spread cream cheese mixture over walnuts in bottom of pie shell.

For the filling: Preheat oven to 425°F. In a large mixing bowl, stir together sweet potato, eggs and yolk, brown sugar, maple syrup, milk, cinnamon, cloves, ginger, and salt until well blended. Pour mixture over cream cheese layer. Protect edge of pie with foil to prevent overbrowning. Bake at 425°F for 10 minutes. Reduce oven temperature to 350°F and bake 30 to 40 minutes or until center is set. Cool pie completely.

For the icing: In a small bowl, blend together cream cheese, powdered sugar, and milk until smooth. Drizzle or pipe over the top of cooled pie.

Pipe or dollop a ring of whipped topping around edge of pie; Sprinkle with chopped walnuts and pastry cutouts, if desired. Chill until ready to serve.

Maple Sweet Potato Surprise Pie

SWEET POTATO PRALINE PIE WITH MARSHMALLOW MERINGUE

Marles Riessland, Riverdale, NE
2005 APC Crisco National Pie Championships Amateur Division 2nd Place Sweet Potato

CRUST
1 cup pastry flour
2 cups all-purpose flour
1 teaspoon salt
1 teaspoon sugar
½ teaspoon baking powder
1 cup plus 1 tablespoon butter-
   flavored shortening, chilled
1/3 cup ice water
1 tablespoon vinegar
1 egg, beaten

FILLING
3 eggs, beaten
½ cup sugar
½ cup brown sugar
1 teaspoon cinnamon

½ teaspoon ginger
¼ teaspoon cloves
¼ teaspoon salt
2 cups mashed cooked sweet
   potatoes
½ cup milk
1 cup half and half

TOPPING
½ cup flour
½ cup chopped pecans
¼ cup packed brown sugar
3 tablespoons butter, softened
Meringue
2 egg whites
Dash of salt
2/3 cup marshmallow crème

For the crust: In a large bowl, combine the flour, salt, sugar, and baking powder. Cut in shortening with a pastry blender until the mixture resembles coarse meal. In a small bowl, mix water and vinegar with the beaten egg. Add the liquid mixture, one tablespoon at a time, to the flour mixture, tossing with a fork to form a soft dough. Shape into 3 discs. Wrap in plastic wrap and chill in the refrigerator. When ready, roll out one disc and line a 9-inch pie dish.

For the filling: Heat oven to 400°F. In a large bowl, beat eggs. Add sugars, spices, and salt. Stir in sweet potatoes. Mix well. Gradually stir in milk and half and half. Pour mixture into 9-inch unbaked pie shell. Bake 15 minutes at 400°F. Reduce oven temperature to 350°F. Bake 35 minutes.

For the topping: Combine all ingredients. Remove pie from oven and sprinkle topping over filling. Return pie to oven and bake 20 minutes longer or until center is set.

For the meringue: Preheat oven to 350°F. Beat egg whites and salt until stiff peaks form. Add marshmallow crème gradually. Make wreath of meringue on pie top, sealing edges to crust. Bake for 12 to 15 minutes until lightly browned.

STREUSEL-TOPPED SWEET POTATO PIE

Sarah Spaugh, Winston-Salem, NC
2005 APC Crisco National Pie Championships Amateur Division 1st Place Sweet Potato

CRUST
2 cups all-purpose flour
¾ teaspoon salt
⅔ cup butter-flavored Crisco
  shortening
5 to 6 tablespoons cold water

FILLING
3 to 4 sweet potatoes, cooked and
  peeled (2 cups mashed)
½ cup caramel sauce or ice cream
  topping
¾ teaspoon ground cinnamon

2 tablespoons melted butter
¾ cup whole milk
2 eggs
½ cup brown sugar
½ cup pure vanilla extract
¼ teaspoon salt

STREUSEL TOPPING
½ cup brown sugar
½ cup unsifted flour
¼ cup cold butter
¼ cup chopped pecans

For the crust: Combine flour and salt in a medium bowl. Cut in Crisco until flour is blended to form pea-sized crumbs. Sprinkle the cold water over the mixture and toss lightly with a fork until the dough forms a ball. Roll out the pastry and place it in a 9-inch pie plate.

For the filling: Preheat oven to 400°F. Spread the caramel sauce in the bottom of the unbaked pie crust. Mash the potatoes. Lightly beat the eggs. Add sugar to the eggs. Beat together and add to potatoes. Add and combine remaining ingredients. Pour into crust. Bake at 400°F for 15 minutes. Reduce heat to 350°F and bake for 30 more minutes. Remove the pie and sprinkle on the topping.

For the streusel topping: In a medium bowl, combine the brown sugar and flour. Cut in the butter until mixture is crumbly. Add the pecans. Sprinkle over pie. Bake for 10 to 15 minutes more or until the topping is golden brown. You may serve with whipped cream.

Streusel-Topped Sweet Potato Pie

SWEET POTATO PIE

Christine Montalvo, Windsor Heights, IA
2008 APC Crisco National Pie Championships Amateur Division 1ˢᵗ Place Sweet Potato

CRUST

2 cups all-purpose flour
1 cup cake flour
½ teaspoon salt
⅓ cup ice water
1 cup butter-flavored Crisco, frozen
    and cut into small pieces
1 large egg
1 teaspoon apple cider vinegar

FILLING

1 cup baked sweet potato (peeled),
    packed
3 eggs, slightly beaten
(2) 3 oz. packages cream cheese,
    softened
½ cup brown sugar
½ cup sugar
1 teaspoon vanilla
¼ cup butter, melted and cooled

For the crust: In food processor, combine the flours and salt. Add the shortening pieces and pulse until dough resembles coarse crumbs. Set aside. In a small bowl, beat together the egg, vinegar, and water. Add egg mixture to the flour mixture and combine with a fork, just until the dough comes together. Do not overmix. Form dough into 2 discs, wrap in plastic, and chill for at least one hour or overnight. Roll out one piece of pie crust into a 12-inch circle. Fit into a 9-inch deep-dish pie pan and flute edges. Set aside.

For the filling: Preheat oven to 350°F. Mash sweet potatoes. Add all the other ingredients to sweet potatoes and mix with mixer and beat until smooth. Pour into pie shell. Bake for 20 to 30 minutes or until set. Remove from oven. Cool completely. Garnish with whipped cream.

SWEET POTATO PIE WITH PECAN TOPPING

Tricia Largay, Brewer, ME
2010 APC Crisco National Pie Championships Amateur Division 2nd Place Sweet Potato

CRUST
1/3 cup plus 1 tablespoon Crisco
   butter-flavored shortening
1 cup all-purpose flour
1/4 teaspoon salt
Pinch of sugar
6 to 7 tablespoons ice-cold water

SWEET POTATO PIE FILLING
4 cups mashed sweet potato (cook
   potato in oven until fork tender)
4 tablespoons melted butter

1/2 cup sugar
1 tablespoon brown sugar
1/4 teaspoon pumpkin pie spice
1 farm fresh egg
1/3 cup evaporated milk

TOPPING
3/4 cup brown sugar
1/3 cup flour
3 tablespoons melted butter
1/2 cup chopped pecans

For the crust: Mix flour, salt, and sugar. Cut in shortening with fingers or fork until mixture resembles small peas. Add just enough water to allow entire mixture to stick together. Roll out on floured waxed paper. Press into 9-inch pie plate.

For the filling: Bake sweet potatoes in oven until tender. Scoop out of peels and place in a large bowl with melted butter. Mix by hand until completely blended. Add egg, sugar, and evaporated milk. Mix until smooth. Pour into prepared pie shell.

For the topping: Preheat oven to 350°F. Place brown sugar and flour in bowl and mix. Add chopped pecans and melted butter. Spread over sweet potato pie. Bake for 50 to 60 minutes or until topping is golden brown.

Serve warm or chilled.

SWEET POTATO PRALINE CLOUD PIE

Beth Campbell, Belleville, WI
2003 APC Crisco National Pie Championships Amateur Division 2003 1st Place Sweet Potato

CRUST
1 cup flour
½ cup shortening
Pinch of salt
¼ cup cold water

FILLING
2 sweet potatoes, baked or boiled
¼ cup butter, softened
1 cup sugar
2 eggs
½ teaspoon cinnamon
¼ teaspoon salt
½ teaspoon nutmeg
¼ teaspoon cloves
¼ teaspoon mace

1 cup evaporated milk
Meringue
¼ teaspoon salt
¼ teaspoon vanilla
1 teaspoon lemon juice
3 egg whites
6 tablespoons sugar

PRALINE TOPPING
2 tablespoons firmly packed dark
    brown sugar
2 tablespoons dark corn syrup
1 tablespoon butter
¼ teaspoon vanilla
⅓ cup chopped pecans

For the crust: Cut shortening into the flour and salt until it is pea-sized pieces, then add cold water, being careful not to over-blend. Chill for 30 minutes. Roll out and place into pie pan.

For the filling: Preheat oven to 350°F. Mash sweet potatoes and combine with all of the other ingredients. Pour into pie shell and bake until firm, about 35 to 40 minutes.

For the meringue: Separate eggs, and add 1st three ingredients to egg whites. Beat until foamy. Add 6 tablespoons sugar to the mixture, one tablespoon at a time. Beat until sugar dissolves.

For the topping: Preheat oven to 350°F. Combine brown sugar, syrup, butter, and vanilla in medium saucepan. Cook and stir on medium heat until butter is melted and mixture is blended. Remove from heat.

Spoon dollops of meringue in ring around outside edge of pie. Sprinkle ⅓ cup chopped pecans over the center of the pie. Drizzle all or part of the praline topping over the nuts, as desired. Bake for 15 minutes or until golden brown. Cool to room temperature before serving. Refrigerate leftover pie.

SWEET POTATO PIE WITH PECAN TOPPING

Carolyn Blakemore, Fairmont, WV
2009 APC Crisco National Pie Championships Amateur Division 1st Place Sweet Potato

CRUST
1½ cups flour, sifted
½ teaspoon salt
½ cup butter-flavored Crisco
3 to 4 tablespoons cold water

FILLING
2½ cups cooked mashed sweet
   potatoes
¾ cup sugar
¼ teaspoon salt
½ teaspoon cinnamon

⅛ teaspoon cloves
¼ teaspoon nutmeg
½ teaspoon ginger
1 teaspoon apple spice
½ teaspoon vanilla
2 eggs, beaten
⅔ cup evaporated milk

TOPPING
¼ cup brown sugar
1 tablespoon butter
¼ cup chopped pecans

For the crust: Combine flour and salt in bowl. Cut in shortening with a pastry blender until crumbly. Sprinkle on water by the tablespoon. Stir with a fork to form a ball. Wrap in waxed paper. Chill, then roll out on waxed paper with floured rolling pin. Lay into a 9-inch pie pan.

For the filling: In a bowl, combine mashed sweet potatoes, sugar, spices, and vanilla. Mix well. Add eggs and milk. Mix well. Pour into pie shell.

For the topping: Preheat oven to 425°F. In a small dish, combine brown sugar and butter. Mix until crumbly. Sprinkle half of pecans on bottom crust. Reserve 2 tablespoons for topping and sprinkle the rest over the pecans on bottom crust. Sprinkle topping and pecans over filling. Cover fluted crust rim with foil strips to bake. Bake in a 425°F oven for 10 minutes. Reduce heat to 350°F for 20 minutes. Cool completely.

AMERICAN PIE COUNCIL EVENTS

National Pie Day

Registered in 1983 by American Pie Council founder Charlie Papazian, National Pie Day on January 23 (Charlie's birthday) has evolved into a day when we celebrate the enjoyment of pie by sharing it with people everywhere On this day, we encourage you to share pies with neighbors, elderly shut-ins, police stations, and fire stations, and anyone you would like to feel special. It is a great day to show someone how much you care. If you don't bake, you can buy a pie to share!

The American Pie Council Crisco National Pie Championships

Founded in 1995, the National Pie Championships were initially held in various parts of the country, but in 2002 we found a new home in Celebration, FL. Since then, the National Pie

Championships has grown to almost 1,000 entries each year. Pies are judged on appearance, flavor, crust, mouth-feel, overall taste, overall impression, and originality. Anyone can enter—from amateurs to professional chefs to commercial bakeries—but only the best pies will win.

The Great American Pie Festival Sponsored by Crisco

The Great American Pie Festival, held in conjunction with the National Pie Championships, originally came into existence because commercial entrants to the National Pie Championships had to bake two pies for every pie they entered—one for a display table and one to judge. It seemed a shame to have the display table pies just sit, so a buffet table was created to give everyone, not just the judges, an opportunity to taste and enjoy the pies. This event quickly became so popular that we decided to ask commercial bakers to bring pies just for the buffet, and the Great American Pie Festival was born. After one year in our new home in Celebration, FL, Crisco became the sponsor of this event. "The partnership between Crisco and the American Pie Council has helped create family traditions, memorable moments and great recipes that will live on as long as people gather together to enjoy a slice of delicious pie," states Maribeth Badertscher, Vice President of Corporate Communications, the J. M. Smucker Company. The festival has many activities including the Never Ending Pie Buffet, baking demonstrations, an entertainment stage, a pie making booth, many children's activities, and, of course, a pie eating contest! Hundreds of people volunteer and thousands now attend the festivities each year, and we hope you become one of them!

Pi(e) Day

Since pie baking is part of our American culture, on Pi(e) Day—March 14 (3.14)— we like to encourage our members to pass along the tradition of pie baking to the younger generation.

SPECIAL THANKS

The goal of the American Pie Council is to raise the awareness, enjoyment, and consumption of pies and to preserve America's pie heritage. The members of the APC, and particularly the Board of Directors, are extremely active toward that goal, and their endless energy makes the APC events continue to grow from year to year. Over 400 volunteers help the APC staff and board to make these events enjoy continued success.

Compiling all the recipes for this cookbook was a big undertaking, and I'd like to thank the APC intern Tricia Davit for her tireless efforts in reviewing and editing recipes. Tricia has been at the American Pie Council for the past two years and helps review all the recipes entered in the National Pie Championships.

In addition, I'd also like to thank my grandchildren for their assistance in the kitchen. Richie and Riley helped baked many pies while Braden endlessly peeled apples and grated zest. I'm happy to continue America's pie heritage through them and know they will carry on the tradition.

Last, but certainly not least, I'd like to thank all of the participants in the APC Crisco National Pie Championships and especially those whose winning recipes are part of this cookbook. It is not an easy task to create an original recipe, and, as you can tell after reading this book, many of our contestants have created more than one. My hats off to the talent, patience, and creativity of the home bakers, commercial manufacturers, and chefs who have supported the APC Crisco National Pie Championships and made it what it is today—the search for the perfect pie.

AMERICAN PIE COUNCIL
BOARD OF DIRECTORS

PHOTOGRAPHY COURTESY OF ...

Sue Ade, Bluffton Today
Brion Price Photography
California Raisin Marketing Board
Patricia Davitt
Emile Henry
Gunnar Soderlind Photography
Linda Hoskins

Linda Hundt
Mary Cilia
Naylet La Rochelle
Rumie A. Martinez
Tye Ridolfi
Jim Siegel

INDEX

A

All American sour cherry pie, 34
Almond cherry pie, 182
Ambrosia pie, 232
Appealing apple caramel pie, 2
Apple leaf pie, 4
Apple pie, 6
    appealing apple caramel pie, 2
    best ever caramel apple
        pecan pie, 8
    brandy, 332
    brightest, 10
    butterscotch pecan, 12
    golden, 14
    grandma Haeh's, 16
    gratz grand apple pecan
        caramel pie, 18
    harvest, 20
    Hilton's, 22
    leaf, 4
    orchard-fresh, 24
    simply divine cinnamon roll
        raisin, 26
    splendid, 28
    sticky toffee pudding, 320
    sweet cider, 30

B

Back to the islands pie, 234
Bananas foster cream pie, 138
Berry. See Fruit & berry
Best ever caramel apple pecan pie, 8
Black bottom cherry pie, 36
Blueberry
    and basil lime pie, 208
    classic pie, 192
    raspberry pie, 184
Blueberry–cranberry pie with pecan
    streusel topping, 186
Blue ridge cherry pie, 38
Brandy apple pie, 332
Brightest apple pie, 10
Bumbleberry pie, 188
Butterscotch
    crunch pie, 116
    pecan apple pie, 12
    pecan custard pie, 178

C

Cajun pecan pie, 212
Californese raisin and nut pie, 298
California raisin harvest, 300
California raisin maple
    crunch pie, 312

California sunshine raisin pie, 302
Caramel-pecan chocolate pie, 60
Caramel toffee turtle, 350
Category five peanut butter pie, 256
Celebration of liberty
    chocolate pie, 336
Cheese pie, celebration, 334
Cherry cherry bang bang pie, 46
Cherry pie
    all American sour, 34
    black bottom, 36
    blue ridge, 38
    cherry cherry bang bang pie, 46
    chocolate cherry cordial pie, 42
    classic, 52
    classic cherry strudel-topped
        pie, 44
    Grammy J's, 48
    I'm so cheery cherry pie, 50
    red raspberry, 190
    streusel pie, 40
    sweet tart, 54
    Tom's cheery cherry berry pie, 56
Chocolate
    caramel nut pie, 62
    caramel-pecan pie, 60

celebration of liberty chocolate pie, 336
cherry cordial pie, 42
chip chipmunk pie, 214
chocolate chip chipmunk pie, 214
chocolate hazelnut crunch pie, 218
chocolate hazelnut dream pie, 144
coffee cup chocolate pie, 240
dark chocolate raspberry glacier pie, 74
dark chocolate raspberry truffle pie, 146
double chocolate caramel macchiato pie, 148
double chocolate raspberry dream pie, 66
German chocolate pie, 76
hazelnut crunch pie, 218
hazelnut dream pie, 144
macadamia nut chocolate chunk pie, 216
oh my ganache! chocolate cream pie, 68
raisin walnut pie, 304
raspberry chocolate mint ribbon pie, 252
raspberry delight, 70
raspberry silk and cream pie, 64
shades of, 78
silky, rich & smooth chocolate pie, 80
three blind mice chocolate cheese pie, 82
toffee pie, 250
white and milk chocolate raspberry mousse, 158
white-bottomed caramel chocolate pecan pie, 228
Chocolate-covered strawberry pie, 236
Citrus
    cream cheese lemon pie, 88
    Girl Scout cookie lemonade pie, 90
    grandma's zesty lemon sponge pie, 92
    key lime–raspberry pie, 94
    lemon–lime meringue pie, 96
    lemon raspberry twist, 98
    mandarin sunrise pie, 100
    orange coconut pie, 102
    raspberry lemonade pie, 104
    razzilicious key lime pie, 106
    support group key lime pie, 108
    U. S. route 1 pie: Florida key lime with Maine blueberries, 110
    when god hands you lemons, make a lemon pie, 112
Classic blueberry pie, 192
Classic cherry pie, 52
Classic cherry strudel-topped pie, 44
Classic Italian tiramisu pie, 238
Coffee cup chocolate pie, 240
Cream cheese
    chocolate hazelnut dream pie, 144
    dark chocolate raspberry truffle pie, 146
    double chocolate caramel macchiato pie, 148
    double strawberry malt shop pie, 154
    lemon pie, 88
    lemon swirl cream cheese pie, 150
    pineapple cream delight, 152
    royal macadamia raspberry pie, 156
    white and milk chocolate raspberry mousse, 158
Cream pie
    bananas foster, 138
    butterscotch crunch pie, 116
    creamy coconut, 118
    creamy guava pie, 140
    hula hula pineapple cream pie with fried pie crust, 120
    island breeze pineapple– blueberry, 122
    Max's coo-coo for coconut, 124
    oh, so sweet, Olivia's maple pie, 126
    Olalla coconut supreme pie, 128
    paradise pineapple, 130
    pina colada pie, 132
    raspberry smoothie, 134
    toasted coconut, 136
Creamy coconut cream pie, 118
Creamy guava pie, 140
Custard pie
    butterscotch pecan, 178
    grandma's egg, 164
    Hawaiian vanilla, 166
    lemon drop, 168
    Linda's luscious raspberry, 170
    luscious southern coconut pie, 172
    put the lime in the coconut, 162
    raisin nut, 174
    supreme caramel–chocolate pie, 176

D

Dark chocolate
    raspberry glacier pie, 74
    raspberry truffle pie, 146
Deep-dish deluxe banana split pie, 242
Deluxe pecan pie, 220
Double chocolate
    caramel macchiato pie, 148
    raspberry dream pie, 66
Double strawberry malt shop pie, 154
Dream date pecan pie, 222

E

The engagement ring, 328

F

Fall splendor-sweet potato pie in a gingerbread crust, 364
Fantastico Neapolitan pie, 352
Farm-fresh pumpkin pie with pecan topping, 276
Flutter nutter peanut butter candy bar pie, 258
Four seasons strawberry–rhubarb pie, 194
Freedom pie, 344
Fresh blueberry caramel crumb pie, 196
Fruit & berry
    almond cherry pie, 182
    blueberry & basil lime pie, 208
    blueberry–cranberry pie with pecan streusel topping, 186
    blueberry raspberry pie, 184
    bumbleberry pie, 188
    cherry red raspberry pie, 190
    classic blueberry pie, 192
    four seasons strawberry–rhubarb pie, 194
    fresh blueberry caramel crumb pie, 196
    fruity fruit pie, 198
    ginger, you're a peach pie, 200
    glazed strawberry cheesecake pie, 202
    razzle dazzle berry pie, 204
    rhubarb–strawberry–raspberry pie, 206
Fruity fruit pie, 198

G

German chocolate pie, 76
Ginger, you're a peach pie, 200
Girl Scout cookie lemonade pie, 90
Glazed strawberry cheesecake pie, 202
Golden apple pie, 14

Golden nugget raisin pie, 306
Grammy J's cherry pie, 48
Grandma Haeh's apple pie, 16
Grandma's egg custard pie, 164
Grandma's pumpkin pie, 278
Grandma's zesty lemon sponge pie, 92
Gratz grand apple pecan caramel pie, 18

H

Harvest apple pie, 20
Harvest pumpkin pie, 280
Hawaiian vanilla custard pie, 166
Helen's apple cider raisin pie, 308
Hilton's apple pie, 22
Holiday cranberry mince pie, 326
Honey crunch pumpkin pie, 282
Hula hula pineapple cream pie with fried pie crust, 120

I

I'm so cheery cherry pie, 50
Island breeze pineapple–blueberry cream pie, 122
It's all about the peanut butter pie, 260

K

Key lime–raspberry pie, 94
KP's berry pie, 338

L

Lemon
    drop custard pie, 168
    pie, 112
    raspberry twist, 98
    swirl cream cheese pie, 150
Lemon–lime meringue pie, 96
Linda's luscious raspberry custard, 170
Lovin my latte pie, 244

"Lovin' spoonful" cinnamon roll raisin custard pie, 310
Luscious southern coconut pie, 172

M

Macadamia nut chocolate chunk pie, 216
Mandarin sunrise pie, 100
Maple-kissed butter pecan celebration pie, 224
Maple peach pecan pie, 226
Maple pecan sweet potato pie, 366
Maple sweet potato surprise pie, 368
Max's coo-coo for coconut cream pie, 124
Momma's mud puddle pie, 346
My big fat Italian strawberry–basil wedding pie, 322

N

Nut
    cajun pecan pie, 212
    chocolate chip chipmunk pie, 214
    chocolate hazelnut crunch pie, 218
    deluxe pecan pie, 220
    dream date pecan pie, 222
    macadamia nut chocolate chunk pie, 216
    maple-kissed butter pecan celebration pie, 224
    maple peach pecan pie, 226
    white-bottomed caramel chocolate pecan pie, 228

O

Octoberfest pie, 286
Oh, so sweet, Olivia's maple pie, 126
Oh my ganache! chocolate cream pie, 68
Olalla coconut supreme pie, 128
Old-fashioned pumpkin pie, 288
Old-world sour cream pie, 314

Open pies
    ambrosia pie, 232
    back to the islands pie, 234
    chocolate-covered strawberry
        pie, 236
    chocolate toffee pie, 250
    classic Italian tiramisu pie, 238
    coffee cup chocolate pie, 240
    deep-dish deluxe banana split
        pie, 242
    lovin my latte pie, 244
    peaches and creamy cranberry
        pie, 246
    raspberry chocolate mint ribbon
        pie, 252
    strawberry thin mint pie, 248
Orange coconut pie, 102
Orchard-fresh apple pie, 24
Oreo peanut butter mousse pie, 262

P

Paradise pineapple cream pie, 130
Peaches and creamy cranberry
    pie, 246
Peanut butter -n- strawberry explosion
    pie, 268
Peanut butter pie
    category five, 256
    flutter nutter peanut butter candy
        bar pie, 258
    it's all about the peanut butter
        pie, 260
    Oreo peanut butter mousse
        pie, 262
    peanut butter -n- strawberry
        explosion pie, 268
    premier, 270
    proposal pie, 266
    the ultimate peanut butter pie, 272
    William's peanut butter paradise
        pie, 264

Pecan maple streusel pumpkin
    pie, 284
Piña colada pie, 132
Pineapple
    cream delight, 152
    hula hula pineapple cream pie with
        fried pie crust, 120
    island breeze pineapple–
        blueberry, 122
    paradise pineapple, 130
    splendid pineapple pie, 358
Premier peanut butter pie, 270
Pumpkin pie
    farm-fresh pumpkin pie with pecan
        topping, 276
    grandma's, 278
    harvest, 280
    honey crunch, 282
    octoberfest pie, 286
    old-fashioned, 288
    pecan maple streusel, 284
    real, 290
    tasty, 292
    walnut crunch, 294
Put the lime in the coconut custard
    pie, 162

R

Raisin
    Californese raisin and nut pie, 298
    California raisin harvest, 300
    California raisin maple crunch
        pie, 312
    California sunshine raisin pie, 302
    chocolate raisin walnut pie, 304
    golden nugget raisin pie, 306
    Helen's apple cider raisin pie, 308
    "lovin' spoonful" cinnamon roll
        raisin custard pie, 310
    nut custard pie, 174
    old-world sour cream pie, 314
    raisin pie delight, 316

Raspberry
    blueberry pie, 184
    cherry red raspberry pie, 190
    chocolate mint ribbon pie, 252
    dark chocolate raspberry glacier
        pie, 74
    dark chocolate raspberry truffle
        pie, 146
    delight, 70
    double chocolate raspberry dream
        pie, 66
    key lime–raspberry pie, 94
    lemonade pie, 104
    lemon raspberry twist, 98
    Linda's luscious raspberry custard
        pie, 170
    rhubarb–strawberry–raspberry
        pie, 206
    royal macadamia raspberry
        pie, 156
    silk and cream pie, 64
    smoothie cream pie, 134
    white and milk chocolate raspberry
        mousse, 158
Razzilicious key lime pie, 106
Razzle dazzle berry pie, 204
Razzle dazzle splenda pie, 354
Real pumpkin pie, 290
Rhubarb–strawberry–raspberry
    pie, 206
Royal macadamia raspberry pie, 156
Royal sapphire blueberry pie, 330

S

Second chance pie, 348
Shades of chocolate, 78
Silky, rich & smooth chocolate pie, 80
Simply divine cinnamon roll raisin
    apple pie, 26
Special categories
    brandy apple pie, 332
    celebration cheese pie, 334

celebration of liberty chocolate
    pie, 336
the engagement ring, 328
holiday cranberry mince pie, 326
KP's berry pie, 338
my big fat Italian strawberry–basil
    wedding pie, 322
royal sapphire blueberry pie, 330
sticky toffee pudding apple
    pie, 320
sunshine pie, 340
vanilla bean Brûlée pie, 324
Special dietary
    caramel toffee turtle, 350
    fantastico Neapolitan pie, 352
    freedom pie, 344
    momma's mud puddle pie, 346
    razzle dazzle splenda pie, 354
    second chance pie, 348
    splenda-did peanut butter pie, 356
    splendid pineapple pie, 358
    strawberry smoothie splenda
        pie, 360
Splenda-did peanut butter pie, 356
Splendid apple pie, 28
Splendid pineapple pie, 358
Sticky toffee pudding apple pie, 320
Strawberry
    chocolate-covered strawberry
        pie, 236
    double strawberry malt shop
        pie, 154

four seasons strawberry–rhubarb
    pie, 194
glazed strawberry cheesecake
    pie, 202
my big fat Italian strawberry–basil
    wedding pie, 322
peanut butter -n- strawberry
    explosion pie, 268
rhubarb–strawberry–raspberry
    pie, 206
smoothie splenda pie, 360
thin mint pie, 248
Streusel-topped sweet potato pie, 372
Sunshine pie, 340
Support group key lime pie, 108
Supreme caramel–chocolate pie, 176
Sweet cider apple pie, 30
Sweet potato pie, 374
    fall splendor-sweet potato pie in a
        gingerbread crust, 364
    maple pecan, 366
    maple sweet potato surprise
        pie, 368
    with pecan topping, 376, 380
    praline cloud pie, 378
    praline pie with marshmallow
        meringue, 370
    streusel-topped, 372
Sweet tart cherry pie, 54

T
Tasty pumpkin pie, 292

Three blind mice chocolate
    cheese pie, 82
Toasted coconut cream pie, 136
Tom's cheery cherry berry pie, 56

U
U. S. route 1 pie: Florida key lime
    with Maine blueberries, 110
The ultimate peanut butter pie, 272

V
Vanilla bean Brûlée pie, 324

W
Walnut
    chocolate raisin pie, 304
    crunch pumpkin pie, 294
When god hands you lemons, make
    a lemon pie, 112
White and milk chocolate raspberry
    mousse, 158
White-bottomed caramel chocolate
    pecan pie, 228
William's peanut butter paradise
    pie, 264